THE
ROAD
TO
NAB END

This family photograph celebrates father coming home on leave early in 1917. I am sitting on mother's knee. Jenny stands in the middle, next to Brenda. Dan is in front.

THE
ROAD
TO
NAB END

A Lancashire Childhood

——◦◦◦——

William Woodruff

——◦◦◦——

ELAND

Published by
ELAND
53 Eland Road, London SW11 5JX

Copyright © 1993 by Helga Woodruff; copyright renewed 1999
First published under the title *Billy Boy* by
Ryburn Publishing Ltd in 1993
First published in this paperback edition 2000

British Library Cataloguing-in-Publication Data.
A catalogue record for this book is available
from the British Library.

ISBN 0 907871 67 4

Printed in Spain by
GraphyCems, Navarra

ABOUT THE AUTHOR

William Woodruff was born in 1916 into a family of Lancashire cotton workers. Leaving school at 13, he became a delivery boy in a grocer's shop. In 1933, with bleak prospects in the north of England, he decided to try his luck in London. In 1936, with the aid of a London County Council Scholarship he went to Oxford University. During the Second World War he fought with the British Army in North Africa and the Mediterranean region. In 1946 Woodruff renewed his academic career. He is a world historian whose work has been widely translated. Woodruff has seven children. He lives in Florida.

By the same author

Vessel of Sadness

Paradise Galore

The Rise of the British Rubber Industry during the Nineteenth Century

Impact of Man:
A Study of Europe's role in the World Economy, 1750–1960

America's Impact on the World:
A Study of the roleof the United States in the World Economy, 1750–1970

The Struggle for World Power, 1500–1980

The Emergence of an International Economy, 1700–1914

A Concise History of the Modern World: 1500 to the present

To the memory of grandmother Bridget
who always called me Billy Boy

Contents

Prologue

T hey said I should not go. They said it was madness for an old man to cross the Atlantic to seek out his birthplace.

"You'll find nothing but ghosts there. Why don't you go and see the Grand Canyon?"

Others thought that anybody over seventy had every right to do as he pleased.

"Time's a-wasting," they said, noting my faulty gait.

So I went.

And when I reached the north of England and came to Blackburn, the town of my birth, and asked the taxi driver to take me to Griffin Street, he eyed me cautiously.

"Are you sure you want to go there?"

"Oh yes, I was born there. I've come a long way to see it."

"You're the boss," he said, taking my bags and holding the door so that I could climb in. A cold north wind - the wind I'd long since forgotten - tugged at my coat. I began to regret having arrived in thin Florida clothing.

3

As we moved off, I caught sight of several high-rise apartment buildings; they were harsh to the eye.

"Council flats," the driver said.

But then came landmarks I'd known as a child. The reddish-brown cathedral dominated the center of town. When my great-grandfather Arne Woodruff fled from Westmorland to Blackburn more than a hundred years ago, there were cows grazing around the church. I wondered if the image of Christ crucified was still inside; the Christ with the big hands: worker's hands.

We passed Queen Victoria's statue on the Parade - it was as ugly as ever, green with age and covered with bird dirt. The statue of Robert Peel, the famous nineteenth-century statesman and cotton manufacturer, stood, equally dirty, at the other side of the cathedral.

As we crossed King William Street, I stared at the clock tower above the Market Hall; a touch of Italy in the north of England. My father, recently arrived from America in 1914, had paraded under that clock before going to war.

The King's Arms pub appeared on our left. Its marble pillars looked like potted meat. As a small child, I'd pressed my back against that 'potted meat' waiting to see the first automobile in my life. Mother had warned me that a motor-car was in town, and that I should watch out for it carefully. "It's coming!" the crowd had shouted. As I turned, I saw a large black beetle with a shiny nose crawling across the cobblestones toward me. Its deep cough and trail of smoke added to my fears. I couldn't have been more amazed had an extinct reptile walked by.

But what was this nagging feeling? The more I stared through the taxi window, the more convinced I became that this was not the town of my birth. Had I come to the wrong place?

Of course not. The grey-roofed factories with their fortress-like walls were still there. So was Hornby's Mill - the mill of my childhood. It seemed so small; its windows were dirty and broken. As we turned a corner, I could see endless rows of weavers' cottages running across the town into the hills. The wet roofs glistened in the evening light; they seemed to be sagging. Using the local supplies of stone, slate, and clay, the cottages had been thrown together in the second half of the nineteenth century when the Lancashire cotton textile industry was booming. Whoever had built them had insisted on uniformity, if not downright ugliness. People lived and died in identical cottages that were little more than barracks.

Except that they looked older, most of the public buildings - the gas works, the chapels and the churches - were unchanged.

I asked the driver to go past the two schools where seventy years ago I had been a pupil. All that was left of St. Philip's, was a gaunt, lonely church tower. It stood there forlorn, an island of stone.

"School fell down, church wasn't needed."

My parents had walked through the cobbled streets to be married at St. Philip's in September 1904, "according to the rights and ceremonies of the Established Church." I had approached this same tower as a small, rather frightened schoolboy of four in 1920.

My other school, St. Peter's, was still standing, though propped up at the sides with metal supports. Its walls had the forbidding appearance that they had had when I looked upon them as a child.

We crossed the Blakewater river still running black.

In the far distance, from a high point, I caught a glimpse of the slag heaps on which I had fought with gangs of other children; they stood pyramid-like against the sky.

Yet the nagging feeling remained. The Blackburn of my childhood had had a forest of red brick chimneys belching great twisting coils of smoke. Where were they? The few chimneys I could see were cold and smokeless. I looked at my watch. It was 5:30. The light was fading. Seventy years ago, at this hour, Blackburn's streets would have been filled with the clip-clap sound of clogs as thousands of factory workers, the women in grey shawls, the men wearing dark caps, hastened home from work. Now there were few people about; they were better dressed - no shawls, few caps, no clogs - but there was no haste in their step. At this hour, the Blackburn into which I was born had been noisy, urgent, crowded, vibrant, alive.

The Blackburn I saw was becalmed - like a demasted ship after a storm.

We stood in what had been Griffin Street and surveyed a windswept, rubble-strewn wasteland covering many acres.

"Slum clearance," the driver mused, picking his teeth. "Had to do it, 'Pakis' were moving in."

I stared at a pile of broken glass and rusty wire where my cottage had been.

"It's a pity you came all the way from America to find everything gone."

"Oh, no," I answered. "On the contrary, ...everything is here."

Chapter I

Griffin Street

The fierce rattling of my bedroom window-pane first roused me from the long sleep of birth. Mr. Smalley, whom we called t' knocker-up man, came with his wire-tipped pole in the dark six mornings a week to shake our window until father stirred and shouted loud enough to be heard in the street below, "We're up!" Mr. Smalley then went next door and rattled the bedroom window of our neighbour, Mr. Morgan, the coal hauler. I often lay in bed listening to Mr. Smalley coming down the street. With his coming, Griffin Street began to stir. Daylight followed.

Not long after t' knocker-up had finished rattling our window-pane, a stream of wood-shodden workers began to hurry past my window on its way to the mills. In the Blackburn of 1916, more than two hundred factory and workshop chimneys were belching smoke by five a.m. Muffled voices and morning greetings flew up from the street. As the gray light grew and the night's bright stars paled, the stream of passers-by, their heads covered with shawls and caps, became a river and then a flood. The clip-clap of their clogs on the cobbles drowned out all other noises. In winter, deadened clogs meant a heavy snow; clogs that rang meant a frost. When it was raining, I looked down on a sea of glistening umbrella tops bobbing up and down on their way to the mill.

Once the flow of workers had subsided, except for the rattle of a cart in the distance, all was still again: still enough, that is, until I heard the last running steps dash by - someone trying to reach the mill before the whistle sounded and the tall iron gates were slammed to. Latecomers never failed to excite me. Sometimes, with nothing on but my gray flannel shirt, I jumped out of bed and, with my face pressed against the cold glass, watched the last workers rush by. "Hurry," I shouted, "you'll make it!" Back in bed, I had visions of them squeezing through the crack in the heavy factory gates before they closed. Those shut out of the mills came traipsing back. I could tell from the ring of their clog-irons that they had failed. Time was a hard master.

I also heard the coming and going of our neighbour, Mr. Morgan, the coal hauler, who left his house later than the mill workers. Mr. Lambert on the other side of our house walked to his job at the gas works with Mr. Morgan. About this time, the lamplighter passed down the street with his long pole with a hook on the end of it, and the street lamps were extinguished.

By mid-morning the stream of clogs had been replaced by a stream of horse-drawn carts, clippety-clopping their way to the railway station with mountains of gray cloth. Some of the cloth, which we called 'duties' - after the Indian word dhotis - was on its way to be bleached, dyed and printed in Manchester twenty-five miles to the south; the bulk of it would then go to Liverpool, thirty-five miles to the south-west, on its way to India, wherever that was. India must have been very important to Blackburn because I seemed to hear more about India as a child than I did about England.

The long columns of horse-drawn carts passed within an arm's reach of our front door. I watched the wind tugging at the tarpaulins. With marked regularity, the buckles smacked against the sides. The journey to the station was a race in which the whip was not spared. I wondered if the horses which did

not move fast enough were shut out of the station as the workers
were shut out of the factories.

As the day wore on, the street echoed to the call of the rag-
and-bone man, who cried his wares from a donkey cart. In
exchange for a handful of rags, a bare bone or two, some old
medicine or pickled-onion bottles, or old newspapers, or any
old piece of metal, he gave mother a donkey stone - a piece of
hard chalk - with which to colour the kitchen hearthstone and
the front doorstep. Everybody knew that the rag-and-bone man
was not as poor as he looked. He was followed by the scissors-
grinder who, for a penny or two, sharpened scissors and knives
amid a shower of sparks with a foot-driven grinding wheel.
There were other peddlers, such as the thread, needles and
ribbon seller, who cried their wares. My favourite was the tinker
who mended pots and pans. Because Griffin Street was one of
the main highways to the mills, there was no lingering in the
street for man or beast until darkness came.

At the end of the working day, as the last empty carts drawn
by froth-covered horses returned to the mills, the tide of
workers, the women walking arm in arm, surged past our
cottage door again, homeward bound. Their step was not as
brisk as it had been at the beginning of the day. After that, apart
from the plaintive shriek of a train in the distance, or the
haunting sound of a lonely concertina being played by a
passerby, silence reigned. To keep up steam, the thump of the
mill engines went on all night, but that didn't bother anybody.
The workers didn't notice noises that brought them bread.

———◄◦►———

Like all the other weaver's cottages, our house was one of an
endless row. The outside was brick; the roof was gray slate. It
had four white-washed rooms, two up and two down. They
were about seven feet high. The front rooms measured nine feet
by nine feet. Tall people had to dip when coming through the
front door. When I was sitting on my father's shoulders, I had
to watch out not to bump my head. The downstairs floors were
made of large flagstones, covered with a scattering of clean sand
that was swept up and renewed weekly. The sand got between

our toes. In winter the stones froze to our feet. The ceilings were the wooden floor boards of the upper rooms. There was a tiny yard at the rear, where the rain sat between the cobbles. Beyond was an alley and another unbroken line of cottages.

My brother Dan and I shared a bedroom with our parents. There were two metal beds with straw mattresses resting on thin metal slats. Sometimes the slats sagged, leaving a pocket into which we sank our hips. Dan and I slept in the same bed. We slept so close to our parents that we could touch them. The nearness of our bodies made us feel safe. No one noticed the lack of privacy. I accepted my parent's love-making long before I understood it. It was as natural as somebody using the pisspot (I didn't know the word chamber-pot until I had left school). It didn't disturb me, or confuse me, or revolt me. Like father's deep snoring, I ignored it. Living in such a confined space meant everybody shared everybody else's joys and sorrows.

I think the straw mattresses must have encouraged bugs, for I recall mother sitting on the side of the bed running her fingers down the seams of blankets and sheets. I didn't find anything strange about her crushing the bugs between her thumb nails, though it did get bloody at times. It was a never-ending battle.

Our clothing, what little we had, hung on the whitewashed walls. As the walls were sometimes damp, sheets of brown paper were slipped between the clothes and the plaster. The pegmat at my bedside protected my feet from the freezing floor. In our house there was one by every bed as well as before the two fireplaces downstairs. They were made from old clothing and could be of all colours. They were not only solid and warm; they meant that no garment, however old, was wasted. The women made them at night, pulling strips of cloth with a rughook through a stiff piece of fabric. Several women would work together, chattering, singing and laughing into the night. The mats were kept clean by beating them against the outside wall.

There was not much else in the bedroom: a lace curtain, a tiny black iron fireplace and an empty orange crate scavanged from the fruit market, which served as a bedside table. The crate's two compartments were brightly painted and decorated with a linen cloth at the front. There were also two pisspots, an open-flame gas light, the flame blue at the bottom, white at the top, and a cracked wooden door with a latch.

My sisters Jenny and Brenda slept in the other bedroom, behind a paper-thin wall. When I was born in 1916, Jenny was eleven and Brenda was six. Dan was four years older than I. Because of the wooden staircase, the back bedroom was smaller than the front bedroom. There was only space for one bed and a large wooden trunk filled with linen and bedding. There was no end to what that trunk contained. My sisters' clothing also hung on the walls.

The kitchen, which was beneath the back bedroom, was the center of family activities. There was ever a din going on there at night. The room contained a plain deal bench that served as a table, two rush-bottomed stand chairs, two foot-stools, two rocking chairs, a cupboard for groceries, hooks for pots and pans, the bread-mug (a large clay bowl with a clay lid in which we kept bread, margarine and other food), and another large clay bowl in which the bread was made. A big earthenware dish could be used for any purpose. As the kitchen was three paces one way and two-and-a-half the other, children didn't sit at table, we stood for meals.

The coal-burning open fire range had an oven at one side and an oblong tank for heating water at the other. The water was rusty because the metal flaked off, but it could be used for cleaning jobs. In front of the fire was a top-bar on which the kettle sang. Steel fire irons stood on the hearth which had a metal surround. The whole range was kept clean with black-lead and ammonia. I don't know how much lead we consumed. Ashes from the fire fell into a stone-lined hole in the floor, and were shovelled into a bucket and thrown into the midden in the backyard. I didn't like the look or the taste of ashes, and kept well away from the hole in the floor when it was being emptied. If a mouse fell in there, it never got out again. Coal was dumped in the kitchen under the stairs, a sack at a time. It kept dry there. It was brought by our neighbour, Mr. Morgan, who staggered through the front room with a hundred pound sack on his back.

The cloud of dust that flew up when Mr. Morgan poured the coal - though on our behalf he was ever careful - took time to settle. The worst thing that could happen was for Mr. Morgan to arrive while we were eating. With a sack of coal being shaken out almost against the dining table, it was impossible not to eat coal dust. No one grumbled. Even a child knew that we couldn't possibly manage without coal.

When done, Mr. Morgan quietly folded his sack, adjusted the leather hood that protected his ears as well as his head, repositioned the studded leather guard, which prevented the coal from digging into his back, picked up his shilling and left. I never knew Mr. Morgan to stand in our kitchen talking - perhaps because he was so dirty.

Above the fireplace was a gas light, which was capped with a one-penny asbestos mantle - about the size and shape of a white clay pipe. Beneath the gas light was a shelf on which sat two red and white earthenware dogs. One of my mother's brothers had given them to her as a wedding present. They came with an unfriendly look and never changed. Some said that's how pot dogs always looked; others said, he'd got them cheap. Time in the house was kept by a steel watch that hung on a hook. Father had got it from the navy, years before. To escape time in Blackburn, you had to go into the country.

Under the window was a stone sink and a slopstone, or draining board. Above the sink was the only tap in the house. Next to the fireplace was a deep, large metal basin called a setpot or copper. It was heated with free orange-box wood, and had a chimney connected to the fireplace. Clean water, water free of rust, was boiled in the setpot. My mother and my sisters washed clothes there. Washing was soaked, boiled, rotated with a wooden dolly, rinsed and starched in this small corner. The steaming wet washing was run through a wringer that stood in the yard and, weather permitting, hung out to dry on the clothesline. How forsaken the washing looked through the window when it was left in the rain. Brought inside, it was flung over a clothes rack, fixed to the ceiling in front of the range. Damp clothing usually hung from the ceiling for half the week. The grown-ups got their heads caught in it.

A single metal gas ring stood next to the setpot for cooking. For the gas there was a penny meter under the stairs. If the light gave out and we didn't have a penny, we used a candle; if we didn't have a candle we sat by the fire and told tales or went to bed.

When you opened the front door and stepped down one step you stood in the street. In winter a heavy curtain was put up to stop drafts. Some people called this room the parlour, but that was putting on airs. There was a lace curtain in front of the window, a gas light, a fireplace with a pegrug in front of it, and a rocking chair at either side. The fire-irons and metal surround were made of brass, not steel as in the kitchen. There were also some stools, and another large chest for clothing and belongings. On the Singer sewing machine in front of the window stood an aspidistra that was periodically washed with soap and water and put out for air. Mother's cut-glass punch bowl stood on a small table against the wall. On the shelf above the fireplace were several framed pictures of relatives. There also was a coloured picture of Blackpool Tower and the Big Wheel. The front room was used for entertaining, for holidays such as Christmas and, if coal was available, at weekends. When my sisters grew up, it became our dance floor. Except on the hottest days of summer, it was too cold to sit there without a fire.

For me, the cobbled yard at the back of the house was another world. It could be traversed with a hop, skip and a jump. Underneath the kitchen window was a tap over a drain where the pisspots stood after being rinsed. In frosty weather the tap froze and the pots had to be washed inside. In one corner was a tiny shelter where the cast iron clothes wringer, brushes and brooms were kept. Another corner contained a pile of cinders, picked by us children from factory tips. Our neighbour Mr. Lambert sometimes added a sack of coke from the gasworks. Coke and peat sods were used in winter to keep the kitchen fire going throughout the night; we called it banking-up. Above the cinders hung a large tin tub that was carried into the kitchen when somebody wanted a bath, which wasn't very often.

There was also a petty in the backyard connected to the main sewer; there was no flushing, no lighting, no seat. We used nothing but newspaper there. In summer it stank, in winter you froze to the board. If you stayed too long, one of the family would call from the backdoor, "Wot yer doin' in t' petty? Are yer makin' yer will?" An odd question, because the working class didn't make wills. My sister Jenny would never go out there at night without a flickering candle. If we had no candle somebody had to go out with her and stand outside the petty door until she was done.

Next to the toilet was a brick, roofed-over midden where we threw our trash. This was shovelled from the back alley into a horse-drawn cart. A door lead into the alley, which had a stone gutter down which rats used to scurry. They frightened me to the point of panic. The yard was enclosed by a rough stone wall.

In summer, the smell of rotting garbage was everywhere. Flies descended in clouds; hence the upset stomachs. Indoors we had penny flypapers. In warm weather, we ate while watching the death throes of flies caught on the flypaper above the dining table. Great buzzing bluebottles were the only ones to escape, and they not often.

———◦———

I learned as a child to avoid talking about the damp and cold in our house. "It's bad enough without having you gassing," my folk grumped. I think the damp worried them more than the cold. There was nothing to stop it rising through the flagstones that covered the floor. It got into people's bones. The washing hanging from the kitchen ceiling didn't help either. The cold was sometimes so severe that it made us forget the damp. When the northwind was blowing and the air was smoking with snow, we went to bed with all the preparations of a military campaign. As the only heat upstairs was that which came from the kitchen through the cracks in the wooden floors, we didn't walk, we dashed to bed, taking care not to get splinters in our feet on the staircase. No praying at the bedside for us. The hot oven shelves, covered with flannel, went into bed first, our clothing followed; every garment that could be found was heaped on top. Sometimes we even used thick layers of newspaper as an extra blanket, which rustled when we turned in bed. Underneath it all, my brother and I kept each other warm.

The kitchen fire was banked up and kept alight throughout the night. That was father's job. If the man-of-the-house was about, nobody else touched the poker. I never ceased to wonder how much interest father took in the fire. You knew his mood from the way he handled the poker, or how he rearranged the coals. I think it gave him great satisfaction and saved him from talking. The house would have been unbearable without keeping the kitchen fire going. Even so, there were nights when it was too cold to sleep. On a really cold morning we had to dress quickly or freeze. We didn't linger in the bedroom, we raced to breakfast. Cold and hunger were the great persuaders.

Curiously enough, we never lit the bedroom fires except on Christmas Eve to welcome Father Christmas who entered our bedrooms by way of the chimney. Every Christmas my brother and I woke in the early hours of Christmas Day to find one or two little gifts at the foot of the bed. What magic to waken and find that Father Christmas had not forgotten us - that somebody cared! In my stocking was an apple or an orange, some nuts, and a shining new penny. Requests for fires in the bedrooms at times other than Christmas were met with: "It isn't really cold enough for fires upstairs," or, with the snow-flakes spinning to earth outside, "It's going to get warmer." The answer that settled all arguments was "Coal's done."

One piercingly cold night - with a thick crust of ice and snow covering the bedroom window - father woke up to use the pisspot. He must have been caught unexpectedly. Perhaps he'd been out drinking. Anyway, to his annoyance, he discovered that the pisspots had been left by the drain in the yard and were now buried under deep snow. Before mother could stop him, he'd shot up the window and was pissing into the street. All would have been well had he not pissed on somebody's head. Even better had the passerby not looked up to see who was opening the window. A great howl arose from the cobbles below. With a freezing wind entering the room, mother choked with anger at father. Father choked with fury at the passerby, whose own fury was waking the street. "What reet have you," father bawled, "to be wanderin' t' streets at this hour? Why can't you watch where ye're goin'?" With that he slammed the window shut. Next morning there was an unusual tension at breakfast.

It took father a long time to live the pissing incident down. In our street such tales quickly got around. I was at a workers' meeting with father some nights later when someone shouted: "Any more bull's eyes, Will?" Everybody roared with laughter, including father, which was not like him. When I told grandmother Bridget about the pissing business she crossed herself.

———◄◦►———

I'd always believed that I had been born in our cottage in Griffin Street.

"Ah, no, Billy," mother said one day, "that's where tha wrang; tha was born in t' mill."

"But that's not what it says on my birth certificate."

I discovered that I was born prematurely in the carding-room of Hornby's cotton mill, which was only a few minutes from Griffin Street. Day long, mother cleaned cotton there. On the morning of my birth she had fainted before one of the cotton grinders.

"It was the telegrams."

"What telegrams?"

"From t' War Office. Dad was in France fighting the war. The first telegram they brought to t'mill. The foreman, Patrick Murphy, read it to me. It said that your dad was killed and that the War Office regretted it. Just a line to change your life. Everybody was real nice. Told me to go home and rest, and to come back when I was ready."

"Did you?"

"Well, when you don't have any money and your husband is dead and you've got four mouths to feed, including your own and your unborn child, you'd better be ready all the time or you'll starve."

"But Dadda wasn't dead."

"No, that's right, he wasn't. A week later another telegram came saying that the first telegram had been a mistake. Two hours after that you arrived. Patrick Murphy delivered you on a heap of cotton against a wall in a corner of the shed. I was in my own bed by the time Dr. Grieves got there. He wrote Griffin Street in your birth certificate. With or without Grieves, it was a fine birth. No commotion. Of course, there was the din of the carding machines and cotton dust falling on us, but no bother, all went well. When he'd delivered you, Mr. Murphy dipped his thumb into one of the fire buckets and baptized you, 'Father, Son and Holy Ghost.' He wrapped you in a sheet and shouted to the other cardroom hands: 'Cum and look! Have you ever seen sich? It's a boy, and a sturdy one at that; worth a drink o' rum and tay, he is.' They came running. 'Oh, a grand bairn, a really grand bairn,' they clucked as they crowded around. 'It's not every day it happens in t' shed. Tha can be reet proud of thiself, Maggie, tha can. Spitten image of his dad. Lucky his dad's alive!'

Later that morning grandmother Bridget came across from Dougdale's mill. The three of us were bundled onto one of the factory's horse-drawn carts. With you held in my arms, we rattled our way through the streets until we reached our cottage. Two days after you were born, I was back at work, slubbing in the mill; cooking, washing and cleaning at home."

———◄○►———

With mother in the mill during the war years, the job of caring for me fell to my sister Jenny, who was eleven years older than I. I think she brought me up more than my mother did. Staying home and keeping house meant the end of her own childhood, and the end also of whatever little schooling she had had. Nobody bothered to enforce the rule that she should have stayed at school until she was fourteen. Several times a day she took me from the wooden box that served as my cradle, wrapped me in a blanket and ran through the streets to the mill, where mother was waiting to suckle me. The suckling done, Jenny then went home again and rocked me to sleep.

Once, when Jenny was unwell and could not take me to the mill, mother ignored the factory regulations and walked out. She had the misfortune to run headlong into the timekeeper at the gate.

"Here, where t' goin'?" he demanded.
"Home, t' feed child, it's clemmin'."
"If tha goes out now, tha stays out!"
Mother returned to the cardroom.

Being in Jenny's care didn't do me any harm; I thrived. She handled me as well as a grown woman. Indeed, one might say that I had a privileged childhood, for Jenny, whom I called Gaga, loved and sang to me all day. She loved me even more when I began to creep about and play with her. She never thought of me as a burden. Only reluctantly did she surrender me to mother at the end of the day. Jenny was pleased when morning came and mother departed, and she could reclaim me as her own.

When in later years I suggested that I'd robbed her of her schooling, she countered: "Playing with a baby brother was much better than going to school, especially here." She never forgave the Blackburn children for having ripped the buttons off her brand-new American coat. After four years at school in the United States, she never forgot America. Later on in life when I met her on the streets and asked "Where to, Jenny?" she would grin and reply, "America."

"I had a dream," she told me one day, "in which I travelled back to America alone in a beautiful gondola."

Jenny not only looked after me; after four o'clock, when my sister Brenda and my brother Dan came home from school, she had to care for them, too. Wearing one of mother's dresses, and one of her wide-brimmed hats held on with a long hat pin, she clowned and acted for us until mother arrived. Then she helped to cook and wash and prepare for still another day.

The wonder is that mother and grandmother Bridget should have gone on working in the mill all day while the Woodruff children ran wild. With father away at war and our savings exhausted, mother had no choice. The war allowance from father was not enough to keep the family going. Her earnings as a slubber in the mill were fifteen shillings a week. Grandmother's savings had gone too and she had to work to stay alive. She had a tiny cottage not far from Griffin Street. For some reason she never lived with us or her other children - not even during the war.

There were times during the war when mother felt that the world was crazy. There'd never been such slaughter. The first casualty lists from the Battle of the Somme in 1916 stunned the whole of Blackburn. The tragedy was on such a scale that people simply couldn't understand it. "Everybody felt they'd been kicked in the belly. You couldn't go out, without having to stop and hold somebody's hand," mother said. "Death was common; black clothing was everywhere. The war frayed everybody's nerves; put everybody's temper on edge. The best went to France and got killed, the rubbish stayed home. One day I bumped into a neighbour who had lost her three sons on the Somme. I held her by the hand and nearly died." Mother wondered whether the war was a scourge sent by God. She remembered vividly the excitement when German Zeppelins first bombed London in May 1915. Innocent people had been killed asleep in bed. What was the world coming to?

Like so many of her generation, mother blamed the war for everything. Whatever misfortunes followed 1914, she put them down to the war. She was convinced that it had changed father for the worse. The man who left her to fight in France in 1914 was not the man who returned in 1918. "My Will never really came home again," she grieved. "Fellow who did come home was somebody else. He'd had t' stuffin' knocked out of him."

———◦———

When Jenny was thirteen, a job became available for her in the mill. "No point in her going back to school for another year," said father. "She needs to learn a skill in t'mill." As a result, I was farmed out to baby-sitters, first to Mrs. Beddle and then to Mrs. Allison, both of whom lived in the vicinity.

Mrs. Beddle was a warm-hearted barrel of a woman, with an unpleasant smell, who seemed to roll about the house rather than walk. As her skirt touched the ground, I could not decide whether she moved on wheels or feet. Her only inheritance from her husband, who had been lost at sea, was a large green parrot called Toby. Mrs. Beddle spoke to the parrot as if she were talking to her dead husband.

"What do you think we should do now, Mr. Beddle?"

Peering through the wires of the cage, Toby blinked a lot before answering. Scratching his head gravely, he ruffled his feathers as if he was about to say something of the utmost importance. He must have had a lot of advice to give, for once started, he squawked and screeched on and on like a cotton grinder. Toby had been to sea and had picked up words that the barrel-like woman said would have been better left behind. 'Well, damn my eyes!' threw her into fits.

One morning when I arrived, the bird was hidden beneath a cloth where he remained silent and unrepentant throughout the day. Mrs. Beddle didn't tell me what he'd said.

She was always strict about my eating habits, and was ever ready to help if I was slow in eating the bread and cheese, or hot-pot, that mother had left for me.

"We mustn't overeat, must we," she warned, as her fork repeatedly stabbed and carried off what I thought was a disproportionate part of my dinner. But then she had almost no resources of her own. Eating my dinner was the only way Mrs. Beddle could stop the stomach growlings that went on all the time.

The other baby-sitter, Mrs. Allison, had a strange way of running to the door while calling "Is that you, Jack? Is that you?" In her haste, she dropped whatever she was doing. The odd thing was that Jack was never there. Nor was anybody else.

"I thow't it was 'im," she said sadly on returning; "I thow't it was 'im."

Then she carried on as though nothing had happened.

The longer I stayed with Mrs. Allison, whose heavy eyebrows and large nose gave her a frightening appearance, and whose ammonia smell was no better than Mrs. Beddle's, the more she ran to the door. One day I told mother about it.

"She's lost her only son," mother explained.

"Is he dead?"

"He just disappeared. Nobody knows where. It's left her a bit queer in t' 'ead. Mrs. Allison is a good woman."

It's just as well she was, for I was left in her care for hours on end.

Chapter II

Noises in the Night

As I was the first to be put to bed, I fell asleep to the drone of voices in the kitchen below. Sometimes I fell asleep listening to Jenny singing. She twittered and chirped like a bird; she never sang a song right through as mother did. The cracks in the bedroom floor were so wide that, except when the adults took an unfair advantage by whispering, I could hear all that was going on. When the whispering had gone on too long, I leapt out of bed, and pressed my ear to a crack to listen to the scandal. In our street everybody knew everybody else's business: who was sick, who was well; who was richer, who was poorer; who had 'got on,' and who had 'gone wrong.'

The cracks were large enough to drop metal washers the size of a penny into the front room below. One night Dan outdid himself by dropping one right down the front of a visitor's dress. Convinced that it was a mouse (it was not unknown for mice to fall from the ceiling), the woman grasped her breast and gave a great scream. There was much commotion before the washer was retrieved. It all ended with father bawling at Dan through the ceiling and threatening him with his belt; though father, like the rest, went into fits of laughter once the woman had left.

If I stayed awake, I could tell what everybody was doing. I knew it was washing night because of water being sloshed about. The whole house became damp; condensation covered the windows. Next morning the plastered walls were streaked with wet.

Ironing night had its slightly burning smell. There was the tell-tale snap of the flat iron lid as a fresh red-hot iron was taken from the fire and placed inside.

Baking night was best of all; it offered tidbits. Mother's knocking on the side of the bread tins to get the loaves out, and the rich smell of freshly baked bread, brought me creeping down the stairs in the hope of claiming my share. Before going to bed, I loved to watch mother and Jenny mix the flour, and (with father's help) knead the dough, roll and pat it before putting it in the bread tins which Brenda then placed in the oven. I was allowed to prick the tops of the loaves with a fork.

When I heard hot coals being pushed under the oven, I knew that roasted potatoes with lots of margarine were in the offing. The most disappointing thing that could happen was to fall asleep before the feast was ready.

Many other noises reached me. I knew from the smells and the rattle of pots and pans that mother was cooking the next day's meal. For her, work was unending. When all else was done, there were clothes to be patched, socks to be darned. I heard the click of her needles, the kettle whistling on the hob, the scrape of the rockers, the squeak of chairs.

I listened to my family playing games and knew who had won. I heard the cups being tossed, the dice thrown, the dominoes clinking, the shuffling of the cards. Sometimes they would play Find-the-Thimble - giving great gleeful shouts when one of them went from warm to hot. I knew from the way that those huddled round the fire jumped back that a gust of wind had come down the chimney and had driven smoke into their eyes. Chairs being picked up and put down again meant that the family and visitors were changing places in the hope of avoiding drafts. Some found shelter where others found nothing but a gale. On a really cold, windy night everybody was entitled to scrape his chair about the floor as much as he saw fit.

For my sisters to jump and squeal at the same time meant that a mouse had run across their feet. The mice were cheeky because they were hungry. They marched out of the holes in the plaster as bold as brass. That's why most families, poor as they were, had to keep a cat. We had no fat mice and no fat people. We didn't have a cat in our house; mother said there was no room for one. We used mousetraps. They haunted me. The sharp crack of the trap would waken me at night, followed by a momentary squeaking in the corner.

Very early, from where I lay, I heard talk of a 'ship coming home.' I puzzled about that particular ship for a long time. It must have been the slowest ship on the seas because it never seemed to arrive. "Aye! Tha'll see when it cums," people shouted, slapping their knees. But it didn't come. The only man whose ship came home was mother's brother, uncle Eric. He was the wonder of the family and they often talked about his doings downstairs.

A thin, self-confident man, uncle Eric was head of the local Mechanics Institute. He knew all about inventions, and was always making speeches. "Uncle Eric," mother said, "has the gift of the gab." He was written up in the newspaper as one of the first in our town to have electricity installed in his house. The rest of us considered it quite an honour.

One night, I was taken to celebrate uncle Eric's triumph. Clutching mother's hand, we followed a little knot of muffled-up relatives. The wind roared over the cold rooftops. We crossed the unmarked boundary that separated the poorer from the richer parts of town. We found uncle Eric waiting for us at his garden gate with a lantern that showed up his bright eyes and the blue veins that ran down his nose. His hair was parted down the middle and shone with oil. As he jumped about with his lamp, shadows flitted among the bushes. He was very proud to have so many visitors. He led us into a dark room where we stood about wondering what was going to happen. Other people followed until the room was quite full.

I didn't share the hearty humour of these people. Even the word 'eeelectricity' sounded sinister to me. It was a word we

27

had never used before. It didn't come easily to the adults. Perhaps, as the doom-sayers warned, we were about to be blown up! Nervously, I held mother's hand and tried not to fidget.

With a slightly tipsy uncle Eric dragging out the drama, and with everyone else shouting "One, two, three!" the room was suddenly flooded with an entirely new and magical light. The light was soft, yet blinding; it made us blink. It reached everywhere, right into the corners of the room. It came from a glittering bulb hanging from the ceiling. There was no flame, or spluttering, or hissing; there was no smell as with gas light. From the look of astonishment on the faces around me, there might have been a thousand bulbs above our heads. The air was suddenly filled with a barrage of congratulatory 'ahs' and 'ums.'

"It's past talking," they said, looking around; "it beats it all."

"Aye, Eric," they chorused, "tha're a one, tha're! Tha should be Mayor!"

"Nay, nay, not Mayor. Eric will have to be our mon in parliament fro' Blackburn."

We all clapped. "Speech!" somebody called.

Never stuck for words, a beaming uncle Eric began by saying that 'eeelectricity' was going to change all our lives. There was no telling the wonders it would bring. With the help of 'eeelectricity,' things would buck up for everybody. None of us would have to work anymore. Electricity would do it for us. In the golden age of electricity that lay ahead, we'd all be rich. Strikes and lock-outs, hunger and poverty were going to be things of the past. Progress would come if we all used our 'eads.

Uncle Eric had certainly used his. He had made a lot of money equipping hospitals with furniture and supplies. He didn't make them, he simply took them from one group of people and sold them to another. He and aunt Pearl had started out quite poor. "Couldn't afford children," mother told me. I hadn't met aunt Pearl before. She had blue rings round her eyes; her lips were painted firebucket red. She had a strange rasping voice. Her fat fingers were laden with jewelry. When I saw how small she was, I found it hard to believe the family story that she had once knocked uncle Eric out with a frying pan. He didn't seem any the worse for it.

As if to acclaim the coming of the golden age, uncle Eric and aunt Pearl served hot meat pies, black puddings that scalded our tongues, and great slabs of cold, potted meat. For 'afters' there was hot rhubarb pie smothered with cream. There was lots of beer. As the food was heaped onto our plates, the talking stopped. Although everyone set to with a good heart to "brass th' guts," it was some time before everything was gone.

When there was nothing left to eat or drink, we picked up sticks and trailed back - some a little unsteadily - to our homes by the mills. Before leaving we all sang 'For he's a jolly good fellow.' Uncle Eric stood there blinking, a contented Cheshire-cat look on his face. Everyone agreed that uncle Eric and aunt Pearl had put on a 'reet luvly do.' The talk going home was more about black puddings than about science.

Two things stick in my mind about that night: one was that uncle Eric was the only man wearing a suit and tie, the other was the large mantelpiece clock decorated with tiny colourful birds. I'd never seen such a clock before.

Many things talked about by the adults downstairs in our house mystified me. The war was one. It had changed everything for the worse in their lives. Much later, I discovered that the war was the Great War of 1914-1918 in which my father had fought. Only then did I connect the many limbless men who hobbled through our streets with the war. I'd no idea that the war had made our neighbour, Mr. Beatty who lived two doors away, the gibbering idiot he was.

On fine days Mrs. Beatty put Mr. Beatty outside the front door to air. He lay in a long patched wicker bed on wheels on the narrow pavement, inches away from the street, jabbering and drooling at passersby. He always had a towel under his chin. When I dared to look at him, I was surprised how strong and big his head was. I didn't dare to look what was under the blanket. His eyes were like a blind man's, they looked directly ahead but didn't see. The carters called and waved their whips at him.

"Up and at 'em," he shouted back, making his wicker bed shake. He shouted it so often that it became his nick-name.

"And how is old Up-and-at-'em?" passersby asked as they took hold of his blanket and waggled one of his stumps. Years had to pass before I learned that 'Up and at 'em' was what British soldiers shouted to each other on the Western Front before going over the top of the trenches. Mr. Beatty went on fighting the Great War until he died. His great comfort was for Mrs. Beatty to sit and read the Bible to him. On Jenny's orders, I crossed the street when she was reading, so as not to disturb.

Nothing in my childhood, not even downright wickedness, was as bad as the war. Everybody knew how the war had come about. The Germans had caused it. The Germans were responsible for most troubles. I think it helped a great deal to have the Germans to blame. Whatever the trouble, if the war and the sickness couldn't be held responsible, then the Germans must have done it. It came as quite a surprise later on to meet Germans who struck me as ordinary people - people who could smile and have a toothache.

The sickness was the influenza epidemic that followed the war, and from which so many people died. Whole families lay sick together. The church bells never stopped tolling; the undertakers were busy night and day. My mother, my sister Jenny and my grandmother Bridget were all stricken by it. So great was the fear of contracting the illness that even my mother's sister Alice had refused to help when father had gone to fetch her. Little did she realize that one day, when on her way to the workhouse, she would seek my mother's assistance. Help came from Dr. Grieves and a good Samaritan woman who walked in off the street. She had seen us in the morning, a dejected group of children huddled in the doorway; we were still there in the late afternoon. "Where's your mother?" she asked Brenda. "She's sick." So the stranger went in and took care of everything. For two or three weeks, she shopped and cooked and fed the whole family and kept the house clean until mother and Jenny could get back on their feet. Then, unpaid, she left as mysteriously as she had come and was never seen by us again.

Provided I stayed awake, not much escaped my ears at night: "Aye, Ah'd really like a drink," said father.

"A good glass of stout would make all the difference," answered mother.

"How much money do we have, Maggie?"

"Fourpence."

"Well, that will buy a glass of beer."

"You go and enjoy the fourpence, Will, it will do you good." I heard her put the coins on the table.

"Nay, if we can't afford a glass each, we'll share it," father replied. "Off tha goes t' Griffin and get it."

I heard mother get a mug, put on her clogs and shawl, and leave the house. I heard her footsteps going down the street toward the pub and coming back again.

"Real gradely," father said, smacking his lips, as they savoured half a glass each.

Neighbours who lifted the latch at night with a shout of "Y'in?" were greeted with laughter. Some 'y'in's' were so loud that they startled me out of my sleep. Having shut the door behind them, because of drafts, visitors usually stood quite still, head cocked, waiting for an invitation to proceed farther. The answering shouts of the family were equally loud; "Cum in, cum ya." Sometimes I could tell who it was by the smell rather than the voice. Visitors were told to make themselves 'at 'ome.'

The habit of shouting sprang from a good-natured exuberance; also the constant clatter of the mill machinery had made many of the workers partly deaf. It was common for people to cup their ear with their hand and shout "Eh?" In the mills they used lip-reading or shouted to be heard. Shouting in our house was common. It never crossed anybody's mind that I was trying to sleep above their heads. Nobody apologized for making a noise. Except for churches and funerals it was unnatural for us to be quiet.

Quiet or loud, I loved their voices: voices slow and melodious; voices sharp and quick; voices full of sorrow; voices full of joy; sweet voices, like Jenny's, which quite spontaneously could break into song and break off again just as quickly; voices which, as the night lengthened, fell silent. Once a subject had been talked to death, custom demanded that the workers should sit back and digest what had been said. I knew when they were ruminating, for the long pauses would be punctuated by isolated remarks like: "By gum! It doesn't bear thinking about," or "Now, what use war that?" or just plain "Eeees!" or "Aiiiis," followed by long meaningful sighs. Minutes later a galaxy of voices were at it again. My people loved talking; eloquence was their birthright. I loved them for it. I never tired of listening, even when I'd no idea what they were talking about. It was the music of the words that mattered.

———◦———

It was from talk in the kitchen that I first learned about Fall River, Massachusetts, where my parents had lived and worked for some years. They had gone in 1906 as steerage passengers to America with my sister Jenny. It took a long time before talk of America made any sense to me. Blackburn was my world. It was one of the first words I learned to write at school. 'Blackburn, Blackburn, Blackburn,' I wrote all over my slate. Later on I heard about London and that the king and queen lived there.

Our neighbours took it for granted that the Lancashire cotton industry started with us, and that cotton was king. Nobody knew how to make textiles like Lancashire folk. Nobody ever would. Father had a different view than those who had never been out of England. He was always telling his fellow weavers that the cotton mills in Fall River were more efficient and that they'd better watch out. Mother said he told his trade union, the Amalgamated Weavers Association, the same story, but they didn't thank him for it. He went on about automatic looms, rings, and mules, and batteries, and goodness knows what other ingenious devices he'd seen in America. His listeners were astonished when he explained that Fall River weavers did not 'kiss the shuttle' to replenish the weft; but that a rotating hopper did it for them. Even more astonished when he told them that in Fall River six, not two, looms were common. "By gum," they said when dad had finished. "It doesn't bear thinking about." Having said that, I suspect they forgot all about it.

The other threat posed to Lancashire came from 't' niggers' who were prepared to work for less money. As far as I could discover, 't' niggers' were poor people who lived in Asia and Africa. My people were simple people, they divided most of the world into 'us and 't' niggers'; in those days racism was a common ill. As my father had been to China, he was expected to be able to talk about 't' niggers' at first hand.

The workers took 't' niggers' no more seriously than they took the challenge posed by the cotton workers of Fall River. 'T' niggers' couldn't match our skill - nobody could. Besides, they were too far away to do us any harm. The idea that 't' niggers' might have begun the cotton industry and might replace us entirely in the cotton trade didn't enter anybody's head. Even in the bleakest days of the 1920's and 1930's, when Lancashire was outcompeted, or shut out of European, American and Asian markets, Lancashire workers never stopped looking on the bright side. Things were 'allus' going to get better. There was "allus a silver lining through each dark cloud shining." "You'll see," they said, slapping their thighs and putting on a brave front, "things are bound to buck up. It's not t' fost time we've had troubles. I mean, what dun yo think we're made of?... Toffee, he, he, he. Cum on, lad, it'll be aw reet!"

Chapter III

Lights and Shadows

The postwar boom in Lancashire cottons meant that there was a job for father when he returned to Griffin Street after the war. Nothing had helped the industry as much as the war. Despite the sky-rocketing price of cotton, brought on by speculators (once the United States had entered the war in 1917), the last year of the war was the most prosperous year in the industry's history.

Properous times meant that we had plenty to eat. Food was something we took seriously. You might say we had a hunger mentality. When we could afford it, we began the day by eating a bowl full of scalding hot oatmeal porridge, made with water, served with a little salt. Nothing could fill you up like porridge. "Gives you a lining." Even when mother was working in the mill, no morning passed but what she did not make the breakfast. Porridge was followed by chunks of home-made bread, covered with Maggy Ann (margarine), beef-dripping, syrup, or jam. Coarse fish was cheap, a week's supply for one person might cost sixpence, and we ate a lot of it. Bought just before it 'went off,' it was obtained at rock-bottom prices. Even at breakfast it was customary to gnaw upon a leftover cold haddock or kipper. We children were told to watch out for bones. Weak tea was drunk, piping hot, without sugar and milk, in great quantities. Other than mother's milk, the only milk I knew until I was in my teens was canned Nestle's milk and blue milk (milk with the cream skimmed off), which was doled into our jug out of a churn brought on a cart from a farm. We knew when the milkman arrived because he shouted: "Fresh milk, fresh milk," in the street.

Dinners were the hot-pots taken to the mills and eaten between noon and one o'clock. Supper was eaten when the family came home - usually physically drained - at the end of the day. Mother decided what to cook or serve cold. Supper could be anything: left-over stew, porridge, fish and chips, toasted crumpets, boiled or baked cod, cold sausage meat, cold tripe doused with lots of vinegar, cheese, pickles - how we loved pickles and beetroot - or a sheep's head boiled in the setpot with barley and peas. The butcher mesmerized me when he split the sheep's head with his cleaver. Crash! ... and out came the brains. If we didn't have a sheep's head, mother might make soup from fish heads and tails, or from a ham bone, or a cowheel, or bits of meat, with herbs and lots of potatoes and vegetables. There was always plenty of bread.

Sunday breakfast was a feast. There was time to cook eggs, bacon, sausages, tomatoes, sweetbreads, kidneys and anything else that could be heaped into the frying pan and onto a plate.

Sunday dinners were very special. It took the concerted efforts of mother, Jenny and Brenda to prepare them. In the affluent years, we had roast beef, or a shoulder or a leg of lamb, with several vegetables. In addition, there was pudding, fruit and balm cakes, dripping with treacle. We weren't fussy about foods that dripped. There was no table linen to be spoiled, only a newspaper. In very cold weather, mother prepared a great cauldron of broth, often with a neck of mutton. I used to watch it cooking on the gas ring, bubbling and popping like an active volcano. I was addicted to its smell; I put my head over the side and breathed it in. With a bit of luck, there was no telling what the brimming ladle might bring to the surface. Being the youngest, I got more than my share of the yellow, greasy, delicious dumplings that were fished up. They were so slippery that you had to be careful or they'd jump off your plate onto the sanded floor.

It was usually at this point that aunt Alice would come down the street and put her gaunt, hungry face around the door. Perhaps she'd smelled the broth. After mother and Alice had made friendly noises, auntie would leave with a brimming jug of hot broth. It always happened this way. I remember aunt Alice well because - except for grandmother Bridget - she was the only relative who regularly came in and out of our house.

The richer we were, the more we ate; when we could afford it, we gorged. On Pancake Tuesdays and Hot-Cross-Bun Good Fridays we children did nothing but eat. I suppose, in good times, before the bottom dropped out of Lancashire textiles in the early 1920's, that is where our money went. We even bought fancy nuts, which father cracked for us with his granite-like teeth. Nobody was accused of gluttony. Few bothered about their waistlines, not even my sisters. We didn't shy away from fatty meat. If we did, father quickly ate it. Food that the rest of us might not be able to stomach, he'd swallow at one go. All meals with us were favourite meals. There was an earthy naturalness about our eating. There was a vigour about it; "'unger's t'best sauce." We champed and chewed with relish. The smacking of lips, belching and sucking of fingers were all ignored, so was slurping hot tea out of a saucer. To eat and drink one's fill was to be blessed.

When there was plenty of good food on the table, those who talked were hushed. "Let food stop your gob," father used to say. We thanked nobody for our meals, except ourselves, silently. Mother was a good cook, but she didn't expect thanks. "Oh, go on, " she'd say if anybody offered praise. I'm told that the rich were brought up to leave a little on their plates. For us, that would have been sinful. We were taught to polish our plates, using a handful of bread as a wiper. We needed no encouragement. We didn't need a dog in our house to eat the scraps. We ate them, even if they'd been dropped on the floor.

It was while we had money to spare that Mr. Levy, the pawnbroker, who owned t' pop shop a few streets away, persuaded my father to take a large-horned phonograph off his hands. It was called a Victrola. "American - a chance in a lifetime," he'd told father. The phonograph was one of the first of its kind, and everyone was overwhelmed by it. Mother had her misgivings. "It's not like father to chuck money about, I don't know what's come over him."

The first I knew about the machine was when it startled me out of my sleep. I was spellbound by the strange, whining voice singing in the room below. As the voice continued to whine for most of that night and the next and the next, the spell did not last; especially as there was only one scratched cylinder with only two songs: 'Take a Pair of Sparkling Eyes' and 'Just a Little Love, a Little Kiss.' The woman who denied the singer 'Just a Little Love, a Little Kiss,' must have been pretty hard-hearted. Without a little love, the poor fellow died on father's phonograph in agony every night. Soon I knew the words by heart. In spite of Dan's contempt, I often sang myself to sleep with them. 'Just a Little Love, a Little Kiss, I'd give my whole life for this...'

My father took great pride in being the only owner of a phonograph in the street. Neighbours put it down to his having lived in America. It must have been unusual to own such a machine, because our house was invaded by strangely silent people all standing and listening. Others put their head round the door hoping to be asked in. There was even talk about buying a second cylinder, or a third. "A penny from each of you will go a long way," father told a crowded house.

There was no telling how many cylinders we might have bought if neighbours had come forward with their money. None did. They crowded into our cottage and listened to the new marvel, but declined to pay for it. The phonograph was put up for sale. Nobody bought it. At a considerable loss, it went back to t' pop shop.

We seemed to make a habit of taking things back to Mr. Levy. He was good-natured about it, and never held us to the last penny. Some years later, my parents obtained a used banjo from him as a Christmas present for me. I loved it. I played 'Little Brown Jug,' the only thing I could play, from morning till night until my family was quite ready to throw me and the banjo through the door. The last time I saw it was in Mr. Levy's window. I regretted losing it.

———◁◦▷———

The prosperity of the textile industry after 1918 knew no bounds. In the early part of 1920 mill profits were higher than they'd ever been. Speculators borrowed money to buy stocks and shares which they promptly sold at a profit. Shares sold at ten pounds one day could fetch fifteen the next. The more speculation, the higher the inflated values became. Without contributing a single constructive idea to the industry's welfare, the manufacturers and the money-spinners enriched themselves. There were accounts in the newspapers of manufacturers playing dice at five pounds a throw. For a stake of £1.500, three manufacturers ran a motorcar race from Blackpool to East Lancashire. While madness reigned, some manufacturers sold out at inflated prices and became wealthy country gentlemen. Others hung on, buying up businesses with borrowed money they could not possibly repay. Much of this money came from the banks.

No matter what gains the factory owners made, my family's wages stayed at rock bottom. Father got between one pound and thirty shillings a week.

When the crash came in March 1920, and the industry collapsed, the banks found themselves the owners of much of the Lancashire textile industry and refused to pour good money after bad. Neither the employers nor the workers recognized Lancashire's changed position. Both sides believed that they were facing temporary problems; that prosperity would return. The employers blamed the workers and the government; the workers blamed the employers. It didn't occur to anybody that Lancashire's world supremacy in cotton textile production had come to an end. The Lancashire cotton industry had got so used to the idea of industrial growth that it was mentally incapable of dealing with industrial decline. Uncertainty, misery and bankruptcy grew. Wishing, working and fighting each other changed nothing.

What the crash in March 1920 meant for the workers was not the loss of profits, but hunger. Out of hunger and social distress sprang the British Communist Party. Some months after the crash, father lost his job in the mill. It came as a great shock to him to be thrown out of work; a greater shock when mother and the rest of the family fell out of work too. Keeping a steady job in cottons in the following years became almost impossible. Life for us had always been uncertain; now it became doubly so.

Under the National Insurance Act of 1920, father received fifteen shillings a week for fifteen weeks; mother was paid five shillings for a shorter period. Children were expected to survive on one shilling per week - twelve pennies. But soon these small amounts were all gone. Any benefits father obtained from his trade union also ran out. Things became so bad that mother lost her cut-glass punch bowl to Mr. Levy at t' pop shop. She called it 'my American punch bowl.' Standing on a small table in the front room against the whitewashed wall to catch the eye of any visitor, its glass cups hanging on polished silver hooks, the bowl enchanted me. The sun didn't often come into our front room, but when it did, the punch bowl magically came alive with a hundred blue-tipped twinkling lights. Although I cannot remember it being used for its true purpose, mother washed and polished it endlessly. It must have been heart-breaking when she had to surrender it. She never said anything when it was carried from the house, but I knew that with its departure she had lost a symbol of better times. I think the punch bowl was a token of the superior life that she had once lived.

It was a demoralizing blow for father to find himself on the scrapheap, especially as he felt that everybody had a duty, as well as a right, to work. "We mun work," he'd say. I could tell from his sighing in bed at night that the lack of work was affecting his sleep. It gnawed at his heart. It was not like him to turn and toss so. Sometimes, on a moonlit night, I'd waken to see him sitting up in bed staring at the door, muttering to himself. He simply did not understand why the mills should be standing idle. The town offered to retrain him and other unemployed weavers as shorthand-typists, but he rejected the scheme as a farce, which it was. There was any number of shorthand-typists in town looking for work.

The bottom was reached when, in exchange for a few cigarettes, which he then bartered for food, father sat in the kitchen and stitched mail bags. He had joined the navy in the age of sail and knew how to use a needle. Even with a piece of leather across his palm, I could tell from watching him that stitching mailbags by hand was a very hard job. He also tried to survive by mending the clogs and shoes of our neighbours. He bought the cokers, soles, pegs, nails and blacking from Woolworths. His bench was a three-footed last which he held between his knees. Except that he was in his own kitchen, and hungrier, he was doing exactly what the prisoners were doing in the local jail. I never heard him say it, but everybody knew that it was at times like this that he most regretted having left America.

Father refused to accept the idea that there were no jobs available. His brand of despair was tinged with expectation. Sometimes, in the early hours, I would watch his shadowy figure slip out of the bedroom. He was a great believer in the early-bird business. For a few minutes he would shuffle about downstairs, taking a long drink from the tap. Then I'd hear him unlock and lift the latch of the front door as he went out in the dark to search for work. I heard the echo of his clogs as he hurried down the deserted street. Slowly, the night swallowed him up. By seven o'clock he would be standing with a crowd of others outside a mill in one of the surrounding towns, hoping to catch the foreman's eye. Perhaps this would be his lucky day. Many hours later, he would return footsore and hungry, chilled to the bone, a defeated look on his face. On his way home he'd pass equally exhausted workers going the other way, looking for the job that didn't exist. The next morning, wet or fine, he was off again on what mother called his 'fool's errand.'

His 'fool's errand' ended one morning in a dramatic way. He had gone off as usual into the dark night looking for work. We all thought he'd struck it lucky when he didn't return at the usual time. But we were wrong. He came back later that morning looking an awful sight. He'd got himself into a desperate fight with some pickets outside a mill at Padiham where there was a strike. They had taken him for a 'knobstick' (strike breaker), and had almost killed him. Now that was ironic because the only thing he ever belonged to was a trade union. They'd beaten him so hard that he could hardly walk. Thank goodness they didn't break his arms, which sometimes happened. Somebody must have brought him back to town and dropped him off in our street.

He arrived home his hair stiff and matted with dried blood. Jenny was horrified at the sight. She ran upstairs. "He was still alive when he got home," mother said, "but only just." His breath was shallow and laboured; his ribs were going in and out like bellows. His face was the size of a large pumpkin; he was black and blue all over where they'd kicked him with their clogs; some of his wounds were gaping. On entering the house, he dripped blood all through the 'best room.' Brenda had to clean it up. Mother wanted him to go to the hospital or to Dr. Grieves, but he refused. So mother and Brenda did what they could for him with iodine and bandages. He didn't complain when they dabbed his open wounds. It took him weeks to recover. After that, instead of going out on a 'fool's errand,' he sat by the fire, pale and glowering. I kept well out of his way. Because the wounds should have been stitched, some scars stayed with him for the rest of his days.

Unlike mother, father seemed oblivious of the famine that now stared us in the face. Tight-mouthed, he kept his thoughts to himself and went on doggedly. If anybody asked him in the street how he was, his reply was always the same, "I'm nicely!" It was a lie, of course, but it would have shamed him to tell the truth. He never seemed to realize that his family was getting hungrier and hungrier. It was something that one was not supposed to notice. There was work and there was no work. If you worked you ate. If there was no work you went hungry. You didn't beg and you didn't steal; the unwritten code excluded both. You didn't complain, whine or whimper; it was a matter of pride. As for the rich, by his lights, it was their job to leave the poor alone. Charity from 'them' would have hurt.

Fortunately for us, it was an attitude that mother didn't share. Although she had been married to father for many years, she had a different code. Come what may, she was not going to see her children starve. Father's unemployment benefits having expired, she kept at him to apply for public relief. He refused. There was a struggle between them and a number of 'scenes.' "Very well," said mother, putting on her shawl and clogs, "I'll take thi place in t' bread queue and shame thee." Father went. He was angry at being bested. By the time he got through the door, he was black-faced.

The rest of us sat or stood around the bare table and waited. We didn't have energy for anything else. We were insensitive to anything except food. Our bellies pained for it. Jenny took it hard. Robbed of all spirit, she sat there listless.

Mother had no energy either, but she forced herself to talk about the wonderful meal that father had gone for, and how delicious it would be. She began by pretending to serve a thick, nourishing broth with many dumplings. "Sit up," she said, "and eat it while it's hot." She followed this with cutlets of veal - "Something special. For once I didn't get the cheapest." She served vegetables and roasted potatoes soaked in sizzling fat by the potful. She was so convincing the way she heaped our plates and pressed us to have seconds. She also dreamed up side dishes of hard boiled eggs, herrings, sausages and pig's trotters. Finally, she served cheese, fruit, nuts and dates. "If you eat slowly, you'll make room." My, how she made our mouths water!

Much later father returned, carrying a bulky Tate & Lyle sugar sack under his arm. He had the air of a thief. He handed the bundle to mother and left the house. She could make him bring the stuff, but she couldn't make him eat it. "Ah won't touch it," he said defiantly. How his body carried on without food, none of us knew. Mother worried about him.

With the rest of us watching, mother shook the contents of the sack onto the table. There were two large prison-made loaves of bread that looked as if they'd been dragged through the mud. There were several tins of corned beef, one of which had its side bashed in, a packet of tea, a pound of sugar, a can of condensed milk, some mouldy cheese, a strip of fatty bacon, some margarine that had strands of felt mixed with it, some Lyle's Syrup, a bottle of H.P. sauce and some salt.

We forgot the feast mother had promised and polished off the lot on the spot. It at least rid us of our aching hollows. The next several days we queued up at the churches and the soup kitchens in the streets. After that father was sent back for more public relief and still more. The items never varied, they were horrid, but they kept us alive. Just.

Perhaps it was the shame of going for 'charity bread' that made father redouble his efforts to find work. One morning, he came rushing into the house to tell us that he'd been made a town labourer and to ask for my help.

"Ah 've bin told t' wash Victoria," he announced.

"T' queen?" my mother asked in a startled voice.

"Go on with you, girl. No, t' statue on t' Parade."

Father and I left the house for the center of town. He led the way carrying a long ladder. I followed with an empty bucket, brushes and rags.

"'Ello! Wert'a goin' wit ladder?" neighbours shouted as we went by.

"T' wash t' queen."

This response produced a surprised look on their faces. "By gaw! They're goin' t' wash t' queen," they shouted to each other.

Father got tired of satisfying people's curiosity and left it to me. I didn't tire. I loved the questions. It made me feel important. To every "Wert'a goin'?" I proudly bawled back: "T' wash t' queen!" and marched on, head high.

When we arrived beneath the statue we could understand why it needed a wash. Most of the head and dour face were covered with bird droppings. The marble crown, scepter and orb were all filthy. Unveiled in September 1905, in commemoration of Queen Victoria, who had died in 1901, this was the first good scrubbing the statue would have.

Pestered by a group of unemployed workers, who shouted advice from the foot of the ladder: "Tha're a proper gobbin, tha're. Tha missing great patches of shit." It took father and me the whole day to make an impression on the dirt. We started from the head and worked down. First we had to scrape off the muck. Then father took a hedgehog brush to the queen and scrubbed. While I carried endless buckets of water up the ladder from a nearby faucet, he hung onto Victoria's head, back, front and sides, and continued to scrape, rub and scrub as if his life depended on it. Yet I knew he hated it. Like his mother Selma, who lived in Fall River, he disliked royalty.

As night came, we left Victoria glowing clean. Father still looked dour; he didn't say a word in returning the ladder and going home. It's said in the family that he never walked past that statue again. He preferred to go out of his way round the cathedral rather than relive his moment of shame. I have a suspicion that the scrubbing of Victoria was for him the blackest day of the Great Depression.

Alas, there was a limit to the number of statues that needed scrubbing, and father was soon out of work again. So were the rest of the family.

———◇———

During these lean times, when I was five and my brother Dan was nine, he confided to me that he was not going hungry any more. We were going to steal food together. Tom Tat's grocery shop around the corner was bursting with food. Dan's plan was simple. He told me about it in whispers when we were in bed one night. On the first really dark night he'd push me through the window above Tom Tat's shop door. The window was always left slightly ajar. I was to jump down inside the shop and open the door, so that we could help ourselves. "What could be easier?"

I was horrified at the thought. Stealing with us was associated with going to jail. Caught stealing, you were invariably sent down. Visions of my going to jail passed before my eyes. I lay there in the dark, breathless.

"But that's stealing," I said.

"It's not. It's the toffs that steal from us. This is taking what's ours."

"Tom Tat isn't a toff; he's like us."

"Ye're a coward," Dan hissed. "Ye're a yellow belly. If ye don't join me I'll eat yer liver. If ye tell anyone, I'll drown thee in t' canal." He got quite worked up about his proposed raid on Tom Tat's and then fell asleep.

I was too terrified to sleep. Over and over, I asked myself what I should do? Should I tell Brenda? If I did, I might finish up in the canal. Even when I dozed, I woke up sweating. In my fevered imagination, I was already in jail. In my dream I didn't seem to have a choice between the jail and the canal.

Dan became obsessed with the idea of robbing Tom Tat's. "What's wrang with us eating until we bust?" He kept at me for about a week, his hissing and his threats getting worse all the time. He even took me round the corner to study the fly-spotted window. It was open a crack. "Ye don't have te steal if ye don't want to, but I can't get in unless ye help me open the door. Ye're small enough to be hoisted up there. Only ye can get through the crack." He kept at me so hard that I began to wish that the deed was done and finished with.

The next Sunday night was pitch dark. Our parents were out. Only my sister Jenny and her boyfriend, Gordon Weall, were in the house.

"Come on!" ordered Dan, making for the door.

I was on the point of making a desperate, last-minute appeal to Jenny and Gordon; instead I slunk after my brother into the dark night.

Two minutes later we were in the shop doorway. Dan took a look up and down the empty street. All was quiet at the Tat's house next to the shop.

"Quick!" Dan ordered, offering me his back. Although I was choking with fear, I knew what to do; we'd practiced it a dozen times. I also knew from staring at them in the daytime where the lock and the two bolts were at the other side of the door. I'd made up my mind that once I'd opened the door, I'd grab my clogs and run.

I put my stockinged feet on his shoulders; he hoisted me up to the window. Reaching up, I silently pushed the window inward. Still resting on Dan's shoulders, I gingerly began to get my head and shoulders through the opening. My weight now rested on the sill. All that remained was for me to draw back the top bolt, wriggle through the open window, and drop to the floor. I could smell cheese, but couldn't see it.

"Haste!" Dan whispered impatiently. "What are yer making?"

"I'm stuck!"

"Stuck?"

With my head and shoulders over one side of the door frame and my legs down the other, I could neither go forward nor backward. Somehow my jersey and gray flannel shirt had become twisted into a hard knot. I was held in a vice. The more I struggled, the more firmly I was held. I broke into a sweat.

"Get through!" Dan hissed.

"I can't, I'm wedged."

"You've got to." He reached up and pushed the soles of my feet as hard as he could.

"I can't," I repeated, my head swimming. "Pull me back. I'm choking." My body trembled; beads of sweat blinded me.

After hesitating, Dan jumped up and hung onto my feet. The pain was awful. I thought he was going to pull my legs out of joint.

"Ouch, stop it!" Dan pulled harder. My body didn't budge.

"Ouch! Ouch!" I sobbed.

"Shut yer gob!" Moments later, I heard his clogs echoing down the street. He had deserted me.

Turning and twisting, I made one last panic-driven effort to break free. I expected Tom Tat to come shouting out of his house at any moment.

The next thing I knew, Gordon was standing on a small stool. He had me by the calves.

"Shush, Billy," he whispered as he undid the knot in my clothing and gently eased me free. Once he had me out of the window, the three of us ran home, double-quick.

That night I lay in bed quaking. I swore I'd never do anything for my brother again. While Gordon and Jenny gave Dan a piece of their mind, they said nothing to father for I heard no more of it. I wonder what the Tat's said when they found their window wide open the next morning. It didn't stay ajar anymore.

———◦———

It was about this time, with things as bad as they could be, and with everybody in the house out of work, that mother and

I - miracle of miracles - took the train to Blackpool, twenty-five miles away. I was baffled; I couldn't believe my luck. It was summer, the weather was warm.

I knew about Blackpool as soon as I could stand. It was a pleasure resort on the Lancashire coast. Its clean, sharp air, and its endless sands were famous. Some of the first greeting cards I ever saw came from there. Against the smoke-filled air of our town, the cards glittered with sun and colour. We had pictures of Blackpool Tower and the Big Wheel on the mantelpiece in our front room. The identical pictures were in everybody's cottage. Everybody who went to Blackpool came back chewing 'Blackpool Rock.' The very mention of Blackpool stirred the imagination of any child in Blackburn.

I don't know if father or grandmother Bridget knew what was going on. All I know is that we were on our way to Blackpool. In the train I couldn't contain myself, I hopped and jumped about with excitement. Until then I'd never seen the sea. I stuck my head out of the window most of the way to catch the first glimpse of Blackpool Tower soaring above the flat landscape. Mother was every bit as excited. I thought we might have been going to relatives, especially as we had no money - mother said we were going to friends - but I never saw relatives or friends. We did see people from Blackburn, but mother avoided them.

Mother and I shared a single bed which stood in a room the size of a cupboard on a landing in a lodging house. The place stank of cabbages and haddock. But it was, after all, Blackpool. The only person mother introduced me to was a big-breasted, fish-eyed woman who seemed to own the place. Her face was covered with paint. She wore such a tall, glossy black wig, that I kept my eye on it hoping it would fall off. She also wore a lot of artificial jewelry that hung down to her waist, and clinked as she moved about. Her earrings were long enough and large enough to swing like the pendulum of a clock. She held my hands and breathed pickled onions all over me. She grunted, but I don't think she ever spoke to me.

For the first few hours mother ran me off my feet. I was overwhelmed by the tower. It gave me a crick in the neck to stare at it, hundreds and hundreds of feet above our heads. We went to the top and looked down on the ant-like people scurrying about in the streets. Before us lay a vast expanse of sand, sea and sky, all of which ended in a far haze. I'd never seen such unending space. I'd heard about the sea - here it was stretching before me. The ships in the distance were the first I'd ever seen.

I don't know whether it was the excitement of riding in an elevator for the first time, or the height of the tower, or the food we'd eaten in the street below, or my fear that anything as tall as the tower must surely fall down - whatever the cause, I felt ill. We sat down until my dizzy turn passed.

After I recovered, we raced together across the sand, at first in our bare feet and then on donkeys. Mother's donkey captured her spirit and went off at full speed careening toward the sea. My donkey wouldn't budge. The more I shouted at it, the longer it stayed and brayed and showed its teeth. By the time I got it to move, mother was on her way back, her bonny hair streaming in the wind. She was easily the winner. And so we went on, going from one thing to another until we returned to our lodgings exhausted.

The moment we got back, I began to feel uneasy. I didn't know why; I just knew that something was not right. It began when mother asked me to wait for her on the bench in front of the house. She had to meet someone inside 'on business.' I was told to stay there until she reappeared. So I sat there alone, in the sun, swinging my legs, and wondering what it could be that kept her so long. I'd no idea whether something good or bad was happening, and it worried me. When she came out, I wondered if I should ask.

I sat there for part of the next day and the next. I became weary of sitting alone on that horrid bench. I'd never been so lonely. I was puzzled at the men who came out of the house with mother. They were strangers. They all wore suits and polished shoes. They weren't weavers, that's for sure. Some were furtive, others hearty. "Tha're a grand lad," they said giving me a tanner (6p) or a dodger (3p), which was a lot of money. I was at a loss to know why dodgers and tanners were being showered upon me. In Blackburn we didn't have any money. What money we had, we knew not to waste. At Blackpool everybody was chucking it about.

Mother must have been puzzled too, because after a couple of days she woke up at night and cried her eyes out, hiding her face in a towel. "Oh Billy," she sobbed, "Oh Billy." She was in real pain. I didn't know what to do. It frightened me. By then I'd come to notice strange smells in the room, and there were half-burned cigarette ends on the floor.

The next morning everything was fine again. The crying was forgotten. Once away from the lodging house, mother's natural happiness returned. She went from being sad, to being intensely happy. She skipped about, made fun, and laughed. She took me everywhere. We visited the circus, the aquarium and the fairground. We bought knick-knacks, and listened to the Punch and Judy show and the minstrels on the pier singing: 'Oh, I do like to be beside the seaside, Oh, I do like to be beside the sea...' We listened to the hoarse bawling of the barkers selling boat rides, and went in a boat as far as Morecombe Bay. Having done everything, we sat on top of a tram and rode up and down the sea front, mother's hair blowing in the wind.

We seemed to eat whenever the mood took us. We didn't eat with the fish-eyed woman with the clinking jewelry. For our food we went from street cart to street cart, stuffing ourselves. There's nothing we didn't try. We had blackpuddings and Irish roasted potatoes, too hot to hold. We also had apples and oranges, Eccles cakes and lots of cups of tea. Mother fed such quantities of food into me that I could hardly stir. How wonderful it was to be rich!

We ate one meal in the Winter Gardens. Mother was excited about it, but I was nervous. Until I grew up, it was the only meal I ever shared with her in a restaurant. There was a great 'to do' before we got there. We had to get into better clothes, and wear shoes - all of which we got from a pop shop. I had to have my hair slicked down. When we were all ready, we entered this big restaurant. I've no idea what we ate. I do remember a band playing. There were many toffs there, crowds of them wearing fancy dresses and suits. I was nervous. It was a new experience for me to see so many people dressed up with nothing to do except gorge and laugh. I'd never known mother to dress so well or to be so relaxed. Her face and hair shone. She didn't talk much; she seemed to be in a dream. She only woke up when the bill came, and the waiter pressed her for a tip. When we came out we stood and watched the coloured fairy lights flicking on and off. What an exciting, colourful world it was! Why wasn't Blackburn like this?

If only we could have been free of that dreadful lodging house, mother and I would have stayed at Blackpool for ever. Instead, after an unforgettable week, we were back in the train headed for home. How drab Blackburn looked when we arrived. One could smell the poverty and the troubled times. Being summer, the smells were worse.

———◆———

Things got so bad in the early 1920s that the number of hungry-eyed tramps coming through our street grew. Dressed in rags, black with sweat, feet in the gutter, fidgeting and scratching, they'd wait until mother or other kind souls gave them butties (bread) and tea. Smells were common among the poor, but the tramps had what we called a 'ripe' smell; they reeked.

Thirst and hunger satisfied, they'd throw their string-tied packages over their shoulder and move off with the same steady slouch with which they'd come. I often wondered what their odd-shaped newspaper-wrapped packages contained.

As times got worse, the poor began to steal from the poor - something unheard of. I have reason to know. One evening as the light was fading, Brenda and I were playing with a new ball on the kitchen floor. The ball rolled into the front room where it came to rest behind a rocking chair in a corner. I ran after it, bent down, and put my hand round the back of the chair. To my horror, my fingers touched somebody's ankle; in a daze, I felt a trouser leg. Something moved. Fearful, I put my head round the chair and looked into the face of a pockmarked scarecrow of a man crouched there. A long, blue scar ran down one side of his face. His eyes and mouth had a hungry look. He smelled abominably. I jumped back as if I'd been bitten. With an oath, the man flung me aside and ran from the house into the street. Someone ran after him, but he'd gone. We never saw him again. I was left trembling and white. As we had nothing worth stealing, he must have been looking for bread, or was hoping to break into and take the pennies from our gas meter.

Somehow my family kept on weathering the storm. Aunt Alice didn't. She had got poorer, older and more ragged. Nobody gave her help. A spinster, there was no one upon whom she could make a claim. Her mother was too poor. People looked the other way, their pity for her unstirred. Either to take her mind off her troubles, or to pick up a bit of extra food, she'd started going to funerals. She never missed a good funeral and was always willing to talk about them. She'd got into the habit of sitting in the cemetery. She said she found peace there. The day came when she couldn't pay her rent. Having been thrown out of her cottage, she turned up with a bundle under her arm.

I knew that I ought to feel sorry for aunt Alice. She was going blind.

Father didn't. He wouldn't hear of her moving in with us. "We've got all t' mouths we can feed," he said. "What's wrong with your brothers helping? Eric's got the money and the space. It's scandalous his turning you away."

"He didn't," said aunt Alice, "Pearl did."

"If his wife won't have you, then Eric should help with money."

"Well, I'll tell you this," aunt Alice wept, "I thowt one of you would take me in. I didn't think you'd put me in t' work'ouse. You've got 'earts of stone, that's what."

I was brought up to believe that the workhouse was a prison for the poor.

Mother cried when Alice left.

———◄○►———

Deep poverty introduced a degree of fear in the house. Mother worried where the next meal was coming from. We all worried about it. We went to bed hungry and slept badly.

I woke from a troubled sleep early one morning to see father going downstairs. For some reason, I crept after him. My brother and my sisters were still asleep. By the time I reached the bottom step, father's dishevelled figure was crouched before the kitchen fire. There was a tweedy smell of peat. Although the fire had been banked up all night, the house was bitterly cold. As I drew my flannel shirt closer to my body, my feet froze on the sanded floor.

Father was holding something which he was wiping with a towel. It looked like a white doll; but the doll had blood on it. Father's shadowy figure danced on the kitchen wall. "Cum now, cum now," he muttered.

I knew that something was wrong. Mother had been crying in the night. Father had been downstairs several times. I had no idea that a life and death struggle had been going on; even less where the baby had come from. I had by now made up my mind that it was a baby not a doll that father was holding. I found it hard to believe that the baby had come out of the bedroom. I'd been told that storks brought them. Jenny had said they were found under flowers; Brenda believed they arrived in Dr. Grieves' bag. While I watched, I heard Dougdale's factory hooter at the end of the street emit a piercing whistle. I also heard t' knocker-up man coming down the row.

"Tell t' knocker-up we're awake," father ordered. He had not failed to see me standing in the shadows.

"Yes, Dadda." I slipped on my clogs, which were kept at the foot of the stairs, and ran to the street door. Having turned the key, I opened the door long enough to yell into the wind: "We're up." Mr. Smalley waved his rod and turned away.

By the time I got back to the kitchen, the gas lamp had been lit. It hissed reproachfully. The pot dogs on the mantle reflected its glow. A little wasted thing with a monkey's face lay on one of the rocking chairs. Father was standing with his back to the fire, looking at it dejectedly. "He's a goner," he murmured. I knew that a 'goner' meant that the baby was dead. Confused, a cold shiver running down my back, I crept away.

Father didn't go to the mill that day. Nor did mother; she stayed in bed. During the morning Dr. Grieves drove up with his horse and gig, followed by his brown and white spaniel, Joy.

That afternoon, the dead baby with the monkey's face was placed into a plain box of undressed pine. Until evening the coffin stood on top of the folded sewing machine under the front window. The paper blind had been pulled down. The aspidistra that usually stood there had been placed on the floor. I tried to look into the box, but the lid was nailed down.

That evening, after the flood of homeward-bound workers had swept past the house, grandmother Bridget lifted the latch and came in. Mrs. Morgan also arrived. There was loud whispering with mother upstairs. Mrs. Fothergill, a woman dressed in black who cared for the chapel down the street, kept on at father about sprinklin'. "Did you sprinkle him?" she kept asking. "Are you sure? You know what happens to an unsprinkled soul, Will." I'm sure that sprinklin' never entered my father's head. He didn't sprinkle my brother while I was there.

The glances and the whisperings that went on made me think that the grown-ups were hiding something. They seemed furtive. No one could tell me what had happened to my brother except that he'd 'died.' If he'd had an accident there must surely be someone in the house who could stick him together again, as I did with my toy soldiers. Instead, everybody sat there looking glum and did nothing to help.

Next morning father left with the coffin under his arm. I was desolated that my brother should have been carried off like that. Where was he being taken?

"Straight to heaven," mother assured me.

"You'll see him again in the hereafter," Jenny added.

"But where is heaven and the hereafter?" And if we were going to see him again, why was he put in a box and carried off? How could he find heaven in a little nailed coffin, without a name, without food, without flowers and a funeral, and all alone? It took me years to realize that, without death benefit insurance, a 'proper burial' for him was beyond our means.

His death left me afraid. Death was evidently something that neither Dr. Grieves nor anyone else could fix. It was permanent as nothing else in my life had been before. It was the first time that the truth struck home. It was days before I stopped worrying about my brother. It was just as well that he was never mentioned again.

When I was a little older, I learned that a 'proper burial' was something that the workers took seriously. They knew what was proper and improper. They had a horror of being cast into a pauper's grave. It meant humiliation and disgrace. It was all very well to tell them that their spirit would enter heaven through the pearly gates; they still wanted to know what was going to happen to their bones. That is why most of them paid a penny a week death dues so that the 'proper' thing would be done when they died. We paid our pennies to a squirrel-like fellow whom we called t' bump man, but who liked to be called by his full name: Mr. Charlie Hetherington.

The wonder is that the penny death dues were enough to keep Mr. Hetherington in clogs. Collecting pennies for the death club, however, was only one of Mr. Hetherington's occupations. His passion was to study the bumps on people's heads. "Give me your head for a minute or two," he would say, "and a penny, and I'll tell you all that you need to know about yourself." Mr. Hetherington's 'reading' of bumps was more reliable than fortune telling, or tossing the cups, or cutting the cards. People said so.

One night father asked Mr. Hetherington to look at our heads. Charlie didn't need persuading. He began with father. He then turned to mother, my sisters, Jenny and Brenda and my brother Dan. From the look on his face, I could tell that - as far as bumps go - my family were an uninteresting lot. Their mental faculties had not produced any unusual changes on their skulls. "As a family, I'm afraid you're a bumpless lot," he said to father. He expected even less of me. Yet the moment his fingers touched my head he became excited. "Oh, look at this." He ran his fingers through my long, fair hair, "I say, have you ever seen anything like it?" he went on triumphantly.

The whole family crowded around. By the light of the hissing gas lamp they scrutinized my scalp. They were mesmerized by what they saw and felt. "Well," said father, following Charlie's fingers with his own, "now I see what it's all about; the bumps are as plain as can be." The family was greatly impressed when Mr. Hetherington announced that with bumps like that I must surely become Prime Minister of England.

"Mm...mm...," said mother, "if he'd been born in Fall River he could have become President of the United States."

———◆◇▶———

The news of Lancashire's hard times in the early 1920's must have reached my grandmother Selma in Fall River, Massachusetts, for she periodically inquired if her grandchildren, Jenny, Brenda, Dan and I, were alive and well. Since leaving America in 1914, there had been the odd exchange of news between Blackburn and Fall River, but I don't think grandmother Selma trusted father's letters.

One day a letter arrived saying that two of her sons were about to visit Blackburn. My American uncles, my father's brothers had emigrated to America with him in 1906. I took the letter from the postman, and it caused quite a stir in the house. My parents went into a frenzy of preparations. Crockery, cutlery, chairs and food were borrowed from relatives and friends. There was such a bustle. Mother planned to serve ham and tongue at the same meal, something unheard of except at a wedding. At the last minute father decided to impress his brothers by serving a two shilling bottle of 'Barrel Bottom' wine - for us a scandalous waste of money. He sent me scurrying through the streets to the vintner, a florin clasped in my hand. The vintner handed me the bottle in a brown paper bag. "Put it under your jacket, lad." The licensing laws were ignored. Anyway, the wine didn't impress the Americans.

Oh, what a stir the arrival of my uncles caused! Having taken one of the few taxis in town, they arrived in Griffin Street red-faced and hearty. They were full of fun and energy. They were much too florid and much too fat to be textile workers. I don't know to which class they belonged, but they weren't working class; later I discovered that Americans didn't belong to any class. They wore strange straw hats and even stranger clothing. They had shirts with attached collars and loud ties, tie-pins and highly polished shoes.

We listened wide-eyed to their talk about America as we ate. "Richest country in the world," they said. I didn't know we were as poor as we were until they started making comparisons.

"You've got to come to America," they repeated. They told me that in Massachusetts they had snow right up to the roof! Jenny and I loved it when they said things like 'OK' and 'Yeah.' Later on my street gang used these words. I didn't know that the Yankees had single-handedly won the Great War until my uncles told me so. I always thought father had done that.

The meal was hardly finished when our house was flooded with people who took it for granted that my uncles knew every member of their families who had migrated to Fall River during the past generation.

On the point of their departure, my uncles pressed into my eager palm a shiny half-crown, enough to keep me in affluence for months. Before I could scuttle away with my fortune, father reached down.

"Nay, nay, Harold" he protested; as he extracted the coin from my unwilling fingers, "tha mustn't chuck tha money at 'im like that. Tha'll be spoiling 'im. Tha can see, he wants for nothing. Tha must be reet out of tha mind, lad." Whereupon, to my profound grief, he handed back the coin.

I knew that there wasn't a word of truth in what father was saying, and the loss of the coin hurt me deeply.

Before climbing into the taxi, my uncles warmly clasped my parents' hands. "You must come back again, Will. Family's roots are at the other side now."

"That's kindly, that's real kindly of thee. I can't tell thee how much Maggie and I appreciate it. Tell mother that we've just got one or two little things to arrange and then we'll be reet over. Tha'll see!" I never did work out what the little things were that he had to arrange, which he never did.

With the whole of Griffin Street gawking, my uncles shook hands all round, patted us children on the head, and tucked us under the chin. They then jumped into the rattling taxi and honked the horn repeatedly, which brought more neighbours running. The taxi swayed down the street followed by a cloud of blue smoke. After that the family and the neighbours sat around like pricked balloons. Everything in Griffin Street was ordinary again.

My parents didn't speak of it, but I wondered if the coming of my rich uncles had not given them pause for thought. After all, if father had remained a tackler in Fall River, instead of returning to Blackburn in 1914, he too could have visited his relatives in England in a straw hat, a fine suit, a loud tie, polished shoes, and a smoke-wrapped taxi.

I think the idea of returning to Fall River gradually fell out of father's reckoning. He must have been poor on coming home from the war. Moreover, the longer he delayed returning to America, the less chance he had. Beset by the severe competition of the newly-established South Carolina cotton mills, Fall River was experiencing the same decline as Blackburn and the other cotton towns in Lancashire had done earlier. Letters from his brothers in Fall River told him so. Naturally, Fall River, like Blackburn, thought the industry was suffering a temporary setback. In addition, America introduced its first generally restrictive immigration act. Emigrating to America was no longer a matter of just catching a ship.

There were other visitors from America, but I came to resent them. They left my parents more in debt than ever. Of course, our American relatives offered to pay for everything, but father wouldn't hear of it. He always put up the same humbug of 'nobody wanting for nothing.' Worse, every visit was followed by the arrival from grandmother Selma of a great parcel of children's summer clothing. Never money, never food, just clothes - clothes that were too thin for our summers. With their coloured stripes, the shirts contrasted sharply with everybody else's drab gray. Dan and I hated them. They shamed us when we wore them to school or in the streets. Other children envied us for having such rich American uncles, but they went into fits of laughter at the sight of the American shirts and dresses. Because of the stripes, the Woodruff children came to be known as the 'Zebra Kids.' Even when my uncles stopped coming to Blackburn, grandmother Selma continued to send the clothing. The ordeal went on for years. It got worse as the stripes got larger. Strangely enough the sizes never changed. Jenny, Brenda and Dan eagerly grew out of them. As I was the smallest member of the family, I regret to say that there was always something that would fit me.

Chapter IV

Family Tree

The visits of my American uncles, and the remarks my parents made about the years they'd spent in the United States, aroused in me a desire to know more about my origins. Over the years, mother tried to answer my questions. Because that kind of thing interested her, she'd made it her business to get it all in her head. Father wasn't half as good. Family history didn't interest him - he focused on the present, not the past. Sometimes mother answered my questions about family history in snatches, sometimes at great length. Bit by bit I pieced it together.

The Woodruff story began long before I was born. It began in the early part of the nineteenth century with my great-great-grandfather George Woodruff, which is as far back as the Woodruff family tree goes. He had had the misfortune to be seized by the army while he was drunk. He fought and died for Britain in Russia in 1856. Mother knew it was 1856 because there was a medal in the family with the date of great-great-grandfather George's death on it. His son Arne was my great-grandfather on father's side. He was born in the late 1840's in Westmorland.

By the time I was born, Arne had become a family legend. Mother often talked about him. She didn't tell his story as if it was dead and done with, but as something that was happening before our very eyes.

Arne had a hard beginning, mother began one day. He not only lost his father, he went and lost his mother too. She sickened and died after the death of her husband in Russia. After that Arne stood alone. Nobody came forward to look after him. As an orphan, he fell into the hands of the parish guardians who sold him to a cotton mill owner high on the moors. Fellow called Crankfit. They say he had a stone where his heart should have been.

Arne was taken by the village beadle to the village green to await the local carrier, Blethley, who would take him to Crankfit's. His few possessions were tied in a large red handkerchief lying at his feet. He wore a cap - from which tufts of straw-coloured hair protruded - and a long dark smock and clogs.

Presently, Blethley came along sitting on his wagon. He was a stocky figure with a clay pipe sticking out from his beard. Arne watched Lucy the bay horse leisurely pull the cart. The cart creaked to a halt.

Removing his pipe, Blethley shouted down, "You Arne, for Crankfit's?"

"That's him," the beadle answered.

"Well then, get up boy," the carter gruffed. "We can't afford to have Lucy standing here all day."

With the beadle pushing and the carter pulling, Arne was hoisted up onto the box next to Blethley behind the horse's tail. On the point of tears, he sat there speechless, clutching his possessions on his knees.

Before the child knew what was happening, the cart with its bundles and packages had rattled around the village maypole, passed the churchyard where his mother now lay, crossed the stream where the salmon were jumping and the ravens were cawing, and left the village behind. Only then did the boy break down and cry. Blethley pulled on his pipe and studied the back of his horse's head.

The man and the boy travelled together for most of that day, passing from green meadow through plowland and pasture to fell. Prompted by a grunt from the carrier, Lucy trundled from one place to the next. In time, Blethley warmed to the child, and told him about the great world beyond the moors. It seemed that Mr. James Blethley had been everywhere.

"Have you ever been to Russia?" Arne asked.

"Russia? Now let's see," the carter answered rubbing the side of his nose.

"That's where my father fought and died in a war," the child went on, while fishing around in his bundle to show the carter a medal.

"Oh, that Russia," Blethley said, turning the medal over in his hand. "Bless me, if you had told me it was that Russia that you was talking about... why..." the carter went on at great length about Russia, telling the wide-eyed boy exactly where his father had been killed. Blethley said he'd fought in the very same battle, on the very same day. And what a battle it had been! Oh, the guns, and the drums, and the flags, and the cries, and the shouts, and the smoke... "'Mazin'," the carter ended.

"Do you have such a medal, Mr. Blethley?"

"Why, of course, but it isn't the sort of thing you carries around."

The hedgerows and fences along which they passed gave way to dry-stone walls that climbed endlessly across the shrouded fells. Here and there graystone cottages straggled unevenly up a valley. Wild smoke blew from their chimneys. Crying curlews and peewits criss-crossed the wagon's trail. The trees gradually became thinner and sparse, the track steeper and stony, the wind stronger and fresher. In the distance a graystone peak stood out like a sentinel. Arne looked down the fells to see specks scattered like white stones which he knew were sheep. In the valley bottom a winding river glinted in the sun. Sometime during the day they stopped at a small inn where Blethley drank a glass of ale and gave Lucy a nose-bag of oats. Arne had some bread and cheese.

When they came out a whole string of pack horses were tied against the inn wall. They were loaded with textile stuff to be worked up by the handloom weavers whose cottages were farther down the slope.

The journey renewed, Blethley talked about a number of things. Yes, he had seen the queen. Yes, he had seen the new-fangled railways in whose coaches people caught their death of cold. Yes, he knew all about the dreadful accident that had occurred when one steam-driven train had crashed into another. "Railways will never be as good as a horse and cart," he confided to the boy. "God never intended railways. You are God-fearin'?" the carrier questioned Arne sharply.

"Oh, yes, Mr. Blethley." His mother had reared him to be God-fearing. She used to say everything was God's will.

"Do you know the town of Blackburn? It's where my aunt Beth lives."

"Yes, I know it. It's full of steam-driven cotton factories with tall chimneys spewing foul smoke. They say this here new-fangled steam business is going to change a lot of things, but I have my doubts. The main thing is that cotton pays well. All the money-hungry people of northern England are making their way to Blackburn. God never intended factories. Factories and steam-driven power looms take the work away from the cottage weavers. Fellows lost their lives for burning factories down. In 1812 at West-Houghton they hung three men and a boy of fourteen for doin' it. Lad went to the gallows calling for his mother."

Arne shuddered. "Couldn't she save him?"

"Not likely. Come to think of it, not long after, in the 1820's I think it was, there was a dreadful rampage at Blackburn itself. Thousands of workers armed with pikes, hammers and crowbars smashed every power loom they could find. By nightfall there wasn't one left."

"Were there more hangings?"

"Oh my word, yes. Others were sent to Van Dieman's Land."

"Where is that?"

"I can't actually say. All I know is that it's a long way from here and you don't come back." There was a pause. "Factories and power looms were soon back in Blackburn," the carter concluded. "'Mazin'."

The carter knew so much about everything that Arne resolved to tell everyone he met that he'd had the uncommon luck to have travelled with the world-famous Mr. James Blethley.

That afternoon they met a cartload of orphans being delivered to another mill on the fells. There was a wild-eyed idiot among them who stuck his tongue out as he went by.

"Did you ever carry such?" the boy asked.

"The pity I did," the man replied. "They were so young - one was five, the others eight to eleven - and so tired; when I got them to the mill I couldn't waken them. They'd been on the road for days. God never intended that either."

"Why do children have to work in factories, Mr. Blethley?"

"They're cheap and nimble, there's plenty of them, and they don't have anyone to protect them. That's why. God never intended it, I'll swear." Blethley cleared his throat and spat out of the cart.

They heard the creaking of Crankfit's waterwheel long before they got there.

"No steam here," said Blethley.

They topped a ridge to see a mill spread out before them. The main building was solidly built in stone and slate. Oblong, it had three levels. Its narrow windows looked out across a pond. Nearby were two other buildings, both of them smaller. The windows of one of the buildings were barred. Beyond and around the mill, as far as the eye could see, stretched the lonely, windswept moors. A blue haze rested on the distant hills. There was not a tree in sight.

"Watch your step with Crankfit," Blethley warned as they approached the building, "whatever you say, he's bound to 'av' a fit."

Crankfit was at the gate to meet them. He was dressed in a long black coat and a stove pipe hat. Except for the sharpest eyes, his face was lost in a thicket of beard and hair.

"You're late," he barked at the boy as Arne jumped down from the cart and stood before him.

Remembering Blethley's warning, Arne kept a still tongue.

"Is this all there is of him?" Crankfit walked around the child, studying him from all sides. "Fat lot of work he'll do. He's stunted, that what he is!"

"He's all I was given," the carter explained, looking at Arne as if he was seeing him for the first time.

Crankfit sniffed at Blethley's papers like a bloodhound. "Humph! I suppose I'd better take him. I swear they're getting smaller and smaller all the time." He grumped and added his signature.

The dreadful conditions under which great-grandfather Arne lived and worked at Crankfit's, caused him to run away. After many adventures he found his aunt Beth in Blackburn. She adopted him and taught him how to weave. When he grew up Arne married a mill-girl called Eva Anders. They had a child who became grandfather William. Grandfather William was killed in the mill long before I was born.

———◆———

Over the years, mother also told me about her side of the family. I learned about her parents, my grandmother Bridget Gorman Kenyon, and my grandfather, Thomas Kenyon, who had died when mother was very young.

Bridget Gorman was born in County Clare, Ireland, the only daughter of a landed family. We hardly knew anything about her people. Her meeting with my grandfather, Thomas Kenyon, was the event that was to shape the rest of her life. Bridget's relatives held that her meeting with Thomas ruined her. There was little to recommend the Englishman to them. Yet he was darkly handsome, well-dressed and dashing, with a fine mustache. Grandmother Bridget once told me, that it was the mustache that had made her fall in love. He had a good job with an English insurance company, which explains his visit to Ireland. But he was much older than Bridget's seventeen years. Worse, Thomas was a Protestant, Bridget was a Catholic.

Mother said that Bridget's father and brothers (their warnings to the would-be suitor to pack his bags having gone unheeded) had chased Thomas from the village. Bridget was in danger of making a poor marriage in an alien land. Bridget's father had forbidden her to see the Englishman again. The jovial recklessness he detected in Thomas was not to his liking.

But Bridget was a wild, lawless thing; she was tired of piano and singing lessons, and going to church. She had found her Prince Charming and was eager to fly away.

There was another motive. Bridget had been 'promised' to a neighbour's son - a Catholic boy, rich by County Clare standards - whom she could not stand. The more distance she could put between him and her, the better. Fully aware that to marry Thomas was to sever relations with her family and become a social outcast, Bridget eloped and fled to England as grandfather Thomas Kenyon's Protestant bride.

Revelation followed. Bridget discovered that Thomas already had three children from a previous marriage. Also, although fairly well off, he was much less affluent than he had made himself out to be.

Having made her bed, Bridget lay in it. From the tales I've heard she had a happy life with my grandfather Thomas. He was a generous man, and easy to live with. She was a good wife and a good mother. She had four children of her own, Edward, Eric, Alice and my mother, Maggie. Maggie, the youngest, was born in Blackburn in May 1884.

Bridget's happiness lasted until Thomas died suddenly ten years later. The day after her husband's funeral, Bridget found that her total financial resources consisted of money she had in her purse. To her surprise, she was not only a widow but a pauper. Unknown to Bridget, grandfather Thomas had spent his savings; for some time he had been borrowing against his retirement and pension funds.

Time only added to her troubles. With no money coming in, she scrimped and scraped until all her resources, including her furniture, had gone. She went into cheaper housing. She appealed to her husband's relatives. Her brother-in-law, John Kenyon at Bamber Bridge, gave her some help, but he had two small daughters of his own and was not as prosperous at that time as he was to become; he couldn't go on helping Bridget forever. From Thomas' boon-companions, some of whom had helped him to spend his money, came nothing.

With no one else to turn to - her frantic appeals to her family in County Clare had gone unanswered - with no funds of her own, and with a dread that her children would finish up in the workhouse, Bridget took the only course open to her: she found foster-homes for her children with people whom she trusted. That is how my mother was 'farmed out' to friends who owned a small pasture farm on the edge of town.

Ironically, soon after that, Bridget found employment looking after the children of a local merchant. She worked hard and saved hard in the hope that she would one day be able to get her family together again. But the merchant's business failed. The merchant's wife, who had become close to Bridget, died. Within a year, Bridget had been thrown back again on her own resources.

After many unsuccessful attempts to obtain suitable work, Bridget finished up as a slubber, cleaning cotton, which was one of the dirtiest and least skilled occupations in textile manufacture. Slubbers or cardroom hands were looked down on. Coarse and degrading, was how Bridget described the work. For a woman as refined as my grandmother, it must have been a wrench to have had to enter the mill.

Yet Bridget got by. Nobody heard her complain. Brought up soft, she was as tough as steel. I never heard her say a word against the way things had turned out, or against her husband for leaving her destitute. "How was he to know he would die when he did?" she said. "He didn't spend the money on himself." Anyway, my grandfather was dead and you didn't speak ill of the dead.

One day mother summed up her feelings about Bridget. "She's quality," she said,"... royal. Her trouble is, she's cum down in t' world...right down, I mean."

There was a pause.

"A lot of us have."

On other occasions mother told me more about the Woodruffs. My father's father, my grandfather William, the child of my great-grandfather Arne and his wife Eva Anders, had been born at Witton, a sub-district of Blackburn in the 1860's. He had been a day-labourer on the land, but had entered the mills to get some ready cash to pay off a debt.

In the mill, grandfather William met a weaver, Selma Nilson, whom he later married, and who became my grandmother Selma. They had thirteen children, two of whom died in childhood. Grandmother Selma was to have a great influence on the destiny of the Woodruffs.

Mother told me that Selma's father had run foul of the law as a boy and had narrowly missed being one of the last convicts shipped to Australia in the 1840's. The injustice of the whole thing - the boy had been accused of stealing some bedding - the savagery of the sentence, coupled with the hardships he had suffered in jail, had left a deep scar on the Nilson family.

During the industrial unrest of the late 1880s, Selma had been accused of assaulting a policeman during a strike. In the witness-box she had denied assaulting anybody. She swore that she had never seen the policeman before. "It's rotten sods like you," she'd shouted at the magistrate, "who make our life hell. Ah'm just as good as thi are." Because of the uproar she caused, grandmother Selma had been sent to jail. The Nilsons were surprised she didn't get three years for carrying on as she did. Guilty or not, her experience in jail soured her of Britain and British authority for the rest of her life. On her release, she would have gladly left the country had she had the money to do so.

"You know, Billy," mother once said, "your grandmother Selma got her wish to escape from England in a strange and tragic way. In 1905 your dad's father, your grandfather William of Witton, was killed when a steel-tipped weaving shuttle flew out of the shuttle race and entered his chest. He had been bending down at the side of the loom when it happened. A knife could not have killed him quicker. Your grandmother Selma was left a widow with eleven children, your father was one of them. I don't know how much money Selma received from the mill-owner by way of workmen's compensation and employer's liability, but it was enough to pay for her family's emigration to America. We emigrated with her from Blackburn to Fall River, Massachusetts in 1906."

"How old were you when you went to America?"

"I was twenty-two. Your father was twenty-three; he was born in 1883 at Witton. We sailed in the summer of 1906. We'd been married two years previously at St. Philip's. Your sister Jenny was about one. Three of grandmother Selma's children remained in Blackburn. They were already married and wanted to stay. Your dad was the oldest of Selma's family to go to America. He'd already sailed with the navy around the world."

"How old were the others?"

"Your grandmother Selma, I think, was in her late forties. Your uncle Peter was six and your aunt Amy was thirteen. Brian, Andrew, Edward, Harold and Paul were in between. The youngest, Peter, was my favourite. They were true Woodruffs - tough as nails."

Mother said that some of Selma's family had tried to dissuade her from going. One night she had heard Selma and Selma's brother Joshua going on hammer and tongs about it.

'You're going to a place you know nothing about,' Joshua had argued. 'It's plain madness to go off like this with seven young children. Here you've got food and a roof, and you'll have the insurance money. Over there you'll be starving in the streets before you know where you are. Anyway, why do you want to run away? England's the best country there ever was. It's plain daft to leave it as you're doing.'"

"And what was grandmother Selma's answer?"

"She said 'Joshua, you're prattlin' like a gobbin. You've never been the one with brains in our family. You talk about risk. William and I have slaved our guts out here, knowing nothing but risk. You talk about us becoming beggars at t' other side. Tell me any Blackburn family that's gone over and become beggars. None of them have come back with their tails between their legs. Everybody I've ever heard of who went to America became rich; you know that. Our brother Mat and his wife Hessie in Fall River have done very well, thank you. They won't see us starve. And don't give me that old buck about love of country. That kind of talk is for the toffs. You keep the country, Joshua, I'll take the money. Frankly, I don't care whether God saves our gracious king or not. I'm tired of the whole rotten lot. I'm concerned to save my family. I know where our bread is buttered and nothing's going to stop me.'

"I'll tell you more about your grandmother Selma some other time," mother said.

Chapter V

American Interlude

I was in my teens before mother told me in detail about the Woodruff migration to America.

The moment grandmother Selma knew she was going to get a lump sum in compensation for her husband's death, she set her face toward America. She'd always been talking about following her brother Mat Nilson who had gone to America years before. Now her chance had come. My father, who had learned to read and write in the navy, wrote a letter to Mat who was working in a cotton mill in Fall River. From there everything led on.

Father read Mat's reply to Selma who couldn't read. Family and neighbours came together to hear it. Mat wrote that there was plenty of work for Lancashire folk in Fall River; the living was good and the pay much higher. 'Tha can lose nothing by coming to America,' his letter ended. Mat's letter encouraged my parents to go with Selma to America, even though my sister Jenny was just a baby.

Selma then got in touch with her nephew Henry Nilson, who worked in a shipping office in Liverpool. He came up with a

June crossing on an American ship, the 'Elizabeth,' which offered the best accommodation for the lowest price. "The only cheaper way to go to America, Auntie, is to swim."

By borrowing money, Selma paid her deposit on the June sailing. She never doubted that the employer's liability money would come through.

Getting ready to leave wasn't much of a problem. Selma packed food in a wicker hamper, bedding in clean sacks, and the rest in straw valises. Most of the clothes the family had were already on their backs.

For two weeks, before she was due to sail, Selma basked in the sun by her front door, arms across her belly, beaming with happiness, and exchanging gossip with all who had the time to stop and talk.

"Then tha's got the death money?" passersby queried, hoping to find out what unheard-of sum had come her way. The more Selma refused to talk about it, the larger the sum became. Rumour made the figure large enough to take the whole of Griffin Street to America.

The street gave them a send-off on a Sunday afternoon when the mills were shut. As the weather was fine, tables were brought outside. Bunting and coloured streamers were hung from the houses. "May you Prosper," were chalked in large letters on grandmother Selma's cottage. There was lots of food and drink.

One of father's friends from the mill, Adam Sims and his wife Emily, had also decided to migrate. Although the Sims had only been married four months, Emily, a mere slip of a girl, was large with her first child. It worried grandmother Selma.

Everybody enjoyed themselves at the treat. There were lots of toasts. Nobody got Selma to her feet. She'd drunk so much that she didn't have any legs. By the time they sang "We'll take a cup of kindness now for the sake of old lang syne," she had to use both bench and table to prop herself up. That night she slept where she fell, in her clothes. Selma was never one for losing sleep.

Before sunrise the next day she'd stripped her cottage clean. "It's not much to leave behind," she said as she took a last look. All the seven Woodruff children were eager to be off. The Sims stood outside with their baggage. Alongside them were the new tenants who had turned up before first light. They sat on their boxes in the street talking in low voices.

A friend of Selma's, Joe Moss, had offered to take them the thirty miles to Liverpool in his cart. His only desire was to do a good turn. As soon as he arrived, the baggage and the bedding were loaded up. Despite the early hour, there was a lot of shouting, hugging and weeping as the migrants climbed onto the cart. "We'll never see each other again on this earth," grandmother Bridget sobbed, clinging to Jenny.

Selma sat next to Joe Moss, clutching a flat leather bag fastened to her waist. The women wore dark blouses and long dark skirts that wouldn't show dirt. They also had straw bonnets, a farewell gift from the pawnbroker Mr. Levy. Being a warm morning, their shawls were thrown back on their shoulders.

At a shout of "Giddup," the cart began to rumble down Griffin Street. This was the signal for the new tenants to rush into Selma's cottage, dragging their possessions after them. As the departure coincided with the morning rush to the mills, Joe and his horse had to fight against the tide of workers going the other way.

"Lucky old devil you are, Selma," shouted those who knew her. "Don't forget us." Others just stared, waved vaguely, and shouted: "Ta, Ta!"

Relatives and friends followed the cart as far as the Griffin pub. Grandmother Bridget stood on the steps waving and weeping until the cart had passed out of sight.

The freedom to suddenly break a fixed pattern of life, to break out of the ranks of the army of workers and go their own way came as a shock to the adults. They had expected to work in the mills forever. Until now, someone else had organized their lives. They felt easier once the canyons of brick had been left behind.

With the sun peeping over the moors, and the sounds and sights and smells of the countryside bearing in upon them, they reached the top of a hill where they looked back at the town they were leaving for good. Despite the smoke haze that hung over the valley, they were able to make out the spire of the parish church of St. Mary and the railway station. The rest was a dense mass of factories, cottages and smoking factory chimneys.

The children preferred going to America to going to school. Every now and then, with great screams, they raced through a hole in the hedgerows to chase a rabbit. Once they caught a hedgehog which Selma ordered them to let go. When tired, the children came running back to the cart, climbed aboard and slept on the bedding. Sometimes the grown-ups burst into song.

Later that morning they met a labourer working by himself on the road.

"And where might ye all be goin'?" he asked as he rested on his spade and wiped his brow with his sleeve.

"To America."

"America? That's a mighty long way to go with a horse'n cart."

"But we're not," the children cried. "we're going on a ship."

"Ye are, are ye? Well, by y'r leave, I'll be hoppin' on the cart and joinin' ye. Ah well, that's the kind of world it is; some mend the roads, others go to America. I'll be thinkin' of ye all the way. May God watch over ye."

On looking back, they saw the man waving his cap.

They spent the night at a farm near Hesketh with the carter's relatives, the Mosses - red-faced, jovial farming people who not only gave them shelter in one of the barns, but a huge, warming evening meal as well. After everyone had washed under the pump, the stew was served with great lumps of fresh bread and a bucket of fresh milk. The children gorged. Fussed by Adam, Emily Sims, who said grace, ate as eagerly as the rest. The meal was accompanied by the sound of thrushes singing their last song of the day.

A cock perched on one of the beams above their heads woke them the next morning. After a huge breakfast, the migrants set their backs to the rising sun and their faces to the Irish Sea. The day was cool and fresh. The Mosses walked a little way with them to wave good-bye.

After a day-long journey, the travelers were met by Henry Nilson at an inn outside Liverpool. He'd cleared their papers at the port. He struck them as a bit of a toff; he wore a suit and tie. The departure of the 'Elizabeth' had been delayed, but he'd found temporary shelter for them.

Shortly afterward they climbed a rise and saw the sea. They'd no idea that so much water and sky existed. They expected to see America in the distance.

Having avoided the town, they came to a shed by a quiet beach not far from the end of the quay. Seagulls perched on the tin roof. Farther on they could see crowds moving about. Behind the shed was a salt marsh that rang with bird song.

It took some time for Henry to open the doors, which were fastened by several locks. Tired after two days on the road, they all poured into the shed intent on finding a place to sleep. Selma and Maggie removed the shutters and threw everything open to the warm breeze. Adam and Will emptied the cart. Joe unhitched his horse and let it crop the grass. The children gathered sticks to cook the evening meal.

An hour later only Joe, Will and Maggie were awake to watch the sun slip into the sea. Swifts and swallows wove a graceful pattern in the fading light. They didn't feel like sleep; instead they sat on the steps, stretching, yawning and yarning, watching the water endlessly rising and falling and listening to the crickets. Now and again they heard the hoot of a ship.

They were wakened in the early hours by Emily's stifled cries of pain. Selma told Henry to get a doctor quickly.

"No doctor will come here at this hour, Aunt Selma."

As the first fingers of light crept across the morning sky, Emily Sims died in childbirth. A calm stillness prevailed, broken only by Adam's sobs.

The next day city officials tiptoed in and out of the shed. "You have our sympathy, Mr. Sims." For their services they charged several gold coins which Adam took from a drawstring pouch around his neck.

The night after the funeral, Selma took Adam aside. "What do you intend to do, Adam? Ar' te going back with Joe to Blackburn tomorrow, or ar' te going to board the ship with us? Tha'll have to make up thi mind quick."

"I already have. Emily wouldn't want me to turn back now."

Later that night, Henry beckoned Selma outside. "Listen, when you get to New York, they're going to ask you a lot of questions. They'll ask you if you've ever been in jail. You've got to watch that one. All you have to do is to say no and smile. They're not going to stop a widow with seven children."

"I 'ope not."

"Another thing, if they ask you about fumigation, when you reach the 'Elizabeth' you'd better act daft. You've got to get on that ship. Dust everybody with the Keating's Insect Powder you've brought before you board."

Early the next day they went down the busy quayside to where the 'Elizabeth' was moored directly opposite the Customs House. The three-masted ship was alive with activity.

Amy was surprised how small it was. "Do you really think that's going to get us to America?"

"It's got to," Selma said. "They 'ave our money."

Sheltered from the sun by a wide awning, they spent a dreary day sitting on their valises waiting to embark. The younger children fretted and cried, the older children found it torture to have to sit still.

Only when the hatches had been battened down were the passengers allowed to cross the gangplank to the main deck. First Class boarded first. "With toffs like that aboard we should be safe," Selma commented.

The Woodruffs were escorted by sailors to the steerage quarters. Their bunks were between the communal kitchen and the toilet, both areas already smelly. Except for sheets placed over string, there was no privacy. Baggage was stowed on the floor. Their tickets simply provided for somewhere to sleep, cook, and wash.

The sound of the ship's windlasses recovering the anchors caused everyone to rush on deck. Henry was still on the quayside. He shouted messages that no one could hear; he continued to wave his hat as the 'Elizabeth' - pushed by a battered-looking tug - threaded its way past other vessels out to sea.

Only when the land was disappearing did my mother wonder if she would ever see England again. "I pray I've done the right thing," she said, "and that all our dreams will come true in America."

It took the Woodruffs a long time to find their sea legs - longer still to get used to the confined steerage quarters and the unbelievable medley of human beings. Except when the sea was rough, they spent the day on deck. Once on board ship, Adam Sims withdrew into himself. He was often seen motionless - hands on rail - gazing across the sea. The grown-ups understood and left him alone.

Maggie used to say that it was the fine weather that saved them. There were nights when it was warm enough to take a blanket on deck and fall asleep with the wind singing in the rigging. Her most vivid memory of the journey was the night storm that terrified her and the children, and left most of the passengers prostrate. The ordeal ended with someone vomiting all over Selma's head.

Not even the storm affected Selma's appetite. Day after day, she sat on deck, at the foot of a mast, eating and hacking wedges from a loaf of bread. "We're going to the land of the free," she told the children. "Once across, we'll all be rich." She rubbed her fat hands gleefully and ate some more.

Selma had always been one for her belly. My father had come home one night when he was in his teens in Blackburn to find his siblings locked out of the house. Several of them had their hungry faces glued to the kitchen window.

"What's up?"

"Mam's eatin' our dinner."

He had looked through the window to see his mother eating several chops.

"There just wasn't enough to go round," she explained. "Better a few chops for me than too little for everybody else."

Two nights before they reached New York, Adam Sims disappeared. After a long search, all they found was his empty moleskin purse. The captain concluded that Adam had been stunned, robbed, and cast into the sea. "It's happened before," he said.

Although Adam's empty purse pointed to murder, he was listed as a suicide. Suicide would make it easier for everybody to avoid being held up in New York.

On the last night Selma stayed on deck. When at dawn the coast began to rise out of the sea, she rushed downstairs and brought up the children. Together they gaped at the sun-kissed city hovering on the horizon. Selma was jubilant; others just stared at the shore, tears streaming down their faces. Henry Nilson had told Selma that if they made a landfall early, they'd stand a chance of getting through to Fall River that night.

Accompanied by a growing number of other vessels, and a burst of whistles and sirens, they approached a large statue of a lady with a lamp. "Ellis Island!" someone shouted. With much clanking and clatter the vessel docked. They'd reached the land of promise.

There followed a day of agony. After being tagged with a number, the Woodruffs joined the flood of other steerage passengers making their way to a large building. "Everybody's afraid they're going to shut the doors," Selma said as she urged the children to keep up.

Once through the vast doors, they climbed a long flight of stairs to a great hall, in which there was unbelievable uproar and confusion. In addition to the thousands of milling, bewildered immigrants, there were hundreds of officials bellowing out numbers and messages in every language.

The Woodruffs joined an endless line that moved between wooden rails. Doctors in blue uniforms with grave looks gave them cursory examinations. While asking questions, they examined hands, face, hair, and eyes. The Woodruffs passed the medical officials in record time; they were all good stock.

After another long wait, Selma was asked questions by a uniformed man with an impassive face.

"Where were you born?"

"England."

"Who paid your passage?"

"I did."

"Do you have any money? Let me see it."

Selma fumbled in her bag. As Henry had instructed, she produced five pounds (twenty-five dollars) to prevent her becoming a public charge.

"How many dependents?"

"Seven."

"Ever been in prison?"

"Now, what, I ask you, would a widow with seven children be doing in jail?"

"Yuh, sure. Can you read or write?"

Coached by Henry, Selma knew that there was no legal obligation to be able to do either. Nor would they test her. "I manage," she answered.

"Do you have any relatives here?"

"Yes, in Fall River, where I'm going."

"What skills do you have?"

"I'm a weaver."

"Is there a job waiting for you?" was the last question asked. For reasons which Selma never understood, to have answered "yes" would have been fatal. Henry had told her to say "No," so she said "No," which at least was the truth. There was a law that was meant to discourage the recruiting of unskilled workers in Europe.

After several gruelling hours, the migrants' names were checked against the ship's manifest. They were given landing cards, after which they pushed open a door marked New York and emerged in the fresh air. While Maggie felt like collapsing, Selma glowed. Before leaving the building, Selma and Will changed some money. They had been warned from Fall River to make sure that they were not cheated. Selma was puzzled by the strange coins, but rattled them together in her hands to show her delight.

Will went for tickets for the ferry from Ellis Island to the mainland and the train to Boston. They saw the train long before it pulled into the station. Having sounded a deep-throated warning, it crawled toward them. It was the first train whistle that Maggie heard in the New World. She thought it sad. Years later she used to say that all American train whistles sounded sad.

There followed one of the worst free-for-alls the Woodruffs had ever experienced. To get a seat one had to push and jostle somebody else out of the way. Thanks to Selma's muscular arms and thighs, the Woodruffs obtained seats together. Mother was worn out protecting her baby, Jenny.

All the passengers cheered when at long last the train got under way. The faster it went, the more they enjoyed the breeze coming through the open windows.

My mother's first impression of America was something of a let-down. The train passed miles of dilapidated, grimy-looking tenements with people and washing everywhere. She thought the sky was larger; everything looked twice as big. More of the houses were built with wood than brick. She was surprised at the number of negroes. Nobody had ever seen a black face in Blackburn. For hours the train hurried through a sprawling, tree-lined countryside where the farmers were still getting in the hay.

By the afternoon, the crowded coach looked as if it had been occupied for weeks. Shoes, packages, suitcases, discarded food, banana skins and orange peel, rolling bottles and crawling infants littered the floor. Despite the open windows, a heavy, rancid smell of unwashed humanity filled the swaying car.

In Boston they caught the train to Newport, which stopped at Fall River, fifty miles away. The Newport train gave them their first close look at Americans. They seemed taller; a surprising number wore suits and shiny shoes. They talked in loud voices as the train jolted along, calling across the aisles in a rude kind of way. There was nothing cowed about them. Some of them showed an interest in the Woodruff children.

The Woodruffs caught sight of Fall River as the light was fading. "There it is," a Fall River passenger told them, as he pointed to the town's famous landmarks, the double onion domes of St. Anne's Church and the double spires of Notre Dame Church. They caught glimpses of great factory-like buildings topping the wayside trees. Quickly they got their things together. Children were wakened and ordered to hang on to each other.

As the train stopped, the Woodruffs jumped down. Selma stood in the middle of the crowded platform with her brood around her. Maggie, holding Jenny, stood next to her crying uncontrollably. Her body still swayed with the movement of the vessel left long behind.

After standing there for some time and wondering what they should do, a group of strangers approached. "Excuse me, are you from Blackburn?" one of the men asked.

"That we are," Selma replied.

"Well, you've cum at last," Selma's brother Mat said as he gave her a hug. "This is my wife Hessie, we've been looking for you all afternoon."

"By gum, am I pleased to see you!" Selma cried. Her face became bright red with pleasure.

There were other Nilsons there, as well as several Woodruffs. They were all eager to meet their relatives. Some of them had migrated to Fall River twenty years earlier, most had been born there. There was talk about Blackburn and the sorry fate of the Sims, but not much else. Even Selma, who had born the ordeal of the journey best of all, and who had not once been seasick, was too tired to talk. Nobody asked them if they'd had a pleasant voyage.

From family history I know that my grandmother Selma and her children prospered in Fall River. As she had predicted, America proved to be the place where most of their dreams came true.

My parents also did well. For the next eight years, my father earned more money as a 'tackler,' or overseer, at the Fleetwood Mills, than he would ever do again. His pay was much higher. For a fifty hour week - from 7 till 5 weekdays, half-day Saturday till 1 - he earned as much as $18-$20; several times his Blackburn pay of £1 to 30 shillings for almost the same hours. What he got depended on his own rather than trade union bargaining power.

My parents had their own apartment in a tenement in County Street. It was better than anything they'd known in Blackburn. It was more spacious, it had great bay windows, hardwood floors, and high ceilings. The roof didn't leak. There also was an indoor toilet. My sister Brenda was born in County Street on 19th September, 1910. Yet Brenda's birth certificate states that she was born on 28th September. I puzzled over this until my sister explained that mother had changed the 19th to the 28th, so that it coincided with the date of her wedding anniversary. The date of mother's marriage was important to her. My brother Dan was born in the same house in January 1912.

In the early 1900's, when my parents arrived there, Fall River, which stands at the mouth of the Taunton River in southeastern Massachusetts, was the largest concentrated area of cotton textile manufacture in the United States, if not in the world. It was called 'spindle city,' or 'the Blackburn of America.' The scale of operations came as a shock to my parents. There were thousands of looms instead of hundreds. For the first time my father had to operate automatic looms and 'batteries,' a device that changed the weft in the shuttle automatically. Spinning differed as well as weaving. The Americans used the faster ring spinning process. Everything from raw cotton to the dyeing of the finished cloth was under the same roof.

Offsetting the higher rates of pay was the absence of workers' compensation. Father had one of his weavers drawn into the machinery and lose two fingers, infection spread and the girl died. Her wages were sent to her family and that was that.

To people coming from England, the ethnic variety of Fall River in the 1900's came as a shock. Most of the population must have been foreign born. There was a babel of tongues. My people were used to English, Irish, Welsh and Scots, but not to French Canadians, Poles, Russians, Lithuanians, Syrians, Armenians, Greeks, Portuguese, Puerto Ricans, Canary Islanders, Italians, Spaniards, Germans, and Swedes; all of whom they called 'foreigners.' Because they spoke English, my parents considered themselves superior. It was not uncommon for 'Anglos,' who had just got off the boat from England, to tell 'dirty foreigners' to go home.

The favourable treatment given to English-speaking workers explains why mother had no trouble getting a cardroom job as a 'doffer,' filling and emptying the carding machines. Without weaving or spinning skills, there was little else she could do. Father became a 'tackler' or overseer. The outstanding advantage he had was skill and a strong sense of pride of craft.

For him nearly all the industrial processes and terms were the same. For the other migrants, many of whom were peasants, cotton manufacture was a completely alien way of life.

Mother was fascinated by the young Polish and Italian workers who sang and danced in the aisles during factory breaks. Father said that they didn't have cold English blood. Mother thought that the workers were livelier, much better dressed, and money-wise, better off.

One thing that my parents could not get over was the amount of theft in the mills. As an overseer, father found himself losing yards and yards of cloth. One thief he caught was blacklisted and run out of town. It was cheaper than sending him to jail.

To her dying day, mother remembered the breathtaking views across the Taunton River to the countryside beyond, and the visit of President Taft in 1911. She'd waved to him.

There is one thing certain, my parents didn't have to fight over pennies in Fall River. For the first time in their lives they could save. Relative to what they'd known in Blackburn, they'd become rich. So rich that they were able to pay for grandmother Bridget's crossing of the Altantic to join them. Bridget came into her own in Fall River. She became the assistant manager in one of the better hotels. It wasn't long before she had her own apartment. At long last, fortune had smiled on all of them. I don't know whether this made any of my family any happier, but it spared them the anguish over money they'd know later on.

Chapter VI

Return to England

In the summer of 1914, grandmother Bridget returned to England, travelling first-class with a party from Fall River touring Britain. She sailed on the transatlantic liner 'Carmania' - the same vessel that my parents would use later that summer. As she was extending her trip to stay with her grown-up children in Blackburn, the date of her return was left open.

By now she was in her early fifties and still attractive. My parents went to the station to see her off. They said she looked like a queen. On the 'Carmania,' Bridget danced from New York to Liverpool.

The wonder is that having visited her children in Blackburn she didn't dance all the way back again. There was nothing to stop her. All that was needed in those days was a strong stomach and money, and she had both.

I never understood why my parents followed her to England in the summer of 1914. Things could not have been going better for them in the United States. Father was earning more money as a tackler than he would ever earn again.

I was never able to get either of my parents to talk about the return journey. I can only assume that it pained them to mention it. I know that in the summer of 1914 they travelled second-class with my sisters Jenny and Brenda, and my brother Dan. My sisters remembered the fuss and bother of getting ready to leave Fall River; grandmother Selma and several uncles coming to the railway station to see them off; everybody crying; the great liner 'Carmania,' from whose bowels they hardly ever saw the sea; being met by grandmother Bridget and several Woodruffs at Blackburn in the pouring rain. My parents returned to Griffin Street, the street from which they had migrated eight years before. My sisters were put to bed that night crying their eyes out to go home to Fall River. They didn't realize that they would never see America again.

I suspect that my mother's homesickness for England was the chief reason for my family's return. Mother never became part of the New World. I think she kept at father about going back to England until he eventually gave in. It could not have been for the want of the company of Lancashire folk. Indeed, my parents talked Lancashire dialect to Lancashire people in Fall River so much that they adopted few Americanisms.

Grandmother Selma may have been another reason for their leaving - perhaps a major reason. I never heard mother express any warmth toward her. While she admired Selma's toughness in migrating as a widow with so many children, she couldn't stand her domineering ways. Selma liked to interfere. There were times when mother wondered whether Jenny, Brenda and Dan were her children or Selma's. Selma also got on mother's nerves with her criticism of England.

When Selma heard rumours of my parents' decision to return to Britain in 1914, she couldn't believe it. Having taken all the trouble to escape from what she called 'Babylon,' here was her eldest son, of his own free will, going back again.

Father knew what Selma's reactions would be. That is why he told mother to break the news. Many years later I asked mother what grandmother Selma had said.

"Nothing," mother answered quietly. "She simply took hold of my hair with one hand and flattened me with the other. One blow from her was enough. Then she spat on the ground and walked away." Selma never forgave father for taking her three grandchildren back to England.

If it had been up to him, I'm sure that father wouldn't have returned. More than mother, he knew at which side of the Atlantic he was better off. "It's better for the likes of us at t' other side," he said to me one day. I sensed that he had made a mistake in leaving America; there was a touch of conscience about it. I think that at the back of his mind, he hoped one day to return. There would always be a job for him in Fall River. While cotton textiles were booming, he went on hoping to make the crossing again.

Until his death, father remained the black sheep of the Fall River Woodruffs. As a boy, he had given his mother a lot of trouble in running away to sea. She'd had to bail him out of the navy because he was underage. He came home in high feather, as brazen as could be; as soon as he was old enough, he went off with the navy again.

I have often wondered why father ran off to war shortly after he reached Blackburn in 1914. Of course, he acted no more strangely than many other men at the time. In 1914 madness prevailed. Shamefaced, he had come home one day to announce that he had joined up. Mother was dumbstruck. She thought he was deserting her. Not so much as by her leave, either. She argued with him; pleaded with him. How could she manage without him? What need did he have to get involved? The war was not for his age. Heavens name, he was thirty-one. He had a family to think of. Instead of his going to France they should take the first ship back to America. President Wilson had pledged that America would stay out of the war. Silently he had stared past her and persisted. His silence had choked her. She had not managed to budge him. His worry was that he might not get to France in time. Like the rest of England he turned a deaf ear to Lord Kitchener's warning that the war would last three years.

A week later, in front of the Town Hall, she attended a ceremony for the men who had volunteered to go to the front. She took the three children, Jenny, Brenda and Dan. There were lots of flags and bunting. A large Union Jack flapped above their heads. The mayor, wearing an ermine-trimmed robe, a cocked hat and his chain of office, made a speech about the wickedness of the Hun, and the need to fight for freedom and liberty, for king and country. To the children's delight, a band played. And then, with orders ringing out, and with much stamping of feet and slapping of rifle butts, the men marched off to the railway station.

On the way home, the children waved small Union Jacks they had been given. Tears blinded Maggie to what was going on. The world, her world at least, had gone stark raving mad. After six weeks training in England, father was sent to France. Later, father said that when he'd got his rifle, he had felt like two men. Like being on a horse.

The war played a primary role in preventing my parents, even if they had intended it, from returning to America. In August 1914 the sea lanes around Britain were mined. In the winter, Hartlepool and Scarborough on the North Sea coast were shelled. A German submarine attack on the 'Carmania' - the ship in which they had sailed - must have come as a great shock to them. In February 1915 Germany declared that the waters around the British Isles were a war zone. To cap it all, in May 1915, the Lusitania was sunk off Ireland.

Father's running off to the war convinced mother that she had made a great mistake in returning to Blackburn. The truth struck her like someone hitting her in the face. In comparison to Fall River, Blackburn looked dowdy and run down. She found herself ensnared in the very life from which they had escaped.

"Then why," I asked her, "after so many years in America did you return to England?"

"I wanted to smell the lilies of the valley," she replied, which I suppose was a symbolic way of saying that she wanted to return to her roots. I know she would not have left America had she known that father was going to run off to fight in France.

I once asked my sister Brenda how she explained father's returning to England and his running off to the war.

"Father was a gaumless creature," she said. "He had the head and brains of a brass knob. He didn't foresee anything because he never thought about anything. He was a grand worker, nobody better, but where brains were concerned he was lost."

Father's dashing off to war made things hard for mother. She had three children to care for. When her savings ran out, she was forced to go and work in the mills.

Mother rarely saw father for the next four years. When he came home on leave, he had changed - the old jauntiness had gone; he was thinner and there was a troubled look about him. "There's going to be nobody left to fight," he had said. His leave in 1916 had meant a second honeymoon for my parents. My birth on 12 September 1916, and naming me William after him, spoke of the joy they had known.

Father certainly paid a price for his actions. He fought for three years as a private with the infantry until he was gassed at the third battle of Ypres late in 1917. The Germans had released gas by shellfire which had caught the British unawares. The soldiers had panicked; clutching their throats and screaming with pain, they had fallen where they stood. Father was a great runner and had taken to his heels. He was one of the last to fall, one of the first to be picked up and treated. He was invalided out of the army in 1918.

As so many others, he came home disillusioned. His experiences had shattered any desire he might have had for change and adventure. He returned to Griffin Street a sick man. Both body and mind were affected. For years he had a racking cough from the gassing.

When he was in a talking mood, he once told me about seeing the king in France. It was a great honour to see the king.

"You never saw such a cleaning up in the hospital as went on beforehand," he said. "One day, the place looked like a slaughterhouse; the next, there were flowers everywhere. They brought in a giant orderly who picked up the patients and shuffled them about like dolls. Anybody who stank or looked horrible had to go.

'That's him,' somebody called, as the king entered the ward. A long crocodile of people followed him. They moved so quickly that anybody on crutches had to hobble noisily out of the way. Here and there the king stopped, pinned a medal onto somebody's shirt, and mumbled something. He looked bewildered. At least he had the gumption not to stick his nose behind the curtains where the German wounded lay. Once he'd gone with 'Three cheers for the king,' the giant orderly shuffled the patients back again. The next day the ward was its usual bloody self."

"Were you bucked up by the visit?" I asked.

"I felt the same after he left as when he came. I'm not a king's man, you know."

By the time father left the front, a great disillusionment had settled on the battlefield. Phrases like self-sacrifice and sacred duty were not heard any more. There no longer was fraternizing with the German troops as there had been on that first Christmas in 1914. Anybody who fraternized was brought up sharp - very sharp. Bellyachers were silenced. To get a 'Blighty' - a wound that would take one home out of the carnage - or to be killed was the only escape. His regiment had come close to mutiny. They sent a staff colonel with a red band on his hat to talk them around. Gave them a good raking over, he did. 'Where is your love of country?' he asked them. Told them they were fighting for freedom. Father felt like telling him back that the only freedom they had was the freedom to get killed. First whiff of cordite, the colonel was gone.

By 1918 father was glad to be rid of his gun and uniform. After that he had to learn the hard way that the politicians' promise of a 'Land Fit for Heroes' was pie-crust thick.

I can remember nothing of my father's homecoming, or of the rejoicing that signalled the end of the war, the greatest war there had ever been. My first dim memory of father is the glee he took in throwing me against the ceiling. It was a short distance, but to me it seemed quite far. "One, two, three, whoops!" he called out, against mother's protests. He also rasped my cheek with his coarse beard. The more I squirmed, the harder he rasped.

Having spent several months recovering from the gassing, father returned to his job in the mills. On the surface, the family life he had known before the war was resumed.

Father's recklessness in volunteering to fight for Britain in 1914 was the last straw for my American grandmother Selma. Yet she had not hesitated to encourage her other sons to fight for the United States once America had entered the war. There used to be a newspaper cutting in the family showing a picture of Selma with her sons in uniform sitting on her porch in Fall River under the stars and stripes. The accompanying article, which I read as a boy in Lancashire, declared that she had more sons serving in the United States Army and Navy than any other mother in Massachusetts.

Grandmother Selma lived into her late nineties.

Chapter VII

World Outside my Door

As soon as I was able to toddle, Jenny took me to the Morgan's next door. Later, I used to run in and out of the Morgan's house. Mrs. Morgan sometimes took her daughter Annie and me to the horse trough outside the Griffin pub at the end of our street. The horses were watered there, and how deeply they drank; great draughts that I was sure would empty the trough. Withdrawing their heads, they shook their wet all over us. People drank from a dented metal cup attached by a chain to the spout from which poured a steady stream of water.

The Morgans never had more than the one child, Annie. Their house was tidy and clean and smelled as good as it looked. Mrs. Morgan had a part-time job washing dishes at the Bull Hotel in town; Mr. Morgan hauled coal. They could not have had much money to spare, yet I felt warm and secure there. I liked the bright red geranium Mrs. Morgan kept in her window.

The Morgans were a strange contrast. He was a muscular fellow, with strong arms and big hands. He used to stand before the mirror at the kitchen sink and, with the tap running, comb his thick, black hair until it hung in a straight line above his eyes. I used to watch him and wait for him to part his hair, but he never did. I knew Mr. Morgan for years and he never parted his hair. Everybody else did. His side-whiskers luxuriated down his face like a garden gone wild. His wife was small, fair and slim. The one thing the couple had in common was their sense of humour. They were forever cheery.

In their house, I sensed the warmest love and affection. In the evening, when Mr. Morgan came home, black as the coal he had carried on his back all day, Mrs. Morgan used to jump up to greet him. It pleased me the way Mrs. Morgan kept touching her husband. She had a way of reaching up and gently running her hand across his coal-blackened face. He responded by showing his gleaming white teeth.

Sometimes on a Sunday, Mr. Morgan - his layers of coaldust scrubbed off - took Annie and me to visit Molly, a big black horse with a star on her forehead. It was not really his horse, but he said it was. Molly lived in a dark hole in the side of a large building in town. I don't know how she put up with the dirt and the smell. She cheered up when we unlocked the door and allowed a flood of light to rush in. Mr. Morgan placed his head against Molly's and soothingly asked her how she felt and told her how glad he was to see her again. He then gave her a carrot. Molly responded by rubbing her head against Mr. Morgan's waistcoat. She looked at him with knowing eyes and quivering nostrils in a way that she didn't look at us. Before we left, Annie and I were allowed to sit on Molly's back and pat her neck. If it pleased her, the horse turned round and tickled us with her soft, wet muzzle. The final treat came on the moment of departure. Mr. Morgan lifted us up and allowed us to take a handful of oats from Molly's bin. We were allowed to take as much as one hand could grasp. All the way home we chewed on Molly's oats.

When I was a little older, my parents took me to the open air market in town. Unless we went on the penny tram, and which we never used if father was in charge, we were faced by what to me was an endless march through all kinds of weather. Once, when father and I were coming home through a blizzard, which had struck unusually late in the year and had fallen upon us suddenly, I shouted to him that we should take the tram home.

He didn't even turn round. "Tha won't melt" he shouted into the wind, as he continued to clump his way along the snow-covered pavement. With the bitter snow-laden wind stinging my eyes and pricking my face, I followed as best I could. Alongside us, steaming horses and snow-covered carts, piled high with empty beer barrels, plunged through the dirty puddles and the growing slush. My heart sank as I watched the tram, on which I had set all my hopes, lurch past. Screaming its protest at the weather, and I hoped at father too, it faded into the gloom where its yellow eye flickered and died. In desperation, I followed the snowman who trudged on before me. The usual crowds of people had vanished.

By the time we reached home, father and I were covered from head to foot with snow. The sidewalks had long since disappeared from view. Other than to stamp our feet and shake ourselves like dogs, we entered the cottage as if nothing had happened. Until our clothing dried, we stood on newspapers before a roaring fire drinking hot tea. My sisters had been bundled upstairs. Although we were both steaming like sheets taken out of the boiling set pot, nothing was said about our nakedness or the weather.

Every Saturday night, when they were in work, my parents went to their favourite pub. Sober from Monday to Saturday, they broke out and made up for lost time. If there was no one to look after me, I was taken along too. With other young children, mostly by myself, I wore out the night sitting in the pub kitchen, which stank of stale beer and cigarette smoke. "Sit still and keep your hands off everything," the pub-keeper's wife ordered. Any dog or cat there fled to some hidden corner from which they hissed and growled at me for the rest of the night. Their noise was drowned only by the clash of glasses, the shouts, the wild laughter, and the snatches of song coming from the bar. 'Meet me in love's sweet garden, down where the roses grow...' 'Oh, you beautiful doll, you great, big beautiful doll...' People drank more if they sang.

Occasionally, I escaped into a picture book that the pub-keeper's wife thrust into my hands. I knew better than to say that she had given me the same book for the past three weeks. I also whiled away the hours by listening to the bar piano. When all else failed, I'd make a dream world of the fire, or watch the second hand twitch its way across the face of the Westminster Chime clock standing in the corner. It came as a relief when I heard the cry "Time, gentlemen, please." After that, amid muttered farewells to those who had left the pub with us, and who seemed reluctant to go home, we walked through the dark streets, my parents discussing the latest gossip. There was always something that caught their fancy. In time, as they often changed their 'favourite' pub, I came to know most of the pub kitchens in Blackburn.

One night all monotony vanished when a fight broke out in the bar. I knew from the dreadful things being shouted that somebody had run off with somebody else's wife. There was such bawling and screaming and smashing of glasses and furniture that I feared for my parents' lives. With distraught faces, they rushed into the kitchen, scooped me up and fled into the night. We never drank there again.

On occasions I was lucky enough to go with my parents to the music hall at the Theater Royal. I peered down from the gods on the most exciting scenes. The music, the flood-lit stage, the sparkle and the glitter of the occasion intoxicated me. Everything that happened belonged to another world. Nobody in our street talked like the actors did, nobody was so cheeky or so swaggering. They came right up to the edge of the stage and talked to us as if they'd known us all our life. Then they got everybody to sing 'Ta-ra-ra-boom-de-ay' until the windows rattled. I believed everything I saw. I felt cheated when the audience booed and threw rotten tomatoes. That's when the magic fled and I noticed the fleas.

When money was short we went to 'penny readings,' where we sat on a hard bench in a cold warehouse. The reader, Mr. Peck, was a gray-haired, gaunt-faced elderly gentleman who wore a threadbare suit and a winged collar, and whose teeth kept slipping. He first told us in his own words what the story was about, and then filled in by reading from the text. I recall only the hard seat and the cold.

———◦►———

Some of the happiest moments I had were those spent with my sister Jenny. She looked after me, even after she started working in the mills. She was the first to take me on a community outing into the countryside. One Sunday morning we boarded a horse-drawn coal barge which leisurely made its way on the canal past the crowded housing, the mills and the slag heaps into the open countryside. We sat on newspapers to protect our clothing from the grime. The adults made light of a dog that floated by with a distended belly.

Once we had left the vile smell of the town and the black poisonous water behind, we were surrounded by meadows alive with birds and insects. The water became clear enough to watch the pike hunt their prey. Breathing deeply, we filled our lungs with fresh air. The cuckoo called from distant woods. Listless, flat-topped brown hills touched with shreds of clouds sat all around us. Wildflowers filled the banks. When we passed somebody we knew on the towpath, a shouting match occurred. A boisterous repartee was expected. The trick was to make sure you got in the last word.

It was high-spirited self-entertainment all the way. It was taken for granted that anybody who had a banjo, or a concertina, a harmonica, or a tin whistle would bring it with him. Everybody was expected to do something, even if it was just to join in the singing, or cheer and clap.

My sister's young man Gordon Weall was a proper clown. He had brought a false nose, false teeth and a wig, and in no time at all had the whole barge shaking. Once started, laughter with Lancashire people was infectious. They laughed and laughed until they gasped for breath, and tears ran down their cheeks. They laughed with a determination to wring the last bit of pleasure out of it. "A good laugh beats all thi medicine," they said.

We ate and drank at noon at a pub in the countryside - the horse knew where to find it. It was the first time I got a sip of beer.

The day gone, we wended our way home again as the lowing cattle left the fields.

Best of all was the first 'sharabang' trip I made with Jenny and Gordon. The 'sharabang' was a long, open cart in which we sat on benches with our backs to the sides. There was a wide step at the rear. Behind us, down the length of the wagon, was a rolled tarpaulin that could be pulled over our heads in case of rain. The driver sat up on a box behind his two horses, his whip standing in its rest. It was never used. Mr. Beatty in his wicker bed, this time without the wheels, was placed in the middle of the cart against our legs. Everybody had his place, nobody was neglected. With so many giving a hand, there was no trouble getting the basket in and out. When we went into a pub, Mr. Beatty went with us.

We started the trip at dawn one summer's day, coming together in front of The Griffin. The younger women wore colourful dresses with wide-brimmed straw hats held on with ribbons. The older women had a kerchief wrapped tightly around their heads and fastened under the chin. Everybody brought their own food. There was a lot of shouting and laughter before we got away.

We spent the whole day in country lanes, passing through woods with the bright sun piercing the boughs; other times crossing open fields; still other times we experienced the great silence of the moors, a silence broken only by the cries of the pewits and the curlews, and the chatter of rushing streams. Once we crossed a great stone bridge that led to a sleepy village where friendly people standing in doorways passed the time of day with us. Every now and again, as we jolted through the ruts, we were bounced about, or thrown backward and forward as if we were riding a wave. "Whoa!" everybody yelled, as we lurched forward: "Whoa!" when we were thrown back again, while laughing ourselves hoarse. In the hilliest parts, the young got out and pushed. No setback was allowed to interfere with our merrymaking. When we struck an especially deep hole, we hung on to Mr. Beatty's basket and rolled with him while he drooled. Mrs. Beatty was for ever attentive to Mr. Beatty, wiping his face, feeding him, and sheltering him from the sun. You'd wonder how she could have been as happy as she was.

As a result of my sister's pleading, I was allowed to sit up front on a high box next to Mr. Fisher, the driver. I was proud to sit next to Mr. Fisher, but I'm not sure that he had the same feelings toward me. He sat like a stone at my side, towering above me. He was the only man wearing a bowler hat. The grown-ups called it his 'badge of office.' He never took his eyes off the road, never turned round to see what was going on behind him, never acknowledged that I was there. At least he seemed deaf to anything I said to him - especially when I asked if I could hold the reins. Later on he gave me the reins and told me to start the cart. I swelled with pride at the opportunity. However, his two horses, Polly and George, both reddish-brown giants, ignored my "Giddups!" They wouldn't budge. Finally, they looked round at me so pitifully that I could do little else but hand the reins back.

What fascinated me about Mr. Fisher was his ability to carry on a conversation with his horses and his passengers at the same time. As he never looked back, I was never sure if he was talking to the horses or the passengers.

"You're a sly one, you are, you want it your way." And then without moving his head or his body, or even taking a breath, he went on: "No there's been no change in Sarah's condition. One says its rheumatics, another says its water. I'll tell ye one thing, that there medicine she's got now is sheer poison. I know, because I tried a drop. If that doesn't do it, nothing will. What did I tell you," he continued without a pause, "I knew you'd leave it to him." I could only think that 'you' was Polly, the horse. "For all the good you're doing, you might as well sit up here with us." And then without any sign that he was changing the conversation: "No its the red, murky stuff; bottle should be marked kill or cure; can't say I'm drawn to it."

And so the day went on until we'd visited our last pub and everyone was warm and merry back in the 'sharabang.' The horses knew when the homeward journey began - they pulled harder. Everybody took it for granted that we'd sing ourselves home. As the light faded, and the 'sharabang' rattled on, we sang:

> Come lasses and lads, get leave of your dads,
> And away to the maypole hie,
> For ev'ry fair has a sweetheart there,
> And the fiddler's standing by...

and

> Buy my caller herrin. They're bonnie fish and halesome farin'.
> Buy my caller herrin. Just new-drawn frae the Forth.
> When ye were sleepin' on your pillows, dream'd ye aught of
> our poor fellows,
> Darklin' as they faced the billows, all to fill our woven
> willows?...

and

> In Dublin's fair city, where the girls are so pretty,
> I first set my eyes on sweet Molly Malone.
> She wheeled a wheelbarrow through streets broad and narrow,
> Crying, 'Cockles and mussels, alive, alive, oh!'...

We sang the songs we all knew. Although it was Sunday, we sang few hymns; although when crossing a moor, we sang 'Out on an Ocean all Boundless We Ride.' Sometimes the men led, sometimes the women; sometimes there was two-part harmony, sometimes three- or four-part. Whoever was moved to sing, sang. I noticed how still everyone in the 'sharabang' became when the rich voices fell silent.

In the stillness I listened to the jingle of the harness and the whispering sounds in the darkening hedgerows and meadows around us. I watched Mr. Fisher's lamps of flickering yellow patches light our way.

And then, after a mile or two, unheralded, soaring to the sky, came Patrick Mulroony's voice singing Danny Boy.

> Oh Danny boy, the pipes, the pipes are calling
> From glen to glen, and down the mountain side.
> The summer's gone, and all the leaves are falling
> 'T is you, 't is you must go and I must bide.

Out of the dusk, his brother Mike joined in from the other end of the cart:

But come ye back when summer's in the meadow
Or all the valley's hushed and white with snow
'T is I'll be here in sunshine or in shadow
Oh Danny boy, oh Danny boy, I love you so.

But when ye come and all the flowers are dying,
And I am dead, as all the flowers must die,
Ye come and find the place where I am lying,
And kneel and say an ave where I lie.

And I shall hear, though soft you tread above me,
And in the dark my soul will wake and see.
For you'll bend down and tell me that you love me.
And I shall sleep in peace until you come to me.

There was no strain; no difficulty keeping the other's pace. The two men just opened their mouths and in high, soft, flowing voices sang like birds. Everybody joined in toward the end. By the light of the stars I saw Mrs. Mulroony and my sister Jenny weeping, though I knew I should not have looked. Few things can be as beautiful as a cart full of simple people harmoniously singing their way home through the gloaming with gladness in their hearts.

Later I watched Mr. Fisher play a game in the dark with Mr. Beatty. Without moving his seat, Mr. Fisher reached back until he could grab some part of Mr. Beatty. Having got hold of him, he pretended to shake him like a terrier shakes a rat. "Grrrr," he went. Mr. Beatty must have known who it was, for he gave the same squeal of delight every time it happened.

Mrs. Beatty enjoyed it too. "Oh! Oh!" she cried every time Mr. Fisher's hand approached, "we must stop him, Eric, mustn't we?" Between these attacks, she wiped her husband's dribble and played with his hair.

The grown-ups said that Mr. Beatty and Mr. Fisher had gone off as young men in 1914 to fight the war in France. Mr. Beatty had been hit with a shell. He would have bled to death had Mr. Fisher not scooped up what was left of him and, risking his own life, run back through the mud looking for help. Mr. Fisher, they said, had saved Mr. Beatty's life. Some said that was a good thing; others didn't seem so sure. They looked down their noses, and studied their clogs and said, "Mm...mm," in a serious grown-up way.

By the time we got back to the Griffin, I was fast asleep across Mr. Fisher's knees. I don't know how long I had been there. He held me up while everybody stood and sang:

> Praise God, from whom all blessings flow.
> Praise Him all creatures here below;
> Praise Him above, ye heav'nly host;
> Praise Father, Son, and Holy Ghost.

Chapter VIII

Schooling

Because my parents did not want to go on paying a baby-sitter, at the age of four I was sent to St. Philip's school round the corner from where we lived. As I was to turn five several weeks later, nobody took any notice of my age. The law was ignored.

On my first schoolday Brenda took me by the hand and left me in my classroom. Our caps and coats hung on hooks on the walls. Because of the occasional outbreak of head lice, Brenda had told me to keep my cap separate from the others. I think I was smaller than most of my companions, and I was afraid. I had good reason to be.

I discovered that my schoolmates were a wild lot. Newcomers were roughed up by bullies who ran in a pack. No sooner had I got into the schoolyard for the morning break than several bullies knocked me down. I expected my brother to defend me. He didn't, although he was quick with his fists. His walking away from me on that occasion coloured my view of him for the rest of my life.

With my ears ringing from the first blows, I appealed to the older children in the playground to help me. Instead they took pleasure in watching me get bashed. As I was small, I tried to seize their legs and topple them. One or two kicks in the face with steel-capped clogs put a stop to that. By then, with stars dancing before my eyes, I didn't know where I was, or where the school was. In a blind, crying rage all I could do was to hang on to one of my opponents and, in a tangle and a tussle, have the wind knocked out of me. Every time I broke free and managed to get to my feet, weeping and gasping for breath, I was thrown down again.

Only when my face was covered with blood was I allowed to scramble through the pack and run in search of my sister Brenda, who I knew was playing in the girl's yard next door. She was horrified when she saw my swollen lips and puffed-up face. "I'll murder them for this, Billy," she hissed as she took me home. I must have been a ghastly sight when my parents came home that night. Mother was shocked. "Tha's been at it agin," was father's only comment.

Back to school I went the next day.

A week or so later, before my wounds had healed, three bullies grabbed me in the playground again. My earlier terror was renewed. At first I managed to break away, but they recaptured me and dragged me down. At that moment a fury landed in our midst. It was Brenda. "I'll show you," she shouted, "hurting our Billy! Take that...and that...and that!" Like a wild animal she rained blows upon them until they pleaded for mercy. They got none. Everybody in the school yard was deeply impressed with Brenda. Henceforth, as long as I stayed at St. Philip's, I may not have been popular, which priggish-like I sought to be, but at least no one dreamt of touching me again.

My teacher at St. Philip's was Mr. Manners, a small man with a thin waist. He had large, thoughtful gray eyes and a hollow face concealed behind a pepper and salt mustache. He wore a stiff, high collar and a dark suit that, like his bald head, shone with age. His nephew Joe had a swollen, misshapen face and a cast in one eye. He sat on the front row directly in front of his uncle with nothing better to do than to pick his nose. That was bad. Eating the stuff was revolting. Hardly a day went by without Mr. Manners breaking off lessons to give Joe a slap on the head for his antics.

Joe and Mr. Manners seemed to be tied to each other with an invisible rope. When one stood, the other stood. When one sat down, the other sat down. When one left the room, the other followed, even to the toilet. They came together in the morning; on and off they fought until noon when they sat in the classroom and had their dinner together. The battles were renewed in the afternoon. They left together at night, a weary Mr. Manners muttering to himself in an absentminded sort of way, a radiant Joe. Joe must have thought that life was a funny business, for he was always laughing. When he wasn't laughing, he looked older than his years. He was the only child there in a suit, shirt, tie and shoes. Now and again he would jab one of us with a dirty pen nib to let us know he was still about.

The decorations in Mr. Manners' classroom were meager. There was a stained print of Boadicea, an ancient British queen, and a torn map of the world. Most of the map was painted red, "The British empire, our empire," Mr. Manners assured us. I had no idea why we had such a big empire except that it was taken for granted that we were better than anybody else. On Empire Day (24th May), we sang: "What is the meaning of Empire Day, why do the cannon roar?" The meaning to me was that we got free buns and half-a-day off school. There was also a large Lever Brother's Lifeboy Soap poster, which covered most of the wall at my side. It showed a bar of lathered Lifeboy Soap with a finger that pointed at me. Beneath the finger in great letters were the words WHERE THERE'S DIRT, THERE'S DANGER!

That poster worried me. I took it personally. Why had Mr. Manners sat me there? My neck was no dirtier than the others. Nor did the poster lead me to wash my neck anymore than I was doing. Washing in such a cold, wet climate didn't come easy with us. I never knew anyone who believed that cleanliness was next to godliness. I think we believed in being comfortably dirty.

115

Oddly enough, I got my first book with Lifeboy Soap coupons. It was a one-volume encyclopedia called The Wonderland of Knowledge. My letter to Lever Brothers, sending them the coupons I had saved, was the first letter I ever wrote and I haunted the postman every day after I'd posted it. I was so excited when the package arrived. It was addressed to me, personally. I wouldn't let anyone touch it. I refused to have the string cut and preferred to struggle to untie the knots. After some minutes, I extracted the book from its cardboard box and laid it on the table. It smelled so new and clean. You wouldn't believe it but it was ten-and-a-half inches long, seven-and-a-half inches wide, and one-and-a-half inches thick. I know because I measured it. It must have weighed several pounds. The cover was a treat for the eyes; it was dark blue; in the center was a man reaching out for the sun, the moon and the stars.

I never dreamed that a book could contain so much. It not only offered knowledge, but inspiration. "You are now standing," it said on the title page, "at the Gateway to the Wonderland of Knowledge... the key to your future and the future of the World. For you will learn by the past deeds of Men and Nations what good things to do and what bad things not to do. You will be inspired by the nobility and perseverance of those who rose from humble birth to sway by Thought or Deed the destiny of Man. And what they did, you too may do."

I wondered why the author kept stressing the 'humble birth' bit.

"Anybody who gets a book with soap coupons, Billy," my sister Brenda said, "would have to be of humble birth."

The book started by tracing the history of the world. I'd never heard about Ancient Egypt, or the Chaldeans, or the Jews, or the Cretans, but it told me. I'd no idea How Music Began, or of the Seven Giants of Music, or the need for Mighty Music of Our Modern Age, but it told me that too.

There was nothing the book didn't tell me. Having read Music Through the Ages, I plunged into The Romance of Exploration from Marco Polo onward. I didn't realize the world was so big.

After that I tackled the Great Names in English Literature - thirty-two of them. Of the thirty-two I had heard of only two - Shakespeare and Milton, and not much of them either. Writers like the Venerable Bede and Samuel Pepys were eye-openers for me.

There followed the Marvels of Invention. There was even a section on Spinning and Weaving. Then came Wonders of the Insect World. This was the only part of the book that I couldn't get excited about, though I did enjoy the section headed Ogres of the Insect World.

I think by the time the editor had got through with the Ogres, he was ready to pitch anything in and take his pay. I suppose that next to the Bible, the *Wonderland of Knowledge* was the most important book I ever had. Being the only book I owned, I read it and re-read it until I knew it backward. I created my own adventure in learning. The book became my most treasured possession.

Mother opened her eyes with awe when I began to rattle off my knowledge: "Imagine you knowing all that," she said. Father was not struck by it: "What good war all that talk?"

Anyway, back to school and Mr. Manners. I think the poor man must have worked himself to death. He sat at a bare table on a platform in front of us. He stayed with us from morning till night. Behind him was the blackboard. Above his head hung an electric light bulb with a plain shade. Working on the blackboard, he taught us the alphabet, arithmetic and the names of our kings and queens from King Canute on. The moment he turned his back was the signal for students to elbow each other or fart. He also taught us the names of distinguished Englishmen and the battles they had won. We copied these things on our slates and then erased them with a rag. We rarely used ink and paper which cost more. He taught us the names of the local rivers and towns and lots of other things - like spelling - which many of us thought nobody needed to know. We learned by chanting in a sing-song voice, swaying to the letters, words, or numbers. I found it easy to learn by jingles: 'Two pints make one quart, four quarts make one gallon...' or,

'Thirty days hath September, April, June and November. All the rest...'

As Christmas approached, the school was transformed into a magic castle. A feeling of festivity filled the air. I must have been impressionable for I watched transfixed while teachers and students converted dark, crowded classrooms into glittering caves. Fluttering coloured paper streamers, pom-poms, Chinese lanterns, and decorations were hung from walls and ceilings. In the ever-present drafts, the great silver bells swung leisurely above our heads. When the gas lamps were lit in the afternoon, the magic grew.

The closer we got to Christmas, the more things changed. There was no thrashing. The cruel use of the Dunce's hat - which I feared more than anything - was temporarily suspended. Even Mr. Manners and Joe took a rest from fighting. We didn't do a stitch of work. We played leap frog and had snowball fights in the school yard. We formed choirs and produced plays. For the plays we created scenery, properties and costumes out of nothing. It was great fun. I also learned something about language and elocution.

In one of the plays I was chosen to tip-toe into an artist's studio and place my head in the hole another student had made in the artist's canvas. The whole idea was that the artist would fail to notice that his canvas had been damaged and would go on touching up the face - my face - with paint. All I had to do was to put my head into the hole and keep absolutely still.

When the great night came, with most of our parents in attendance, I crept into the artist's studio. Having made sure that the artist was not there, I placed my head into the hole in the canvas. At that point the artist returned with his paints. This was the part we hadn't rehearsed. Instead of applying a dab of paint - as he had been instructed - he began to plaster me with the stuff. Howls of laughter came from the audience. When I opened my mouth to protest, he popped the paint brush right down my throat. By now the audience was uncontrollable. The play was considered a great success, but the taste of paint stayed with me for days.

Just before Christmas, the older boys carried in a Christmas tree dusted with snow. It was so high and so wide that they had difficulty getting it through the doors. I was thrilled when they hung the tree with decorations and candles. It became a mass of colour and light. I had never seen such a beautiful thing. How it contrasted with the dark day! They also brought in the crib with statues of Mary and Joseph, and the Infant Jesus, and the Three Wise Men from the East. There was a cow eating from the manger. These things brought home to me the joy and peace of Christmas for the first time.

While we were singing carols around the tree, a horse-drawn cart arrived laden with wooden crates filled with boxes of chocolates. The news spread like wildfire. Some kind soul had donated a box for every child. We shrieked with delight as box after box was extricated from the wood shavings. Each chocolate box lid was a delight in itself. My box showed a boy and a girl skating down a frozen river with snow-covered cottages lining the banks. It was sheer magic for me to possess such a prize. I kept the lid for ages.

At this time, my brother and sisters took me round the darkened streets singing carols. I carried a Chinese paper lantern with a candle inside. "Christmas is coming," we all chanted, "the goose is getting fat, please put a penny in the old man's hat. If you haven't got a penny, a ha'penny will do. If you haven't got a ha'penny - God bless you." We gave a lot of blessings and received some ha'pennies.

My school years were full of things other than learning. After school and on Saturdays, from the age of six, I ran errands for a neighbour of ours, Mr. Tinworth, who had turned his front room into a grocer's shop. I also delivered groceries for him. I was so small that I found it impossible to lift the baskets off the floor. Once Mr. Tinworth had helped me, I staggered off down the street, carrying the baskets on my hip. The grocer paid my parents one shilling and six-pence per week, of which I received one penny. Some customers gave me a half-penny for carrying their groceries, so I didn't do too badly.

Invariably, I spent the penny I received for my labours on a gob-stopper - a coloured ball of toffee on a stick about the size of a golf ball - which I bought at Mrs. Hudson's tiny sweet shop down the street. She kept the gob-stoppers - upon which her small customers repeatedly choked when the toffee came off the stick - in a big glass jar. I felt important when the jar was brought to the counter and I was allowed to dip my grubby fingers inside to choose the colour I wanted. I liked everything about Mrs. Hudson's shop. I liked the doorbell that announced my arrival, the warm, sugary, toasty smell, and all the shiny good things that were there to be eaten. Most of all I liked Mrs. Hudson because hers was the only shop where my opinion counted. In Mrs. Hudson's shop, the customer, however small, was in charge. Spending my penny was the most important decision of the week.

I must have shopped with Mrs. Hudson for several years. We came to know each other well. She never changed. She was the same sweet, gray-haired old woman when I met her as when I left. I owe it to her that I know so much about confectionery. When I became more affluent, she introduced me to all kinds of chocolate and sugary delights. I think I must have eaten my way through her store. She also taught me to be discerning. Gob-stoppers were all very well when you were a child, but not when you were growing up. Under her guidance, I moved on through a whole gamut of licorice delights, aniseed balls, and teeth-locking toffee, each piece of which had a different animal on the wrapper, until I reached what Mrs. Hudson thought was the industry's masterpiece: colourful packets of candy cigarettes that looked just like the real thing. I never did reach the chocolate pipe and cigar stage. One Christmas I bought from her a black chocolate minstrel playing a banjo. It was a 'Christmas special,' not available at any other time. I ate it - cannibal-like, banjo and all - in one go from head to foot.

Between the ages of six and ten, I was helped in my schoolwork by my sister Brenda and my grandmother Bridget. Brenda was not only at her best in tough spots, she was also highly intelligent. Other than father, she was the only one among us who could handle arithmetic. Grandmother Bridget called figures 'soulless.' Mother, Jenny, Dan and I found figures equally distasteful. It mystified us how Brenda could order figures about the way she did. No matter how many she wrote down, they did exactly what she told them to do. Nor did she ever tire of doing completely dull things with them. I didn't care how long it took to fill a water-butt with a hole in the bottom. With a sum here and a sum there, she was quite happy filling the leaking water-butt for ages. I wondered why the butt should have had a hole in it in the first place. Why didn't somebody fix it? Then she worked out how many freight cars were needed on a train that stretched from London to Edinburgh? Everybody knew there couldn't be such a train. It was ridiculous.

Daft as all this seemed, she always came up with the right answers. "You see how easy it is, Billy," she said, arranging the figures as she wanted them. Well, it did look easy the way she did it, but, with me, the figures went crazy. The moment I touched them they stampeded in every direction; they did awful things; anarchy reigned.

"What on earth are you doing, Billy," Brenda said, taking over. "You've made a dreadful hash of it. It's quite simple, really." Then she lined up the figures again and off they went. They always did what she wanted. The annoying thing was that she didn't seem to try. She was like a good collie dog with sheep. Without any fuss, all the figures finished up in the right pen. "There's nothing to it at all, Billy," she kept saying as she disposed of the last sheep.

There was no end to the problems she could handle. Indeed, she made problems harder than they needed to be. Once I managed to get one right. For a moment she was startled. "Ah, but that's the answer in yards," she gloated, "what would it be in feet, Billy? Come on!" That floored me.

There can be no question but what Brenda was unusually bright. To everyone's surprise, she topped the state examinations for eleven-year-olds in the county. And she did it without a book in the house, and without special coaching. It was a real miracle. Her name was in the newspaper. Jenny showed it to me. It was the first time I'd seen our name in print and it had quite an effect on me. It made me giddy. The next day I expected everyone to stop me in the street and ask me if I was the brother of the girl whose name was in the paper, and who was going to go to the Grammar School in Preston. Nobody did. I became so disappointed that I stopped a number of people to tell them that I was Brenda's brother. I told them how she had won a scholarship to go to a special school for girls at Preston, ten miles away. She was going to ride the train there and back every day without paying. Nobody seemed impressed.

After several days a letter arrived from the school board about Brenda. I heard my parents discussing it in the kitchen.

"Uniforms, including stockings are provided," said father studying a list. "Train fare as well," he continued. "And books and pencils."

"Well, imagine that," said mother, "I reckon they must have money cumin' out of their ears."

There was a pause.

"What's it say about shoes?" asked mother. "Lass can't go to college in clogs."

"Nothing," said father, "nothing."

"It must...look again."

There was a longer pause.

"Mm, aye, tha reet, Maggie, it does. It says that shoes will be black, of plain design, and of good quality."

"Um, they're fussy."

A still longer pause. "Where wa' it t' come fra?" mother asked. "Her feet have long outgrown what shoes she had."

"Well, we can borrow money to buy shoes, or we can leave her where she is," father said finally. "We might be making a fuss about nothing, Maggie. It's not good to put big ideas into young people's heads. What use is there in this learning when she could be doing real work?"

Although I was very young I knew that something was wrong. I wanted to shout through the cracks beneath my bed, "Brenda's name was in the paper! You can't stop her going to Preston because she hasn't got shoes."

But I didn't shout. Nobody did. To my knowledge, not even members of the school board. Why didn't grandmother Bridget intervene? She was, after all, the most educated among us. She was always on to us about 'larnin'.'

Brenda didn't go to Preston. One night when she came back from the lending library, I heard father tell her that they couldn't send her to school because she didn't have shoes, and they couldn't afford to buy them. Brenda didn't throw a fit, which is what I wanted her to do. Apart from a mumbled word or two, she accepted their decision. The matter was never discussed again. A brilliant career was denied her.

I think father was to blame. Somebody, somewhere would surely have paid for the shoes had he gone and asked, but he was too proud to beg. Why didn't he buy a used pair, I wondered. The truth is he wasn't interested in education for his children. It wasn't because Brenda was a girl, I think he would have done the same thing had it been my brother Dan. He never encouraged any of us to better ourselves or to make the best of our talents by schooling. Education and keeping up the family prestige didn't matter in our lives - spinning and weaving did. The mills were our destiny. There was nothing dishonourable in that. What had been good enough for him, and for his father and grandfather, was good enough for us. It's where we belonged. It was our station in life and each should be satisfied with his station. Instead of going on to higher education, Brenda entered the mill at twelve as a half-timer. She became a piecer, an assistant to a spinner.

My debt to grandmother Bridget is even greater than that which I owe to my sister Brenda. Nightly, she taught me to read and write. I think she gave me the attention she should have given my mother when she was my age. Grandmother stood over me while I struggled to link word to word, sentence to sentence on my slate. "Practice makes perfect," she said as I cleaned my slate. Her wrinkled finger followed mine when I tried to read a children's English grammar she had borrowed from the public library. Work done, she would tell me about the library books she had read. She didn't go in for the classics like the Penny Reader, Mr. Peck. She liked to read the novels of the time. She was fond of the books of a writer called Warwick Deeping. I suspect she liked him because he had written a book about an Irish girl called *Kitty*.

She also talked about America. She believed that America was the largest, richest country in the world. Beyond the packed cities and skyscrapers of the American eastern seaboard, she told me, were endless grasslands reaching to high mountains. Everything was big. "One day you will go to America, Billy Boy," she said, as if it had all been arranged. As I got older she became more concerned about what was to become of me. "You can go a long way," she would say, shaking her lace cap at me. "That's if you wish to. But you won't go without 'larnin'.' It's the key that opens all doors."

Chapter IX

Changing Faiths

Because mother could never make up her mind which church she belonged to - someone said she shopped for a new religion like shopping for a new hat - we children were tossed between St. Philip's (Church of England) and St. Peter's (Roman Catholic) schools. We started at St. Philips because it was round the corner from where we lived. Later on one of the priests at St. Peter's took mother to task for having her children at a Protestant school. So to St. Peter's we went.

Father didn't care to which church he belonged, provided he could stay away from it. Mother said that father had believed in a God of love before the war but not after it. The slaughter in France had left him without a mooring. "He floats," she said. Father Prendergast of St. Peter's, whom father disrespectfully called Father 'Spend-the-Brass,' once took him aside for backsliding as a Christian.

"Do you believe in God, Will?" he asked.

"I did until the war," father answered. "Tha'd be surprised if tha'd seen what Ah've seen." After which they shook hands. But they shook hands like two wrestlers: a touch of the hands without any warmth. I felt there was a gulf between them which neither could cross.

Mother once took father to a revival meeting in the hope that it would restore his old faith, but he was just as impassive about religion when he returned as he had been when he left the house.

Unable to get father to anymore revival meetings, mother turned her attention to me. One day we took a train to a station outside Blackburn where we joined up with hundreds of other men, women and children. With banners and flags bobbing up and down above our heads, we inched our way along a narrow country lane toward a turreted church at the top of a hill. The well-trodden ground was carpeted with autumn leaves.

At the sound of a command from the front of the procession, we pilgrims repeatedly fell down on our knees in the mud (the wise ones crouched) and sang a hymn about sin. We sang loudly so that our protestations would be heard at heaven's gate:

> ...All my sins, I now confess them,
> Never will I sin again,
> Never will I sin again.

As we shuffled forward, the more fervent among us struck their breasts, while pouring out their fears and hopes.

> Lord have mercy upon us,
> Christ have mercy upon us.

Only when I caught the eye of a girl about my own age who crouched beside me did I see the funny side of what we were doing. For a moment we had the giggles; she pinched my arm, I pulled her plaits.

Like an incoming tide, the crowd surged onward to the church. Tightly packed, we mounted the steps and passed through the great doors. Except for the flickering red eye of the altar lamp, and the candles and tapers, the church was lit only by the dim light that filtered through the windows. The sweet smell of incense and the warm scent of burning wax was in the air. We dipped our fingers in the font of Holy Water, crossing ourselves before going forward into the church.

The building was ice-cold when we entered, but was soon 'set on fire' by a small, dark-eyed monk in the pulpit. He was dressed in a brown robe tied by a white cord at the waist. His cowl was thrown back. He wore leather sandals. His stubs of hair reminded me of a hedgehog.

The priest began by making the sign of the cross and kissing the crucifix that hung at his side. At one moment thundering, at another whispering, his powerful voice soon echoed throughout the church. Throwing his weight from one foot to the other, while stretching out his arms, he mesmerized me. He must have said some important things about our sins, for he was constantly interrupted with heartfelt cries of: "Alleluia! Alleluia!" In their excitement, the callers seemed to try to outdo each other. The priest responded with still more thundering and whispering. It went on for a long time. It ended by our reciting the Confiteor, the Our Father and the Hail Mary. We left with the monk's blessing.

We did not have to kneel in the mud on the way back to the station. With the church bells tolling, we simply formed up outside and sang our way down the hill, now bathed in sunshine. Everybody was relaxed in the train. People were brighter-faced; they said they felt better for coming. I suppose they'd purged their sins; the wrongs they'd done were forgiven them; they'd won a new beginning.

Anyway, back to Father Prendergast and St. Peter's. Father Prendergast was a fat, jolly man of undoubted sincere piety, who seemed to get fatter as times got worse. Everybody liked him, especially for his short sermons. I liked him too, but I took a dislike to St. Peter's from the start. It was a forlorn building with a large bell in a belfry; the gray stone walls had blackened with age and dirt. A bare cindered yard at the side, from which dust blew most of the time, was the playground.

The best thing about St. Peter's was that Rosie Gill went there. She was my six-year-old sweetheart. She always wore the same old brown woolen hat pulled down at the back, and a gray coat much too long for her. We always held hands. We didn't have much to say to each other, but we were happiest when we were together. One day she showed me an amulet of Mary and

129

the crucified Christ, which hung on a cord around her neck under her blouse. It was a beautiful thing of the brightest colours and had been specially blessed. I knew from the way she drew it up so slowly from out of her dress that I was somebody special.

We were holding hands one afternoon on our way home from school when I had a sudden impulse to look over the stone parapet of the bridge that spanned the Blakewater River. The parapet was about five feet high and was not meant to be climbed by small children. Removing my bulky woolen gloves, and disregarding Rosie's protests, I jumped and clawed my way up the wall until I was able to look down on the river rushing over boulders below.

Before I realized what was happening, one of the bigger boys took me by the heels and heaved me over the parapet into the river. Stark terror possessed me as I fell head first. I hit the water with a loud splash; my face struck the rocks.

Rosie was the only one to come to my help. Dripping with blood, I fought my way to her at the side of the river. Leaning on her, with my teeth chattering, I drunkenly made my way home. Fortunately mother was there. She nearly fainted when she saw me. She didn't console me as Rosie had done, but she washed and bandaged my wounds. When father came home, he showed no sympathy. The way he went on about it, you would have thought that I made a practice of jumping off bridges and breaking my nose. No effort was made, either by teachers or parents, to find the bully and punish him. Scores at that school were settled without the unforgivable act of running to the teachers to tell tales. Tell-tale tits got their tongues slit, or something equally dreadful.

I used to call for Rosie on my way to school. Her home was in the next street. On my arrival, Mr. Gill was always standing with his back to the fire, drinking tea. "What, eh," he greeted me. He drank sip by sip, tasting his tea with great care before swallowing it. His bottom was so large that no heat reached any other part of the room. He wore the same oatmeal-coloured woolen undervest, with three buttons at the top, and the same balloon-like trousers. The vest and pants both looked slept in. His feet were wrapped in slippers made out of an old coat. Mr.

Gill must have eaten a lot of eggs, for there were egg stains from his neck to his waist. Rosie said her father was a sloppy eater and that her mother had given up worrying.

What did arouse my curiosity about Mr. Gill was the strange way he kept peering down the inside of his trousers. He would push the front of his pants away from him as far as his braces would go. Then he looked down into the dark hole he'd made as if there was something moving about there. As I watched him, I wondered if he was trying to discover how much room he had to spare; or whether he had got too hot. After a while I made up my mind that Mr. Gill had a pet rabbit in his pants, and was curious to see what it was up to. I would not have been the least surprised if a rabbit's head had suddenly popped up over the top of Mr. Gill's trousers. I never did ask Rosie what she thought.

In time, I came to realize that there were few men as lovable, or as big-hearted as Willie Gill. He was a thoroughly good-natured man, with a good-humoured face, who was happiest when he was helping others. He had the best of intentions. Little wonder that his fellow-Catholics thought so highly of him. His size made him all the more lovable. He was so large that when he entered our house it became crowded.

In a genteel way, he had reached the last state of shabbiness. In the street he wore the same old coat, stained with snuff. It had come apart under his armpits. His trousers were so thin that his knees showed through. His cracked shoes revealed his bare feet. Above his puffy, red face, with its rheumy eyes and large whiskers, he wore a crushed hat made of wool and bits of fur. It added distinction to an already odd appearance. His hair had never seen a comb. He smelled suspiciously of urine.

Mr. Gill had long since given up working for a living. Any money the Gills had came from Hessie, his thin little wife, whose weak, staring eyes didn't seem to like what she was seeing. Those eyes troubled me as a child. There was a story that Mr. Gill had worked in the mills but had given it up. Some said life had been unkind to him; others said he lacked backbone. Most said he was broke because he spent his time looking after others.

Meanwhile he survived by thinking up the most preposterous schemes to make money. One of these was to sell as fresh tobacco the cigarette ends which we children retrieved for him from the gutters. After taking the paper off, he placed the tobacco in a dish in his window. It was sold as 'Fresh Virginia.' I cannot think how many diseases he must have spread. The really good cigarette ends we found, we smoked ourselves.

———◦———

Mr. Gill first aroused in me the joy of going to Blackpool. It was long before my visit there with mother. One day - wonder of wonders - he suddenly proposed to take ten of us, including me, to Blackpool. Pied-piper fashion, armed with buckets and spades, we eagerly followed his waddling, fat figure to the railway station unable to believe our luck. He had our parents' consent, but we would have followed him anyway. We cheered as the train moved off. We heaped praise on Mr. Gill until his cheeks shone.

We'd gone only two or three stops when Mr. Gill said we had to get out. Puzzled, for we had no idea that Blackpool was so close, we leapt out of the train ready to run into the sea. But while there was plenty of sand, there was no sea. "Tide's out," said Mr. Gill, wrinkling his nose.

"Where's the tower?" everybody demanded.

"They've just moved it," Mr. Gill said, stuffing his shirt back into his trousers.

"Where are the people?" we pressed.

"Gone home."

"Are you sure, this is Blackpool?" I insisted.

"Eh?"

"Mr. Gill, where are we?"

"Little Blackpool. Big Blackpool is farther on."

"But you said you'd take us to Blackpool," I protested.

"You promised us." Some of the children began to cry. The crying got louder and louder.

What with the threatening weather, it looked as if Mr. Gill was going to break down and weep too. Instead, he shuffled in place like an elephant fastened to a stake. "Oh dear," he kept saying, his face past hope. His good-hearted plan to take us off our parents' hands and spend the day digging in a sandpit had misfired.

Had he told us that he was taking us to a sandpit, we would have gone with him gladly. But he'd said Blackpool, and Blackpool was a very different thing. Every suggestion he made, including building sand castles - after all, we had brought buckets and spades - was rejected. By now the children were making quite a din.

Threatened by our spades, Mr. Gill became desperate. "Follow me," he called as he shuffled off, his sail-like trousers flapping in the breeze. "I've just remembered, Blackpool is round the corner." Walking directly behind him, I felt the whole sky was covered by the seat of Mr. Gill's pants.

But the real Blackpool was not round that or any other corner. Turning corners only revealed more broken ground, more empty acres of sand. Tired of searching for the real Blackpool, our protests were renewed.

A vanquished, snuff-stained Mr. Gill led us back to the railway station. Some of the children cried all the way home. It was raining hard by the time we got back to Blackburn. Not knowing what to do with us - our people were still in the mills - he sat us all in his front room, half of which he occupied, and followed our movements with watchful eyes and a nervous cough. He was, after all, surrounded by ten discontented children brandishing spades. At the first mill whistle, which told him that our parents were on their way home, Mr. Gill rushed us out of the house. He never played the role of Pied Piper again.

To return to St. Peter's, I thought the school was as cheerless inside as it was out. The rooms were dark and had little else but rows of wooden desks and benches - the latter polished by the seats of past generations. The walls bristled with wooden pegs on which hung caps and coats. Like St. Philip's, there were the same lights, the same table for the teacher; the same blackboard. Both schools shared a distinguished war record of former students. The Lancashire Fusiliers had won an unmatched seventeen Victoria Crosses in the Great War, the highest military honour Britain could bestow.

In addition to Father Prendergast there was a young curate called Smail. He had come from a rich parish in London, and had a hump on his back, hence his nickname 'Humpty Dumpty.' He must have wondered what he'd fallen into at St. Peter's. He seemed to play no part in school life. Whenever I saw him in the streets he had his head down reading a leather-bound prayer-book. He had downcast eyes. I don't know whether he was a real priest or not. What I do know is that he had a quick temper. Give him cheek - "Smail, Smail, ate a whale," we used to call after him - and the prayer-book hit you like a stone. Everybody I knew gave him a wide berth. Mother said he was 'a fish out of water.'

There also were two nuns. Everybody loved the twinkling, big-boned, innocent Sister Lucy whose face was like a polished apple. I took an instant dislike to the gnarled, thin-lipped Sister Loyola, whom everyone feared. I shrank from her.

When Sister Lucy entered our room everybody looked up, everybody smiled. She had a delightful way of reaching down and gently - ever so gently - pinching your cheek. She was so sweet and cherubic that I felt like standing up and pinching her back. When Sister Loyola entered the room, the class froze. At the end of the day Sister Loyola took Sister Lucy home as though she were dragging her on a halter.

At St. Peter's the teachers were forever talking about sin and hellfire, which gave me nightmares. Whereas the Lifeboy Soap poster had been my constant companion on the wall at St. Philip's, at St. Peter's I sat next to a large picture of Christ with hard, staring eyes, pointing to his exposed, bleeding heart. There was a Cross on the middle of the heart and a fire on top of it. I never lost my fear of the blood. Although I felt a childish loyalty to Christ - Sister Lucy had said that He had suffered terrible things to help us - I found the picture oppressive and avoided Christ's eyes and his pointing finger as much as I could. Elsewhere in the room were pictures of Christ being scourged at the pillar, and Christian martyrs being fed to the lions. The only peaceful thing was a blue statue of the Madonna that stood on a windowsill with its back to the light.

The Catholics were expected to pray all the time. We prayed and prayed. We were forever crossing ourselves and getting down on our knees. Our teacher, Miss Little - she was in fact very large - asked us to pray before class to help us in our work. Now and then, we made the Stations of the Cross in the chapel next to our classroom, to which we had a communicating door. We banged and bumped and snickered as we went down on our knees and got up again, making our way from station to station. I was too small to know what it was all about. Christ's passion and death interested me, but I was bored by the time we reached the last station. Obviously, I lacked reverence and devotion.

When the door leading from our classroom to the chapel was left open, I could see as far as the altar. Compared to our drab room, it was like looking into another world. There was a ceiling studded with golden stars, gleaming metal and stone, polished wood and a mysterious, flickering red light hanging before the tabernacle. Mass was said there to a crowded congregation every Sunday.

The happiest moments were when Father Prendergast wandered into our classroom making the sign of the Cross. He was a kind man who didn't seem to have any purpose other than to tell tales in a slow mellow voice and make fun. His stories had happy endings, like Noah and the Ark, or the fellow who was swallowed by a whale. The pictures of suffering around the room didn't affect his spirits. He had a hearty laugh, which caused the folds of flesh on his neck to glisten. He laughed so much that I feared that his shaking belly would escape from beneath the black belt that held his paunch in place.

One day, during one of his visits, Father Prendergast asked us what we'd like to be when we grew up. I knew it was only meant for fun because we were all destined to work in the mills. Nevertheless, I boldly said I'd like to be a tinker. The tinkers - most of them Gypsies - who mended our pots and pans struck me as wonderfully free; they didn't work in the mills; they came and went as they wished.

For some reason my answer threw Father Prendergast into fits of laughter. Every student in the room joined in. Even Miss

Little (who found Father Prendergast's visits a strain) laughed. I could tell from the trouble Father Prendergast had in adjusting his belt that his rippling belly had broken loose.

There was no laughter when Sister Loyola visited us. She was as serious as Father Prendergast was jolly. She had suffering on the brain. She was always talking about a wrathful God. I wondered if her idea of love wasn't to thrash us all. She left me with a life-long fear of God. I didn't fear Christ. He had given His life for others, and as far as I could tell, was a good man who was now quite dead. He was the Good Shepherd: He was real; I knew Him. God was different; He was full of mystery; He was a strange figure who could pop up anywhere at any time. I never understood why God had sacrificed His son instead of Himself.

Sister Loyola did not like her views challenged, not even by Father Prendergast. Whenever he intervened: "Oh, come now Sister, not everybody must suffer," Sister Loyola's eyes would flash and she would withdraw into a dark, offended silence.

One had to watch out for Sister Loyola. She'd spring a question on you without warning.

"Who is God?"

By rote we answered "God is the Supreme Spirit, who alone exists of Himself, and is infinite in all perfections."

"Who is Jesus Christ?"

"Jesus Christ is God the son made man for us," we chanted back.

"Why did God make you?" was one of her specials. Everybody in the class knew the answer.

"God," we jingled, "made me to know Him, love Him, and serve Him in this world, and to be happy for ever with Him in the next."

"And sin?"

"Sin is an offense against God."

Before she left the room she asked, "What will Christ say to the wicked?"

We could jingle the answer without thinking: "Christ will say to the wicked, 'Depart from me, ye cursed, into everlasting fire'." Hell was final; from everlasting to everlasting.

I loved the words, I loved the imagery, the mystery and the rhythm. I loved parading my knowledge. But I didn't understand a single thing. I never worked out how three gods - God the Father, God the Son and God the Holy Ghost - could be one. The nature of God the Father I simply could not grasp. I was especially confused about the use of the word God. To say 'God' was all right, but to say 'By God' in a loud voice was all wrong. I could tell from the distrustful look in Sister Loyola's eyes that she didn't hold out much hope for me.

"These things you must learn, child," she insisted, "understanding will come later."

I have never forgotten Sister Loyola's sermon on the crucifixion and death of Christ given to the school one Good Friday. We were all assembled in the main hall. Sister Loyola stood against the plaster statue of St. Michael spearing a horned serpent - the devil. Hypnotized by her words, we relived Christ's passion. We shared His agony in the garden. We saw His scourging at the pillar. We watched as a crown of thorns was pressed against His brow. Together we walked with Him as He carried His blood-spattered cross along the Street of Sorrows. Eventually we reached Calvary, where we bided while His feet and hands were pierced most cruelly. With Sister Loyola, we saw the cross being heaved up against the sky. As we looked upon the sagging figure with its bowed head, its haggard face and its stiff, outstretched arms, our sorrow was complete.

While she was talking, a storm had blown up. Papers were scattered and a cloud of dust came through the windows before we could shut them. The blackened sky was split by flashes of lightning. Sister Loyola had just cried out: "And the curtain of the temple was rent from top to bottom," when the whole school was shaken by a crash of thunder. I felt the building rock, my chair shake. I heard the windows rattle. I didn't need convincing that Jesus had just given up the ghost. I was too terrified to believe anything else. To me this was the God of wrath; the God of vengeance; God on the grand scale; only this God could have shaken the school down to its foundations.

Sister Loyola never let the Woodruff children forget that we had come from St. Philip's. She was wary of us on that score.

"All Protestants are heretics," she repeated with a dark look that went right through me.

I wasn't sure what a heretic was, so I screwed up enough courage to ask her: "What is a heretic, please Sister?" The answer was on her lips before I'd finished asking. "A heretic," she intoned, "is someone who has offended God and has been abandoned by Him." That left me more puzzled than ever.

In Sister Loyola's eyes the Woodruff heretics were lucky to have made the change from St. Philip's to St. Peter's. "God is in our church," she said proudly, "not in their's." I knew enough from Sister Lucy's comments that only a fool would not have God on his side. "God," Sister Lucy had assured me, "is all-powerful, all-watching, all-seeing, all-vengeful. No one can fool God." Sister Lucy's religion was simple: fear the Lord and glorify Him every day. "Hold fast to the Cross," she urged me. It was not only the right thing to do, it was the wise thing to do. I don't know what others thought about God, but I kept a still tongue and followed Sister Lucy.

Of course, there was more to St. Peter's than the severity of Sister Loyola. As the chapel was next to our classroom, the air was sweet with incense. We heard the gentle tinkling of a bell. The colourful ceremonies and the sense of mystery overwhelmed my imagination. As long as I went to that school, I was besieged by miracles: seas parted, the dying were healed, ghosts rose, chariots of fire soared through the skies - there was no end to it. The imagery of it all sustained me. At St. Peter's we were eternally being 'washed in the blood of the lamb.' At St. Philip's you never saw a drop of blood; you were washed in Lever Brother's Lifeboy Soap.

The great advantage of being at St. Peter's was that I could take part in the annual Easter procession. Massed Bands came from all over the district. The importance of the procession was measured by the number of bands; brass and silver bands were everything. With their leaders strutting proudly with a long silver stick with a brass ball on top, the bands thumped and pounded, blared, boomed and crashed until you couldn't hear yourself speak. Whether marking time with their polished boots on the cobbles, or on the march, the bandsmen blew their horns and beat their drums until the veins stood out on their necks and the windows rattled. The crowd made way, counted the number of bands, and crossed themselves.

I preferred the hymn:

> Oh, Mary, we crown thee with blossoms today,
> Queen of the angels and Queen of the May...

to the more militant 'Faith of our Fathers' with its deaths in dungeons dark.

It would take a hard heart not to be moved by the spectacle of Mary's garlanded figure rocking above a sea of wide-eyed, young girls carrying bouquets of sweet-smelling lilies of the valley. Dressed in white, stumbling along at their own pace, they contrasted sharply with the sooty walls and the grimy streets.

It was especially moving when the crowds sang their praise to Mary, Queen of the May:

> To live and not to love thee, would fill my heart with shame.
> When wicked men blaspheme thee, I'll love and bless
> thy name...

Alas, there were wicked men about who not only blasphemed Mary's name, but who did their best to disrupt the procession. Most years were peaceful, but then the fighting would break out again like a rash. To my horror, a fight did break out one day when we were passing St. Philips. Protestants were touchy about the Catholics demonstrating before their church.

The fight began with a lot of shouting, which was followed by the throwing of rotten eggs and tomatoes. The throwers took care not to hit the bands, but they did hit us. While I scrambled out of the way, I saw a number of Protestants try to seize the banners. There was a free-for-all right along the street. One pole was broken over somebody's head. Nobody took any notice of the police whistles, or the shouts of the priests.

While the battle raged, the bands continued to march in place, crashing out still another hymn. Disregarding the fact that the faithful, and the not so faithful, were being beaten over the head, and little girls sent screaming, the bands played on. After all, they were being paid.

The battle over, with the Eucharist held high at the front, we all formed up again and continued the march. 'Faith of our Fathers' rang across the town.

After that, the Chief of Police always led the procession. With his medals, bright belt and his white gloves, he was out at the front looking for trouble. Blackburn Protestants had enough gumption not to knock him down.

When a wind got up, the marchers had enough trouble on their hands without protesters. As the wind rose, a shouting match developed between those holding the poles and those, front and aft, who held the guide ropes. "Nay, nay, pull on it tha clown," someone shouted, "pull to t' right; can't tha see what's wanted?" It wasn't unknown for those who carried the big banners that stretched across the street to be lifted off their feet and flung aside. Because of his strength, not his religion, father was sometimes asked to help with the big banner. I knew when they'd slipped the pole into the leather holder that hung between his thighs, that that was one banner that would not blow over.

On one occasion, the wind proved too strong and the image of God Almighty, resplendent in the reddest of robes, who had been soaring above our heads and our hearts, was suddenly wrapped around somebody's head. It was a fate that could befall any of the radiant holy men and women whose portraits rode past at roof top on a full sail. Befittingly, the banner bearing the blue, glittering figure of the Virgin Mary,with its inlaid profusion of lilies and roses, and its golden crown, never suffered such ignominy.

Following the Chief of Police at the head of the line was a resplendent figure who far outshone the arm of the law. He wore a long scarlet, gold-trimmed cloak with a fur collar, striped, sail-like trousers, an Admiral's hat, pointed fore and aft, and polished shoes covered with spats. In his right hand he carried a silver baton. This was the Grand Knight of Columbus, Willie Gill. No longer dishevelled, this was the real Willie Gill. Even his step had changed; he no longer slouched. Everybody knew him and they never failed to express their surprise at the transformation.

"My, what a toff tha are, Willie," they called out. "Tha're a one, tha're."

Twirling his silver stick, Willie revelled in the praise. Such a day took years off his life. Not everything, certainly not the important things in the life of Willie Gill could be expressed in terms of money. There was happiness and dignity and glory to think about. I had to blink when I saw him the next day. It was like a mirage: the emperor had gone, the tramp had returned.

The best thing about the Easter processions, weather permitting, was the eating and drinking that followed. Some Easter picnics became a soggy, treacherous fight against the driving rain. If the weather was fine, having declared their faith to the entire town, the Catholics filed into somebody's meadow where large tents and food awaited them. Led by Mr. Gill, the bands marched through the farm gate, taking care not to step in the cow dung, and then stopped playing. Chin straps were loosened, box hats removed, banners lowered and placed against the trees. For a few minutes people stood around wiping their foreheads and talking. A clap of the hands from the priests was the signal to begin eating. Accompanied by the tinkle of glass, the clatter of plates and the rattle of cutlery, it became a free-for-all.

The tents were full of refreshments. There were plates of bread and margarine. There were pies and cakes, jellies and preserves and buckets of hot water for the teapots. For those who could get to the barrels quick enough, there also was cider.

First time I ever felt tipsy was after drinking a glass of that cider. Either my mates and I had got in the wrong queue, or the people doling it out didn't realize that the drink was intoxicating. I knew something was wrong when my friends' speech thickened. It took a long time for the priests to catch on to what was happening. They thought our weaving about on the grass was funny. Not Father Prendergast. He was too old at the game. The moment he arrived, he took one shocked look at us and boomed: "Serve no more cider! Satan is in the barrel!"

You wondered where such mountains of food for those Easter treats came from and how they could all be eaten. Despite the lean times, a lot of it was provided by the parishioners, the women trying to outdo each other. Each woman watched her own and other people's food to see which was eaten first. Pies and cakes that lingered were no honour to anybody and were quickly disowned.

We children slipped underneath the tables, hidden from sight by the table clothes that reached to the ground. We crawled about there against the shuffling feet and ate like horses. To obtain our share, we periodically reached up and grabbed what we could.

When the serious business of eating and drinking was finished, everybody turned to gossiping or to playing games. We had races, tug-of-war and, while the fiddlers scraped, clog dances by a group called the Cloggers, who laughed shyly as they danced. And when that was done, we sat on benches or on the grass outside the tents, and sang. When the light failed, and the fiddles were stilled, my family had a way of reuniting and wandering home together.

―◦―

One day at school Miss Little sent me with a message to another teacher. It was eleven-thirty and I'd soon be off to the mills to deliver my family's midday meal. When I looked down the massive oak banisters on the main staircase, there wasn't a soul in sight. Apart from the drone of distant voices, all was still. I threw myself headfirst onto the banister and shot down toward the ground floor.

I arrived at the feet of Sister Loyola. There was no mistaking the shiny black shoes, the black gown with its black rosary hanging from waist to knees, and the wooden cross swinging pendulum-like before my eyes. Sister Loyola was a small figure but from that angle she looked enormous. I was seized with terror.

While she held me with her cold eyes, I wished I might fall through a crack. I was so frightened that I could neither move nor breathe. After one of the students had broken his arm, Sister Loyola had threatened dire consequences.

"Don't you know it is forbidden to slide down the banister?"

"Yes," I stammered. My lips and tongue felt dry.

"So you have done it willfully?"

"Yes," I faltered; yet I felt no remorse.

Before I could escape, she had grabbed me by the ear and was dragging me back up the stairs to my classroom. She twisted my ear so savagely that she made me cry.

The moment Miss Little saw Sister Loyola she took off her specs. "Oh, dear," she said. Miss Little did not like violence. If she was forced to punish us, she did so reluctantly and with a light hand. For this she was respected.

"Stop what you're doing!" Sister Loyola ordered the class, "I am about to make an example of someone who willfully disobeys school regulations. Your cane!" she demanded of Miss Little.

"Oh, dear," Miss Little repeated, adjusting her pince-nez.

Still held by the ear, I watched Miss Little go to the cupboard for her bamboo rod. Each teacher had such a cane and used it regularly. If you broke the rules, you were for it. No argument. The cane was administered either on the seat of the pants or on the hands. The rod on the seat of the pants was less painful. With Sister Loyola there was no choice. She went for the hands.

Having let go of my ear, Sister Loyola began to push back her wide sleeves. With my heart thumping, I stood there watching her, fearing the worst. She tested the rod, bending it with her hands. Then to get the feel of the cane, she struck the air several times. Whoosh, whoosh.

"Put up your hand!" she ordered. Her pale face had reddened. Her lips were set in a hard strength of will.

I raised one of my arms, offering my palm.

"Higher!" she ordered, lifting the hand with the tip of the cane.

Every eye was on the cane. Where thrashing was concerned, Sister Loyola had a reputation; it was something worth watching.

I waited, biting my lip.

Suddenly she brought the stick down across my palm and fingers with all her strength. There was a rattle of her cross and beads, and a sting of pain as if my hand had been laid open. I stifled a howl.

She cut me five more times on that hand, each cut worse than the last. I saw and felt the red weals. A shocked Miss Little stood there, hand over her mouth.

Breathing heavily, Sister Loyola demanded the other hand.

"No!" I screamed "No!" Three cuts were the usual punishment. I'd already had six.

Sister Loyola reacted as if I'd struck her across the face. There was a murmur from the class.

"You wicked, wicked boy!" she called threatening me with her stick.

"No!" I repeated defiantly. Shaking with anger and shamed before the class, I felt rebellious, even violent. Before Sister Loyola could recover from her surprise, I lunged forward, struggled with her, and wrenched the cane out of her hand. I then rushed to the open window and flung it into the street. Avoiding Sister Loyola's outstretched hands, I ran from the room. I left my cap and coat behind; I didn't stop running until I reached my mother in the mill. Between tending the clattering machines, she heard me out.

"So much for St. Peter's," she said, doffing another can of cotton. Back to St. Philips we went.

This traipsing backward and forward between St. Philip's and St. Peter's did not do the Woodruff children any harm. Other than to be given strange looks, and to be the subject of nods and whispers, which suggested that the Woodruffs had escaped from a zoo, we were never ostracized because of it. Father Prendergast and the Reverend Reeves of St. Philip's (who was as lean as Father Prendergast was fat) probably took the view that the Woodruffs were not worth fighting over. The Reverend Reeves once asked me: "Do you have the faith, my child?" I must have said something awful for the Reverend lapsed into shocked silence and never bothered me again.

All I cared about was how my street friends took this crossing of religious boundaries. Fortunately, they ignored it.

It says a lot about the privation of the early 1920's that we children were prepared to attend the church or chapel that offered most food. We didn't even worry about the difference between church and chapel. We cast our net widely: Catholic, Church of England, Congregational, Presbyterian, Methodist, Independent, Unitarian, Baptist; we tried them all. Dan had a nose for these things. All we had to do was to follow him. He darted from chapel to church, with a sure knowledge of who was offering what. We were completely unscrupulous about it. We sang anybody's hymns, provided tea and rock buns followed. Accompanied by the organist, and the earnest young preachers with good looks and sonorous voices, we sang "Now thank we all our God," or "Count your blessings, name them one by one, count your blessings, see what God has done," with copious insincerity. We thundered out the words, "I know not, Oh! I know not, what joys await us there, what radiance of glory, what bliss beyond compare," but it meant nothing. Our sole concern was food.

I thought that some of the churches and chapels we visited were severe and dark. There was no beauty in them - no mystery. It made it easier if there were paintings on the walls. While the preacher preached, I could join Moses or some other Old Testament prophet, or lose myself in the maxims painted on the walls, such as: "In everything give thanks," or "Abstain from evil," or "Cast all your care upon Him, for He careth for you," and many more.

Both church and chapel smelled of hymnals, camphor, wax and carbolic soap. I don't know why, but everything had to be scrubbed, rubbed and polished. Scrubbing brushes were common; they were called hedgehogs, and would take the skin off you if you didn't watch out. If a thing didn't shine, as all doorknobs and brasses did, or smell of carbolic soap, as most floors did, it wouldn't do. The constant rubbing, scrubbing and small-tooth combing was the only way to cope with the dirt.

In our search for food, we were compelled to listen to innumerable sermons on sin, mortify ourselves in the long, polished pews, and endlessly repeat the Lord's Prayer   The sermon, usually delivered from a pulpit high above our heads, was literally and physically the price we paid for the refreshments, which at times seemed so far away. I suspected that the preacher was trying out his sermon on us before he gave it at the Sunday service. I really resented it when, on top of everything else, he announced: "We will now lower our heads and examine our conscience." That was all very well for a minute or two, but some of the preachers had a conscience the length of your arm. I think they were stretching it out before handing out the buns. It wasn't my conscience that was troubling me - it was my belly.

I hope there wasn't as much sin in town as the preachers said there was. According to them, the place was awash with big and little sins. The big sins were the ones to watch. If you dropped dead with one of those chalked up against you, you went straight to hell and stayed there - forever. It struck me odd that one of the big sins should have been gluttony. I didn't think my brother and I should stay awake at night watching for that one; not when we couldn't get enough to eat.

Not only did there seem to be a surfeit of sin about; there were so many ways in which the Devil could trap you - even without you knowing it. I was worried when I learned that you could even sin by silence. According to the preachers, you needed eyes in the back of your head to keep up with Satan. If you didn't watch out, he'd nab you and you'd be in hellfire before you knew it.

These sermons not only made me feel hot round the collar, they also puzzled me a lot. I didn't understand why I would go straight to hell for gluttony, but pull down a fairly light sentence for drunkenness. Nor did I understand how God and the devil could keep a proper tally of all the petty and mortal sins that were about.

I expect the preachers knew. I suspect that they also knew what we were up to. They never distributed food and drink until the sermon was over. Although the rock buns they handed out were too hard to be eaten quickly, we speeded things up by dunking them in the hot tea. One afternoon, with Dan's planning, a gang of us collected eight buns and eight cups of tea each from different places of worship. As a count was kept by the ministers and their prim wives of our comings and goings, our multiple appearances must have caused a staggering increase in church attendance.

During my school years, whether at St. Philip's or St. Peter's, I'm afraid I didn't learn much more than how to survive. I suspect that that is all that was expected of me. School was a holding pen until I entered the mills. No teacher ever wasted time talking to me about the love of learning, or that education mattered. Nobody emphasized what good friends books can be. Curiosity was not encouraged.

There were teachers other than Mr. Manners and Miss Little, but I have only dim impressions of what they taught. Teachers at my elementary schools were interchangeable. They taught a bit of everything. I know I must have taken the eleven-year-old examination - the one in which my sister Brenda had distinguished herself - but obviously my efforts did not attract anybody's attention.

There must have been textbooks in my late years at school, yet I cannot remember a single one - not in Mathematics, not in English, not in Geography, not in History. No book ever went home with me. My family never bought school books. There was no homework and no report cards. I never owned a school satchel. What would I have done with it? Nor did I understand why some children went on to the next class while others stayed behind.

I suspect I used school as a place where I could rest before tackling the tasks that awaited me in the real world. My teachers knew I was physically exhausted and were kind enough to leave me alone. None of them ever asked me to go chasing prizes. I was never put under severe mental strain. Nor was I ever encouraged by my parents to take school seriously. When in later years the seed of learning was planted in me, it found a fertile, unworked soil in which to grow.

From the age of ten onward school was incidental. I was up at five to deliver newspapers. I got to school as the bell rang. From nine until eleven-forty-five I dozed; worse still, I think I slept. At eleven-forty-five the teacher gave me a signal, and I ran from school (sometimes with Dan) to deliver my family's dinners in the mills. Dinner hour was from twelve till one. The meal, a stew of meat, potatoes and vegetables, had been cooked by mother the night before, filled into basins, and taken to work in the morning. They were left on a large stove in the mill warehouse. Before noon the basins were hotted up, hence hot-pot. My family could, of course, have collected their own dinners, but they had other things to do, and they were exhausted from having been on their feet for the past four hours. Besides, children were expected to help. I had to move quickly because, as spinners, my sisters did not work in the same mill as my parents. If there were groups of workers standing or squatting against the mill walls when I arrived, I knew I was late.

I collected the dinners from the stove where my family had placed them. I had a knack of distinguishing our basins from scores of others, because ours had a pretty pattern. But one day mother put father's hot-pot in a mud-brown basin. As it was the same as some of the others, I ran off with somebody else's bowl. The way the fellow chased after me through the factory, bawling out that I'd pinched his dinner, you might have thought that his life was at stake. Losing one's dinner was a serious matter.

I ran with each basin in my cap because it was scalding hot. I first went to father, then Jenny, then Brenda. Speed was essential; nobody wanted a cold-pot, not even Jenny and Brenda who seemed to be lathered with sweat from the heat and humidity of the spinning-room. Once I tripped and fell carrying father's dinner. It spilled into my cap: meat, potatoes, carrots, peas, gravy, the lot. All I could do was to scoop it out of my hat back into the bowl and say nothing. He never noticed, but my hat smelled for days. The last two basins were for mother and me. We ate our dinner balancing ourselves on an overturned round sliver can, our backs wedged against the whitewashed wall. We had to cover the hot-pot from the fine dust that fell like a gentle rain.

It wasn't difficult to know when the dinner hour was done. Precisely at one, somebody threw a lever, and with a creak, crack, thump and clatter the whole room began to tremble and shake. Once the machinery became alive and the myriad wheels began to turn, you either jumped up smartly and set about your business, or you found yourself in trouble. The machine was the boss, it wouldn't wait, and it took no excuses. Glad to escape the din, I raced back to school. From one-thiry to four I must have dozed again. After four I ran the streets with the evening edition of the local newspaper. Then I came home and ran errands.

————◦————

Running in and out of the mills daily, I could hardly fail to learn something about textile manufacture. I watched mother breaking up the bales of cotton, clean, blend, whirl and pound them until a continuous sheet of matted tufts called a lap emerged. This was called slubbing. The lap was then fed into the carder which had two rollers covered with fine wire teeth to break up the tufts and separate the individual fibres. From the carder the untwisted rope of cotton (a sliver) was coiled in tall cans. The sliver, about an inch in diameter, was then combed to remove the shorter fibres, drawn across smooth leather-covered rollers, twisted into a long, firm thread, after which it was wound onto large spinning bobbins. This was roving. The bobbins went to the spinner where the threads were blended, drawn and twisted some more. Jenny and Brenda were spinners.

The resulting yarn, both warp and weft, came in all kinds of threadcounts, or thicknesses. It was then woven. My father was a weaver. He spent his life 'kissing the shuttle.' It was called 'kissing the shuttle' because he drew the weft thread from the cop by sucking it through a small hole at one end of the shuttle.

The workers, including my own family, took pride in explaining their work. It was like being admitted to a secret society. They were serious about it. When they talked about cloth, hilarity stopped. Problems that arose in the mill during the day, such as when the weave or pattern was varied, were discussed at night until a solution was found. Men or women were not judged so much by what they did at home but by what they did in the mill. People respected skill. Pride of work meant a lot. Work was everything.

Chapter X

Blackpool Rock

I think the years from the early twenties to the mid-thirties were rather like Lancashire weather: generally awful, with bright periods. One such bright period occurred when my parents suddenly decided to take us to Blackpool.

It must have been in 1924 or 1925, when the textile industry had made a partial recovery from the crash of 1920. Anyway, my people were in jobs, otherwise we wouldn't have had the money.

We went during Wake's Week, a traditional holiday originally linked with the Church. Each cotton town had its own particular Wake's Week when everything was shut down. The mill owners spent the week doing maintenance and stocktaking. The workers - if they had the money - escaped to the hills or the sea. We hoped that the Morgans might join us, but they covered up by saying, "No, we've decided against going away for the week. We're just going for days. There's nothing like your own bed." We knew that talk of going away for days was humbug, but the pretense was kept up.

It was agreed by my family that we'd get away at the crack of dawn on the Saturday morning after the mills had stopped. Until then we children talked and slept Blackpool. Mother slipped me a coin to buy a new bucket and spade. When the day came we were up before dawn straining to go. We searched the sky for the sun. The family's one and only straw valise was got out and filled with food. As the price of food at Blackpool was too high, we took bread, oats, a large can of Lyle's syrup, margarine, cans of milk, fish and pineapple chunks, tea, sugar, eggs marked with our name, a jar of jam, a jar of piccalilli relish, salt and sauce. The clothes we took were on our back. Having left two shillings under the pot dogs on the mantelpiece to pay for iron rations when we returned broke, we locked the door and left the house. The week's rent we took with us to spend in Blackpool.

Father went first, carrying the valise with a leather strap round it, then mother, then us. Our first stop was the King's Arms, where our parents vanished. Jenny, Brenda, Dan and I were left to amuse ourselves on the pub step. Fortunately, the King's Arms had two marble pillars at the entrance that looked like potted meat. Jenny at once took charge. She pretended that the doorway was her shop. The rest of us lined up before an imaginary counter and placed our orders for potted meat. With an imaginary knife, Jenny (with the pub regulars stepping over us) pretended to cut slices off the pillars to feed us.

One customer, a twinkle in his eye, stopped and talked to us.
"What you up to?"
"I've opened a potted meat shop," said Jenny.
"Oh, you 'ave, 'ave you? Where's your folks?"
"Inside."
"Going to Blackpool, are you?" The stranger eyed our buckets and spades.
"Yis," said Brenda.
"How much did you say your potted meat was?"
"It's very special today," said Jenny. "Sixpence a pound."
"Well, I'll take two bob's worth."
With our eyes popping, Jenny 'cut' four pounds of meat according to the customer's order. She 'weighed' it, 'wrapped' it, and 'handed' it to him carefully. The man pretended to put

the packet in his pocket. After that he gave Jenny a real two shilling piece.

"That'll be a tanner each," he said.

"Oh, thank you," we rejoiced.

"Ta, Ta!" he said. "Remember me when you're on't sands."

"Oh, we will," we chorused.

We'd 'eaten' an enormous amount of potted meat by the time our parents emerged. By now they were full of the holiday spirit. There followed further stops at the Lord Derby and The Plough. Each stop increased our fears. What if our parents drank so much that we might never get to the station? What if we had to drag them back to the house drunk? We need not have worried.

I'd noticed for some time that something was dribbling from the valise that father was carrying, but had kept a still tongue. Nothing must prevent us getting on the train. Eventually even father noticed that something was wrong. The procession was halted, the strap undone, the top of the valise lifted.

"It's the bloody syrup," father exploded, staring at the confused heap of syrup-saturated clothes and provisions at his feet. "You wouldn't believe it, the damned stuff's everywhere."

With us all looking on, he separated the can and its lid from the other items in the suitcase. Staring at the empty, two pound tin in disbelief, he said the most awful things about syrup in general and Lyle's syrup in particular. Then he kicked the empty can into the street, slammed the valise shut, fastened the strap, and marched off in a towering rage toward the station. His foul mutterings could be heard yards away.

We children followed, breathing a sigh of relief.

Still dripping syrup, we climbed aboard the train. It was an excursion train and it was packed. It was good humour all the way. Everybody had broken loose. If anybody had talked about cotton on that train he'd have been thrown out onto the track, headfirst.

On arrival in Blackpool we were told to rush past the ticket barrier. Only mother and father had tickets. "If you're caught, act daft," father said. Following Dan and my sisters - Jenny although fifteen was so small that she passed as a child - I dashed past the ticket collectors. They paid no attention to us. Once past the barrier, we waited for our parents at the station entrance. The rich children we saw were clean and tidy, wore respectable clothes, and had clean noses. They shouted respectability. No dashing past the ticket collectors for them.

From the station we walked to a lodging house in the back streets. Father paid for a week on arrival. The family shared one bedroom. There were lots of other Blackburn children in the house with whom we could play.

We abandoned our parents on arrival and only joined them for meals. Sitting on benches, in sand-streaked bathing suits, we ate twice a day with all the other families in a large room downstairs. Everybody squeezed in where they could. Nobody dreamed of grumbling. We'd come from the same town, some from the same street. We belonged together. There wasn't a sad face among us. Old and young, we'd promised ourselves a treat in Wake's Week, and we were not going to be done out of it. The dining-room table and benches rocked with laughter. Every meal was a joyful shouting match.

Aside from the smells, and the queuing for the toilet, everything was bliss. In the dining room the landlady's word was law; nobody answered back. She was skilled at her job, and knew how to get us out of the house when she wanted to. The only subdued person there was the landlady's husband who seemed to do most of the work.

As long as the weather was fine - and it was with us - we spent our time on the beach or paddling in the sea. We ran wild. What the adults did was their business.

A week later, with long faces, and our mouths stuffed with 'Blackpool Rock,' we caught the train home. It seemed to go faster on the return journey. There was no stopping at pubs, or pretending to eat potted meat. Our week of make-believe was over.

After Blackpool, Blackburn air hung like lead.

Chapter XI

Running Wild

I began to run wild from about the age of seven. Our house was so small that my brother and I were happier on the street. To sit around at home was to run the risk of being given a job. As I was the youngest, and Dan had a way of disappearing, I was invariably caught for these jobs. Meat scraps or a soup bone had to be obtained from the butcher. Fish heads and tails had to be collected from the fishmonger. I knew that when I went to the butcher I mustn't fail. "Mam asks if you can let her have some scraps," I'd say. I carried a dodger in case my pleading eyes failed to break down his resistance to part with bits of meat for nothing. I returned with my bundle of scraps wrapped in newspaper. Same with the fish heads. Printer's ink was part of our diet.

Going to the cobbler for new irons on our clogs was another job I had to do. While my family sat at home in their stockinged feet, I sat with other children by the cobbler's last. We slid along the polished bench until our turn came. Grown-ups were served first.

The cobbler lived a few doors away. He sat in his front room, bent over his work, with a gas lamp at his side. The lamp had mirrors around it, which gave an unusually bright light. The whole place smelled of sweaty feet and wood shavings. For front cokers (metal runners attached to the wooden sole) I paid eightpence; for heels fourpence; for a toe cap twopence. With his tools and wood in easy reach, the cobbler cut and shaped new clogs to size. They had a stout leather upper, a wooden sole and a heel strengthened with iron cokers.

I marvelled how the man filled his mouth with nails and wooden fillings, and how he seemed to fire them from his mouth at the clogs - like bullets from a gun. He never missed. When he stood up to shake the shavings off his leather apron, I noticed the stoop of his shoulders. Perhaps because his mouth was full of pegs and nails, he didn't talk much.

Chores finished, I dashed away to join a gang of boys in the often rain-darkened streets. When the paper blinds were drawn, each cottage became a shiny, orange-patched island in the dark. There were usually eight to twelve of us, huddled together in the dark in a mill shed. When it was raining outside, we sat and talked. Our favourite topic was sport. A run of victories for the town's football team, the Rovers, kept us talking for weeks. A child murder up Whalley way occupied us for a month. We were astonished at the dreadful things grown-ups could get up to.

If all else failed, we sat entranced while Shorty Cooke - one of the gang - told us a story that we all knew was a whopping lie. "I don't think you've heard this one," he'd begin. He told his tale so naturally and so convincingly that you wanted to believe him. One of his best tales was the visit he and his father had made to the Cup Final at Wembley in London. He had it all off pat. Yet we knew that he and his dad had never been beyond the tram ride to Whalley Bridge. Shorty ran a firewood business out of an old pram. He sold penny bundles of firewood, which he bought from a dealer in bulk, extracting a stick from each bundle and selling it again.

Often the gang shared a cigarette, passing it from mouth to mouth. Shorty Cooke always had a fag. We suspected he had pilfered them, but we never pressed him. We thought it manly to smoke and, of course, we were men. We inhaled deeply, and took pride in blowing the smoke down our noses. When the mood took us, we carried out raids on neighbouring territory. We didn't use knives; we couldn't afford them, but we did carry catapults, stones and sticks. For a few bruises, we rid ourselves of all our aggression.

Girls didn't take part in our fights; they were kept at home. Until we reached our teens, sex didn't interest us. We preyed on courting couples for the fun of it. Our flashlights were detested by them as they clung to each other against the dark mill walls.

In the nipping cold of winter I kept myself warm with a portable winter warmer - an empty Oxo beef tin, which I first perforated with a nail and then filled with slow-burning cotton waste. I carried the flat tin - half as big as my hand - inside my shirt. Periodically, to keep it nice and hot, I took it out of my shirt and whirled it around on the end of a string. I rarely set myself alight.

On Wednesday nights (market night), I'd run with several mates across the stall-covered town square snatching fruit and vegetables. There were scores of naphtha-lit stalls, selling the same produce. I didn't take the fresh stuff, I took the discarded produce thrown into the bins standing between the stalls. It wasn't as easy as you might think. I had to run, jump, hang on to the bin, reach down, sort out the rotten produce in the half-dark, fill my pockets, and make my escape before a rod descended across the seat of my pants - as it sometimes did. Successful raids ended, I'd crouch beneath a hissing gas lamp and eat enough fruit and vegetables to last the week.

Saturday morning, before I took to going to the reading room in the town library, I usually spent at the stockyards. To earn a penny or two, groups of us would struggle across a bog of steaming manure to help the farmers drive the cattle they'd bought to their farms in the surrounding hills.

When business was slow, we sat on top of a wall gaping through the barred windows of the Summer Street Abattoir to watch the slaughter going on within. We ignored shouts of bugger off. It puzzled me how a powerful bull could be felled with a single blow to its head. One moment there was a mountain of muscle, the next moment a carcass of bones and flesh. Pigs had their throats cut, squealing all the time; after which they were thrown into great tubs of boiling water.

I agonized over the lambs and sheep. With frightened eyes they climbed a death walk in front of where I was sitting. They seemed to appeal to me for help. Instead, I watched them being stabbed through the head. Blood was everywhere. "Look out! Look out!" I shouted, but I never saved one. I didn't understand why they died so meekly. As long as I stared through that window, I refused to accept the inevitability of death. I wanted the animals to kick and fight.

On a Saturday morning, our gang looked in on the open-air market on the town square. For a few pennies, we could buy a 'thoroughbred' puppy, or a rabbit, or a ferret (to catch the rabbit), or a singing bird, or a pocketful of tame mice, or a goldfish in a bowl. 'Real diamonds' cost sixpence each; a 'gold watch' made of brass a shilling; 'new' false teeth or spectacles, whose owners were in the graveyard, two shillings and sixpence. For nothing at all, we watched a man almost kill himself lifting heavy weights.

From the 1920's onward, with the coming of the talking pictures, we spent many Saturday afternoons at the cinema. We paid to get in by handing over two empty, clean, two-pound jam jars. The matinee, solely for children, was a wild affair where a man kept order with a long bamboo pole. If we were caught blowing rice or rock-hard peas at the pianist, or spitting orange pips from the balcony, or whistling too long at the kissing scenes, we ran the risk of getting whacked over the head - a real hard whack.

Talking pictures opened up a new, exciting world for me. With two jam jars, I first saw Charlie Chaplin. It is impossible to convey the impression the earliest films made. It was like seeing the first electric light, or the first automobile. In exchange for two empty jam jars my spirit soared across the great plains of America as far as the Rockies. I jolted along in a covered wagon, gun on knee. There were times when, glued to my seat, I feared the red Indian warriors as much as any white settler had done.

When we children were not at the films, we were watching the town's football team, the Rovers. We got in by sliding across a neighbouring roof. Once in the ground we scattered; better one of us thrown out than the lot. I was crazy about football (soccer). The first time I heard thousands of people - caps in hand - sing 'Abide with Me' was late one afternoon at the Rover's ground. The words of the hymn appeared on a screen. To keep time with the band, one simply followed a little ball that jumped from word to word.

> Abide with me; fast falls the eventide;
> The darkness deepens; Lord with me abide;
> When other helpers fail, and comforts flee,
> Help of the helpless, O, abide with me.
>
> Swift to its close ebbs out life's little day;
> Earth's joys grow dim, its glories pass away;
> Change and decay in all around I see;
> O thou who changest not, abide with me.

The singing gave me gooseflesh.

Everybody but the dead and the dying watched the Rovers. Nothing was allowed to interfere with a game, not even a snowstorm. We'd rush off to a match with our rosettes and rattles as if our lives depended on it. When the Rovers played, the town's honour was at stake. Only Aston Villa had won the Football Association Cup more times than Blackburn - six times against our five. We spent Saturday afternoon at the game and the rest of the week arguing over the result. Next Saturday the madness began all over again. If a player left Blackburn to get better pay elsewhere, we took it as an insult. He'd put money before the game. One year, by illicitly raffling the same two pound bag of sugar over and over again, our street gang equipped our own football team with Rover colours. We played on a nearby tip, using caps for goal posts.

I was eleven when the Rovers won the Football Association Cup at Wembley Stadium in 1928. Few things have provided me with such excitement. The match against Huddersfield was broadcast all over town. My mates and I listened to every word. It was the first time the final had been broadcast by radio from London. We heard the king and queen arrive and the singing and the playing of the massed bands. It came over the radio as real as being on the field with the ninety thousand fans.

It was amazing what Blackburn did. Everybody said we were in for a licking. After all, Huddersfield had a far better record in League football that year than we had. They had a far better team. Their forward line was the best in the country; their center forward, Jackson, was the bane of all goalkeepers. Some said he was as good as Stanley Matthews, the greatest of our football idols. But our eleven finished up beating theirs by three goals to one, just the same.

How did we do it? Well, in the first minute our center-forward, Roscamp, scored a goal by bundling Huddersfield's goalkeeper Mercer, ball and all, into the net. It took our breath away. You could hear the roar of the Blackburn fans all the way from London. After that it was our game. By half-time we had a lead of two goals to none. Huddersfield fought back in the second half, but our half-back, Campbell, bottled up their forward time and again. Only Jackson got past him to score Huddersfield's single goal. Roscamp offset that by scoring the third goal for Blackburn. Puddefoot, another of our heroes, just missed scoring a fourth.

When the final whistle blew, we all danced for joy. The town went mad. It remained mad until long after the victors came home bearing the precious trophy. It had been 37 years since we'd won the cup before. In 1928, we equalled Aston Villa's record. At the station the team was mobbed; traffic was stopped. My mates and I followed the players around the town. Where Association Football was concerned, we were top of the pile.

Most Saturday nights found us at St. Philip's church hall, where they held a weekly sixpenny dance. At the interval, hot tea and meat pies were served. The dance hall had a pork pie smell. Some dancers seemed to enjoy slipping us hot meat pies as much as we enjoyed eating them. Once, when we were very hungry, we set some mice free during the spotlight dance when of the room was in darkness. We helped ourselves during the confusion, and ran for our lives.

To escape from the murky darkness of the streets into the lighted dance hall was the highlight of my week. Unlike some of my companions, who were concerned solely to obtain meat pies, I loved the lights, the music and the air of romance. To see the mill girls prettied up with their curled hair and white dresses, and all the boys in their tight-fitting suits, raised my spirits. Everybody knew everybody else, and it was all very friendly. It was so intimate and intense that there was no room for wallflowers.

Being there every Saturday night, I knew all the dances. My two sisters danced as well as anybody; especially Jenny who danced as light as a feather. If she hadn't had a partner to hang on to, I think she might have flown round the dance hall.

The spot-dance, especially when it was a waltz, was my favourite. The moment the main lights were switched off, and the spotlight was switched on, a hush fell on the room. The ceiling became a mass of tiny twinkling stars. The girls' necklaces, bangles and earrings - all glass - winked in the flashes of light. Everything became remote. With the spotlight darting about the room, I watched the dancers swaying like a gentle wave, to the muffled tap of the drum. "Moonlight and roses bring wonderful memories of you..." Sitting under one of the tables, peeping through the tablecloth, I went on hearing the music long after the band was stilled.

It was a let-down when the lights were turned on again. The moonlight and roses, the princes and princesses had all departed; a pushing, perspiring crowd of cotton workers had taken their place.

With my mates, I also visited the music hall. As they didn't barter seats for jam jars, we either had to furtively make our way in via the endless concrete back steps, from which we tried to slip into the gods, or find a relative or friend to smuggle us in. If we failed to penetrate the theater's defenses, we'd find out where the freaks and curiosities were lodging, and carry out a vigil outside the house in order to watch them for free.

The first of such vigils I made was before a row of houses in Talbot Street several streets away from the theater. We arrived there about forty minutes before curtain time. It was winter, dark and misty. We didn't know where The Tallest Man in the World, The Smallest Man in the World, and The Wild Man from Borneo were staying, but we knew they were there. We decided to divide our forces. Each of us patrolled several houses, ready to give a shout if anything happened. I was told to walk up and down at one end of the street.

I was staring at the front of one of the houses when I felt my hair rising. Peering through the window above the doorway was a man's face. He fixed me with his eyes. A man would have to stand on a ladder to peer through there. I was looking at The Tallest Man in the World.

Instead of raising the alarm, I froze and stared back. Moments later a taxi pulled up at the curb; it was without a roof. The door of the house opened, The Tallest Man in the World lowered his head, hurried down the stone steps, crossed the sidewalk without looking to the left or right, climbed into the open taxi and sat bolt upright. I could have touched him.

He was followed by The Smallest Man in the World, who didn't reach as high as The Tallest Man's knee; yet from the way he bore himself, I knew he was a man not a child. He looked at me as if he didn't like being seen for free. Behind him came The Wild Man from Borneo, complete with skins, feathers, shield and spear. He grinned in my face, but I was too scared to laugh back.

By the time my mates had run from the other end of the street, they saw only the back of the car and the head and shoulders of The Tallest Man in the World. We went back there the next night and the next, until we had had our fill.

One day I was allowed to go on my own to a children's matinee of R. L. Stephenson's *Treasure Island*. Somehow, I'd got two pennies to pay my way into the gods. From up there it was like looking down into a magic kingdom. No man has ever frightened me as much as Long John Silver did. When it was over I rushed into the street and grabbed the first person I saw - a nice old gentleman - to tell him all about it. "I want to warn you against Long John Silver. He's treacherous. He'll stop at nothing." The old man must have understood children. He rested himself on his walking stick and, with a benign look, and the odd "Well!" or "You don't say," heard me out. He seemed as revolted by the treachery of Long John as I.

The floodlit world of the theater was far more real than reality to us. We entered into it, took part in it, even to the extent of shouting warnings to the heroine and hissing the villain. The audience in the gods was completely uninhibited. "Bloody scoundrel thi are, knocking t' lass about like that," somebody bawled. If we shouted too much, someone else yelled "Shut thi gob!"

The trouble with some people is that they went on nursing their grievances long after the play was over. They stood outside the stage door and hissed the actors they didn't like as they left. The villain - however striking - had to watch his step when returning to his lodgings. "Ah could teach thee a lesson or two," they called after him. "A thorough bad un thi are."

When we'd nothing better to do, we flew our linen kites above the mill tip. The wind was always waiting for us. It could change its course so capriciously. Although I plotted and planned against it, I once lost my kite. I often wondered where the wind came from and where it was bound. I envied its freedom to come roaring over the hills and go its way.

Now and again we shared the tip with groups of unemployed workers who, desperate for something to do, played marbles or pitch and toss by the hour. Occasionally they organized a dog and rat fight. After laying bets, the dogs were matched against the rats. The man whose dog killed most rats was the winner. There was no sport in it. The rats never had a chance. From the moment they were let out of the cage, they tried to get away. When the dog went after them they crouched and squealed with fear. I never saw a dog bitten, but I saw a lot of rats killed. Those that escaped and sought refuge in the outer tip were slain by men with picking sticks. It was a cruel sport.

As we grew older, we boys took to chasing each other in and out of the town's clay pits, fighting each other with clay balls. The girls preferred to mold the clay into bread and cakes and play shop. They even made a clay currency. In summer we ran barefoot through abandoned quarries filled with nettles and dandelions, keeping a sharp look-out for broken glass. Alone, or with other gangs, we fought pitched battles along the canals and, if there were no courting couples there, or tramps setting up house, defended the railway tunnels from attack.

Oblivious of danger, we chased each other across single-line railway bridges where it was strictly forbidden to go. One winter day, three friends and I were caught on such a bridge. A coal train was upon us before we knew it, swaying toward us at an alarming speed, puffing blue smoke. We knew that the only safety bay was farther on, beyond our reach. It was too late to run back; the track was frozen and slippery. Terrified, we scrambled over a metal screen and, fully dressed, jumped into the icy canal - that is all except Wilfred Green who fled before the train. As I fell, I felt the train thunder past above my head.

With the other two boys, I dragged myself out of the canal. Our teeth were chattering, our lips were turning blue; ice was forming on our clothing. We lay on the bank for several minutes gasping for breath. In the distance, the train rattled and rumbled on its way.

"We'd better find out where Wilf's got to," one of us said.

We clambered up the steep bank until we reached the track again. Wilfred Green had disappeared.

"Wilf!" we shouted, "Wilf!"

Shivering with cold, we began to walk back across the bridge, puzzled where he'd got to.

We found a lumpy object at the end of the bridge. It was Wilf. He was lying on his belly, at the side of the track. He didn't look like Wilf Green anymore; not the Wilf Green who always came out on top of our fights. He looked like a crumpled, blood-stained sack tossed out of the train. His legs had been severed at the knees. Speechless, we stood and stared.

We had the wind up too much to touch him. Instead, we backed away and fled across the bridge to a signal box. Breathlessly, we told the man in the box what had happened. Then we all ran home, slantwise across the fields.

For a long time Wilfred Green's life hung in the balance. Youth, to say nothing of medical care, pulled him through. In time he was fitted with false legs with which he began life anew. In the hospital, and in the streets later on, he avoided those of us who had been with him when he lost his legs. He wasn't blaming us - at least I don't think so - it was just that he'd begun a new life, which for reasons that he knew best, he didn't want to share with us. Mother said his pride was at stake.

After several weeks of sitting around and wondering whether Wilf would live or die, life went on as before. Undeterred by the near fatality, whole evenings were given up to playing king of the mountain on one of the slag heaps near Nig Lane. The slag heaps were pyramid-shaped piles from disused mines in the Dells End district, well outside the town. Hundreds of feet high, they were a blight on the skyline. Nobody wanted them; nobody knew what to do with them; no grown-ups went near them. Meanwhile they rotted, fumed, and fouled up the local canal and everything else in the vicinity.

The pools of stagnant water that stood at the foot of the tailings fascinated us. They were every colour of the rainbow. We were not afraid of the nettles that grew there. Reciting the words: "Gently stroke a nettle and it will sting you for your pain; grasp it like a man of mettle and it soft as silk will remain," we grabbed a handful and hoped for the best. Everybody had to pass the 'nettle test.'

Slipping and sliding about among the rubble, one gang defended the summit, while the others - no holds barred - tried to dislodge them. It was hard work dragging yourself up to the top and then slithering down again. It also had its dangers; landslides happened on the steep slopes. In summer, if we got too dirty and too hot, and the light was still good, we stripped off and "One, two, three," threw each other into the canal. When the seasons changed and winter came, we deserted the slag heaps and went sledding. Headfirst, we'd come whizzing down the hillsides, disregarding the trees and the great clods of heavy wet snow that fell upon us. The closer to the trees we came, the more exhilarating the ride.

With water everywhere - teeth-chattering cold water even in the summer - we learned to swim young. The canal was a dirty colour, but the river Blakewater or Blackwater that ran through town was worse. Its walled banks by the mills were stained with mill dyes. Although forbidden to children, we one day went wading in the black, murky river by the factories looking for fish. "You shouldn't be in there. It's dangerous!" a woman shouted over a low wall. We took no notice of her. We turned over stone after stone without finding a fish. The river was dead.

In all our wild escapades, we seldom ran foul of the police. For us they had a stigma; we were brought up to distrust and avoid them. We distrusted them because they defended the rich. We avoided them because they used their batons rather than words. We got the 'short end of the stick.'

———◄◦►———

The long summer school holiday was the period of greatest freedom. We fled the factories and the smoking chimneys for the hills, and empty, wind-swept moorlands outside the town. We fled like farm animals escaping from the long winter indoors. Girls and boys went together. Having been shut up, we discovered the sun, the moon and the stars again. The vast expanse of the countryside made us feel free. Our parents didn't bother that we might get lost, or drowned, or gored by a bull, or fall out of a tree, or break our necks. Children were not the focus of their life, work was. Dan avoided these outings, Jenny and Brenda were by now too old. Rosie Gill and Annie Morgan always came.

With a little food in our pockets, and accompanied by birdsong, in a straggling band, we ranged the countryside from morning to night, getting hotter as the day wore on. They were long summer days that never seemed to end. We explored the surrounding villages such as Feniscowles, Riley Green, Copster Green, Tockholes and Ribchester. Every Lancashire child knows that 'chester' means the site of a Roman camp. Ribchester was not just another village; it was the ancient crossroads of Roman communications, one arm of which went from Ilkley Moor in the east to the Fylde in the west, the other arm from Manchester, twenty-five miles to the south, to Carlisle, ninety miles to the north.

We were proud of our link with the Romans. We knew a lot about centurions, and the Roman heavy cavalry, and which legion was where. We relived our Roman history, walking the ancient roads, storming the ancient walls, stirring the pigeons out of the Roman ruins, and with exultant war-whoops, slaying the fiercest of Roman soldiers before they had time to seize their swords or sound their horns. One thing we all knew was that the Romans had built the Wall of Hadrian - seventy-three miles long across northern Britain, one hundred miles to our north.

After keeping guard there for three hundred years, they got tired of our weather and went home. A lot of different people must have followed the Romans in Britain. Yet it is the Romans we remembered best.

When we were not killing Romans, we robbed birds' nests, mimicked bird calls, plucked berries, chased butterflies, fished, rabbited, skimmed pebbles across the water, and ran down the turf-clad banks to swim in the Ribble, at one time the boundary between England and Scotland. That part of our sex education which we had not already acquired in our homes we obtained by following the activities of the stallions and mares, the bulls and cows, the cocks and hens we chanced upon in the fields. Steeped in local lore, we were ever watchful for witches and fairies, especially if a mist was about. We knew that at certain times of the year witches were quite common on Pendle Hill; also that eaves-dropping elves lived in caves, or in the roots of trees, or under large rocks and were best left alone.

We knew the eerie stories connected with certain farms and buildings. Salmesbury Hall was haunted by a white lady. On dark, stormy nights ghostly horesemen rode across the moors. We took it for granted that unseen eyes were watching us as we hurried by. One field we avoided was where a milkmaid had been murdered. Some grown-ups swore that on dark nights she could be heard walking in the meadow, weeping. We knew every grim detail. We also avoided old church yards with their sloping, moss-covered stones, lest we should be caught unawares. Having run ourselves to a standstill, we made a bed on the turf and slept among the daisies.

All summer long, we ran as free as the wind. Provided we closed all farm gates behind us and didn't interfere with the grazing cattle and sheep, we were free to follow a path or a rushing beck (stream) wherever it led. Nobody bothered us. Late in the afternoons, we would look in at a farmhouse to watch them milk. I thought the way the milk squirted from the udders into the pail was magical. I loved the sloshing of milk from one pail to another. To be given a mug of warm milk with cream on top, whose sweet smell was equal to its taste, was to know what paradise was all about. Our best bet for a free drink were men milkers, not women. Naturally, we all drank from the same mug.

The only authority we recognized was that of the older children. If the oldest was a girl, she ruled; it was her job to bring us home safely. In town each child was responsible for its own acts; when roving the countryside we acted as a group. We depended upon each other. Everything had to be shared. There was no 'iffing' and 'butting,' no sticking out. You kept the rules or you didn't go next time.

Before dark we'd be home again, achingly hungry, with grazed knees and elbows, and perhaps a sunburn. We brought with us bundles of nettles for nettle-beer, cresses and docks; armfuls of flowers; and stained linen bags filled with berries. The older children knew which berries to take and which, like the baneberry, to leave alone. Sometimes we'd come home: sodden, wet through, icy-cold, and our clothes full of clinging, prickly burrs. Always our energies were spent, our instincts and our imagination satisfied. Life may have been dangerous - jagged rocks and seemingly bottomless holes in the river were the greatest hazard - but it was never dull. We lived in a world of intense activity; a world in which we didn't have enough time to fit everything in.

The sights, smells, and feelings of those long summer treks were intoxicating. Lying on our backs in the grass, we watched the cloud shadows moving smoke-like across hill and dale. Around us was the bulk of the hills, where the soil lay barren. To get to Whalley Abbey, we had to wade across a sea of bluebells, daffodils, violets, and primroses . We passed hedgerows covered with flowering currants and white hawthorn and damson trees white with blossom. Smoky-faced lambs skittered behind drystone walls that climbed endlessly across the fells into a windy sky. We never went far without smelling lilies of the valley, or new-mown hay, or the peculiar dry smell of the heather at the end of a long hot day. In our ears was the song of the pewit, the curlew, and the lark. The hills echoed to the singing streams and the shrill whistle of the shepherd calling his dogs.

If the weather went against us, we played king of the mountain in one of the cottages after the adults had gone to work. Girls were banished from these games. Armed with pillows, one gang defended the top of the staircase while the other tried to dislodge it. Repeatedly, somebody fell down the stairs without coming to any harm. More damage was done to the pillows than to us.

Sometimes foul weather was disregarded. We went out just the same. During my unfortunate, short-term career as a Wolf Cub Scout, I competed in a fire lighting contest on an island in the Ribble in the pouring rain.

When the signal to begin was given, I ransacked the island for dry twigs and dead grass. I had lit a fire in the rain before, and I knew to start with dead leaves. To the burning leaves I added a tiny stick or two. Until the fire got going, I protected it from the rain with my cap.

My fire was crackling and sending up clouds of sparks before the other fires were lit. I'd used only one of the two matches we'd been given. I must say, the Scout Master didn't like it when I gave him the other match back.

I won because I was determined to win. I wanted to show them that a stained cap, patched pants and a torn jersey had nothing to do with being the best Cub Scout.

I loved every minute I spent with the Scouts. I'd joined them not because my parents said I should, but because scouting seemed to me such a good idea. It was what I was looking for. I loved the knot-tying, the First Aid and all the rest. I really believed in it. My nemesis was the Scout master's mother who used to attend our meetings in St. Alban's Church Hall at the other side of town. There was no Scout troop at St. Peter's or St. Philip's. She and I didn't hit it off. She was always tidying me up, which I resented. She didn't have to keep saying how odd I looked in my ragamuffin outfit. I was tired of her treating me as an ugly duckling. It irked me so. She made it plain that I just didn't fit in, and the sooner I left the better. I suppose I'd jumped into the wrong pond.

"Oh?" was all my parents said when I asked them to buy a scout uniform "Oh?" I did raise tenpence to purchase the Scout necktie and a leather-studded fastener, but that wasn't good enough. I was issued an ultimatum by the serious young man who led us: "Cub Scout cap and a uniform, or out!

I was sad and humiliated when they threw me out. I just didn't feel it was fair, especially as I was enjoying it, and I had won the firelighting contest. "Oh," was all my parents said when I told them that I no longer was a Cub Scout "Oh." For a long time afterward when moving about the town, I followed my troop's way of alternating running with walking. Run a hundred steps, walk a hundred steps, and so on. It made me feel that I was still part of the group.

On an earlier occasion, before I joined the Scouts, Harold Watkins and I had borrowed a bike and cycled down to the Ribble to camp there. I rode on the carrier with a borrowed tent, food, blankets and a pot wedged between me and the saddle. The ride was endless and bumpy. I gripped the seat springs in front of me so hard, and for so long, that I couldn't release my fingers when we got there. I also had severe cramp in my bottom and my legs. I had to run up and down the river bank, flapping my arms, trying to restore my circulation.

As we set up the tent, we watched as swallows skimmed the foaming river, feasting on clouds of gnats. Rings showed the currents' flow.

Harold and I must have been very hungry, because we ate our two day's rations during the first long twilight. Food gone, our troubles began. Unlike the warm day that had preceded it, the night became cold with a chilly breeze. The damp rose from the ground and penetrated our limbs. We sat up at every sound. One moment we were certain that someone was being strangled to death at the water's edge; the next moment somebody seemed to be crying for help from the river. Now and again, an owl hooted close by.

Shaking with cold and fear, we stuck our heads through the tent flap, and looked around. Nothing looked as it had done in daylight. The ground was a wet, misty gray. Mysterious shapes were everywhere. We had a feeling of being completely lost. I wondered out loud whose silly idea it had been for us to be there at all. Harold guardedly suggested that the idea had been mine. I really wasn't up to fighting him, so I let his silly comment pass. Blankets round our shoulders, we struggled from beneath the tent fly and walked up and down the river bank, talking to each other in strange, muffled voices. We agreed that when light came, we'd go home. Only when the blood was flowing again - we'd been walking about as stiff as posts - did we notice the starlit beauty of the sky. Our interest in stars, however, was fleeting. We crept back into our damp tent and slept.

Several hours later, before daybreak, we were wakened by a cow lowing. From the noise it was making it might have been an elephant in mortal agony. Unable to sleep with that din in our ears, we got up to investigate. It was a black and white Jersey lying on the bank closeby. With her big, sad eyes, she seemed to welcome us. While bellowing across the valley, she heaved and strained. When a calf's head popped out from her rear end, I knew why she wailed so.

I'd seen a calf born before, but this birth was no less magical. I stood there awestruck. Despite the early hour, the flies began to swarm. We tried to help the cow by driving them off with our caps. The cow didn't mind. By now she had stopped her lowing and was purring like a large contented cat. We marvelled at the way she cleaned her calf with wet, sloppy licks. Nobody had to tell the calf what to do. It struggled to its wobbly legs from a bed of buttercups and began to feed from its mother's udder. It made us feel glad that we'd come.

Though still before daybreak, I thought we should tell the farmer that he'd got a calf. With the soft light changing from gray to silver, we tramped down the misty bank in the direction of the farm house. The river sang at our side, toppling and turning in the dark shadows. Chewing their cud, other cows placidly ignored our passing. Glittering, dew-soaked cobwebs lay on the tufted grass. Across the fields a plaintive curlew called. The last bats of the night flickered by. At the house there were dogs barking, but no lights. We had to throw stones at the windows to waken the farmer. After several throws, a wild-looking head appeared.

"What's t' want?" the farmer demanded sharply.

"Tha's got a calf," I shouted, disregarding his ugly look.

"Oh, Ah 'av, 'av Ah?"

"Tha 'as."

"Wheer?"

"Down t' bank. He woke us up."

"Tha's woke me up. Cudn't ya 've cum 'n told me after cockcrow?"

"We thowt tha'd want te know."

"Ya did, did ya?"

"Ai, besides, we're goin' 'oom."

"Well, that's summat," said the farmer as he slammed down the window.

"Cheeky bugger," I said to Harold. "He doesn't seem to appreciate us tellin' 'im."

With the sky becoming lighter, we went home, riding through the soft early morning light. As I was riding pillion again, it was as hard riding back as it had been getting there. On arrival, we shamefacedly confessed to having eaten all our food. The only thing we talked about at home was the birth of the calf. Seeing that was worth all the trouble we'd had.

Chapter XII

Siblings

J enny's love for me grew as the years passed. By the time I was eight or nine, she was entering adulthood, and had started courting. I looked on her young men with jealous eyes. I used to think that some of them were not good enough. Whenever one of them came to the house at night, my brother and I were sent to bed. We used to spy on them through the cracks in the floor. The rest of the family went out to keep out of the way. Among the suitors there was John whose hair shone with brilliantine; there was Alec who wooed her with Black Magic chocolates or with fish and chips; and there was Mike who did nothing but sigh. I couldn't work out why Mike came at all. When the sighs became unbearable, my brother and I shouted down: "Go and put a sock in it," which kind of spoiled the atmosphere. Dan and I got into such fits of laughter that we had to pull the blankets over our heads. When there was nothing but silence, we felt impelled to hop out of bed and peer through the cracks to see what was going on.

I preferred it when my sisters invited their friends to dance in our front room. They were crazy about dancing. As fashion dictated, the girls had their hair bobbed, wore short skirts and gartered stockings. There wasn't a lot of space in which to dance - even though what furniture there was had been removed - but nobody worried. Somebody came with a concertina or a banjo and away we went. It was one of the occasions when Dan was willing to join in. In that confined space, we jerked, twisted, and spun to the latest tunes until it made us dizzy.

American dances were popular. I learned to dance the Charleston and the Black Bottom in that little room. The Charleston was the big hit. When the dancers got too hot, they just leaned against the walls or stepped out of the front door and cooled off in the street. Everybody was good-hearted; those were happy times.

On one occasion the dance ended in a fight. I don't know how it began. One moment all was bliss; the next the girls were screaming and the boys were knocking each other down. Dan in the middle of it. Jenny fled upstairs. I knew it was serious when I saw mother grab the rolling pin, the frying pan and the poker - the three deadly weapons in cottage fights - and run upstairs, too. My job was to open and shut the front door, lock and unlock it, as the bodies, some of them with bloodied noses and torn suits, were tossed into the street. The fight wound down with two of the boys wrestling on the sanded floor. Spoiled their shirts and pants, they did.

Being the youngest in the family and the most readily available, I often served as Jenny's courier. It baffled me why I had to keep running with notes between Jenny and her current suitor when they were only several streets apart. I not only had to carry messages, I had to describe in detail what her young man looked like. "Was there any last word?" she asked. There usually was: "Tell her, I'm allus thinking of her neet and day." If I thought a fellow was not really worthy of my sister, I stuck a dart in him whenever I could.

This courier business could go on for weeks with Jenny going into a decline. There were times when she didn't sleep or touch her food. "You're letting your courtin' get the better of you," mother scolded. The courier business, as far as I could see, didn't have the slightest effect. It was just a waste of time, paper and my clog cokers.

My running stopped when Jenny decided on Gordon Weall. Nobody enjoyed life as much as Gordon. People said he laughed right down to his heels. When he walked in one day with the top of his hair shaved off, we went into fits. He must have been one of the first in town to have a crew cut. He looked just like a red Indian brave. Mother was thrilled with him. There was nobody better than Gordon. He was lucky to get Jenny; she was equally lucky to get him. I gave the romance a push whenever I could.

Jenny and he had a wonderful courtship. They were a sunny-tempered pair. When they were both in work and could afford it, they dashed off on a cheap excursion train to Blackpool to dance all night in the Tower Ballroom. They came back at dawn and went straight to work. Fifty miles for a dance! Now that was really living it up. Poor they may have been, but none so joyful.

Like Jenny, Gordon was a giver. In return for my help in his job as a painter, he was generous to a fault. One Easter, when he was in work, he took me to the Easter Fair. The night before I'd watched the long convoy entering the town. The lorries, carts, one-horse caravans (with dogs tied underneath), the animal cages, and the massive steam engines piled high with scaffolding excited me. In no time, the whole square was covered with tents, canvas booths, roundabouts and lookers-on. People came in such numbers that they had to lock arms and jostle their way through the crowds. All was din and bustle.

Gordon spent a whole three shillings on me. Thirty-six pennies! I rode on everything. I think I ate everything too: ice-cream, roasted potatoes, sticks of sugar. We went on the Big Dipper, the Cakewalk, the perilous chairboat swings and the Big Wheel, and shrieked like everybody else. I waved to Gordon excitedly, as my papier-maché horse rose and fell to the accompaniment of piped music from the elaborately decorated steam organ. All was happy shouting and lovely disturbance.

Gordon considered the sideshows of freaks and caged wild animals a real 'swiz' so we avoided them. Instead we watched the contortionists, and listened to the black-faced pill and potion sellers who for tuppence would cure you of the most dreadful illnesses. We tried to avoid the roll-down-the-penny men, who stood ready to pick the pennies from our pockets. To the light of a naked flame, we tried to dislodge a coconut or knock down a wooden effigy of a woman.

We almost went into a booth marked: MODERN AMERICAN ENTERPRISE. REFINED ENTERTAINMENT, but decided against it. We didn't know what 'refined' meant.

At the end of the day, there was the added joy of going home through the littered, crowded streets hanging on to a coconut and a large balloon. A day or two later, with equal bustle, the fair disappeared as quickly as it had come. With it went the wet, trodden paper and the orange peel. Watercarts washed the cobbles free of sweat and stale beer. Normality returned.

Paradoxically, the fair got bigger, better and brighter as times got worse. The bleaker our world, the greater our need of diversion. No depression in trade and industry was allowed to mar it.

———◇———

It was Gordon who introduced me to speed. One day he roared up to our front door on a motorcycle he'd just bought. The big buckskin gloves and goggles he was wearing made him look very daring.

"I was lucky to get it," he said, his face flushed and happy. "It was already sold to a chap who couldn't take delivery. The coppers had other plans for him. I got it just at the right moment."

I must have been somebody special, for I was the first to be invited to ride on the pillion seat. Jenny wouldn't go near the machine. It terrified her.

"What's that strange knocking sound?" I asked, as I clambered aboard.

"Nothing, Billy. Minor adjustment of the carburetor is all it needs. Goes like a bird."

This flying like a bird past houses and park railings was an entirely new experience for both of us. The faster we went, the happier we were. Gordon went so fast that things became a blur. I learned to hang on with my knees and hands as we roared round the bends. We raced across town; we thundered down quiet country lanes leaving a cloud of dust behind. On occasions Gordon avoided obstacles by whizzing around them at the last moment. Another 'minor adjustment,' this time to the brakes, was obviously needed. Meanwhile the strange knocking sound got louder.

Gordon was not satisfied just with speed; he had to do antics. With me off the pillion, and the bike in motion, he hung on to the handlebars while jumping from one side to the other - as he had seen cowboys do with horses in western films. He also rode while standing on the seat. It was hair-raising. He became known as the daredevil of the district. It was Jenny's belief that he would finish up killing himself and her brother. With the potholes and ruts that pitted the roads, she had every reason to be afraid.

The knocking sound, which Gordon was always going to fix, but never did, one day brought our wild riding career to a close. Giving a particularly explosive knock, the engine died. Later the bike was sold for scrap.

———◦———

Brenda took after father, she was a Woodruff: stocky, silent, tough. She didn't flutter about like Jenny, she stomped. She didn't have Jenny's good looks. She had a Woodruff face: strong, square, with the broad brow and thoughtful eyes. She didn't indulge in fairy stories like mother; she dealt with immediate problems. Nor did she sing. She could no more sing than father. One thing certain: she was utterly reliable.

Her joining the Salvation Army at seventeen came as a great surprise to my parents. Father was not against the Salvation Army, no working man was, but he didn't like her going off like that. There were words in the kitchen between Brenda and father. The dispute started innocently enough, but one thing led to another. Neither could bear to hear the other one out. The shouting match ended with father bawling: "Goddamit, go 'n join t' Army if tha must, but stay theer. Ah've 'ad enough of thee."

"Ah will," Brenda flared defiantly. Then she burst into tears, ran upstairs, and slammed her bedroom door. It was so tense and quiet in the kitchen that I could hear father's watch ticking on the fireplace. Moments later, Brenda came storming down the stairs clutching her belongings. Mother tried to grab her as she crashed through the kitchen, but Brenda pushed her aside and was gone.

"See what tha's dun," mother screamed at father, tears running down her face. "Ah 'ope tha satisfied."

Some days later, driven by mother, father went in search of Brenda. I think he bitterly regretted having thrown her out. He found her and they made their peace.

Brenda came home with father carrying her brown paper package, and we all sat together again in our stockinged feet in the kitchen and ate roasted potatoes.

"It's like old times," said mother. It wasn't. Everybody was tense. But time passed and wounds healed. Brenda joined the Salvation Army.

With her scrubbed face, her black bonnet and her red sash, Brenda now attacked sin as fiercely as she had attacked the bullies who had knocked me down at school when I was four.

I found her conversion overwhelming. "Billy," she said to me one day while pressing my hand against her bosom. "Billy, you must declare yourself. Are you for God or for Satan?"

More than anything else, I was for Brenda, so the first thing I did was to stop the harassment our street gang had been giving the Salvation Army. Keeping our distance, so as to avoid being clouted by an overzealous Soldier of Christ, we urchins used to march after the Salvation Army band and parody the Army's favourite hymns:

> You won't go to heaven when you die, Mary Ann,
> Yes you will, no you won't, yes you will, Mary Ann...

We also mocked them with the lines:

> Sally Army sells fish,
> Three-half-pence a dish.
> If you don't like it, don't try it.
> If you don't want it, don't buy it.
> Sally Army sells fish.

We ended with:
> Oh, you're in the Sally Army
> And safe from sin.
> You'll all go to heaven,
> In a corn beef tin.

The worst kind of nonsense, yet we indulged in it repeatedly. Odd that we should have picked on the Salvation Army which did so much to help the poor. Our conduct was a mixture of mischief and hooliganism. Anyway, largely because of me, these attacks ceased after Brenda joined up.

One of the first things Brenda did - to the obvious discomfort of father - was to launch a holy war against drink. The trouble was she went overboard. Unlike her usual steady self, she worked herself up into a frenzy against alcohol. She was indefatigable in persuading people to sign the pledge of abstinence. She also was expert at working the crowd for copper and silver. She was brave the way she stood with her group under the flag in front of the Griffin pub at the end of our street, rattling her tambourine, and selling the Salvation Army newspaper *The War Cry*.

Those drinking in the Griffin took a different view. The pub was one of the few places where the workers could relax. Drink meant conviviality and friendship. For some it meant oblivion from a bleak existence; their only armour against despair. They didn't want anybody spoiling it by reminding them of sin, or by singing temperance songs in the bar.

At first the pub-keeper was good-hearted about it. He saw the funny side. But then he came round to the view that Brenda was trying to rob him of his living; especially with her talk about banishing barmaids. It was embarrassing to father. The pub-keeper was especially sore with her when the Army brought in other contingents from Preston, where the English temperance movement had begun.

Yet Brenda made many converts. She did, after all, labour in a fertile field. At some weddings and funerals people used to drink so much that they forgot why they'd come. Money that should have gone into people's bellies, or on their backs, went down their throats. I often saw shawl-covered mothers, with infants in their arms and toddlers hanging on to their skirts, trying to get their husbands out of the pub late on a Friday night before the weekly earnings had all gone.

One man Brenda saved was Mr. Lambert who lived with his wife next door. Until Brenda got at him, Mr. Lambert spent most of his time working as a labourer at the Gas Works or drinking in the pub. He was known as an irredeemable tosspot. Mrs. Lambert, a bright-eyed badger of a woman, was forever throwing her shawl over her head and running to his rescue. Having picked him up off the pavement, she reeled to and fro with him, doing her best to get him home. She came up the street, staggering under his weight, propping him against the wall while she took a breather. The ordeal was habitual.

It was just as well that Mr. Lambert was a silent rather than a fighting drunk, otherwise, being drunk so often, he would have been killed. We children were rather cruel about it. If Mrs. Lambert had not got to the pub in time, we followed the old man through the street as he struggled home, teasing him, and going into gales of laughter when he clung to one of the gas lamps. He rewarded our unforgivable behaviour with a gurgle or two and a silly grin. He never harmed anybody and was far better than a lot of nasty people I knew.

I've forgotten how long Brenda worked on him before he agreed to sign the pledge. But sign it he did, and a different man he was. He became one of the stalwarts of the Nazarene Chapel. He was one of Brenda's favourite redemptions. She used to say that if she could save Joe Lambert, she could save anybody. "Ate out of my hand, he did."

As long as she remained a Soldier of Christ, Brenda never relaxed in the battle against alcohol. Yet she didn't succeed in converting my parents. Despite her unending call for penitence, they remained faithful to the pub.

———◄○►———

There were others who took the fight against drink into their own hands. My friend Harold Watkins and I one day witnessed his mother being beaten by his father for being drunk. Somebody had run in to tell Mr. Watkins that his wife was coming up the street, tipsy. He ran to meet her and beat her on the head and shoulders until, with a bleeding face, she struggled through her door.

Nobody would have dreamed of intervening; they might have intervened had he not done something about it. "If I wor in your place..." they would start. In such a close society, trollops and drunks among the women had to be contained. What you did in your own cottage was your business; what you did in the street - especially what a woman did in the street - was something else. I knew the Watkins family as well as my own, and I know that Mrs. Watkins didn't get drunk again.

I never did learn all the unwritten laws that told you what you could and could not do with alcohol, or anything else. There were fine lines which you must not cross, and about which you could learn only over time. You simply had to watch for the signals. I found them conflicting. Why did we react so harshly to a drunken trollop in the street, but did little, if anything, to stop two drunken women beating each other to death? I could watch two men fighting and have little reaction; a man and a woman fighting didn't upset me much; but two women fighting, their mouths full of anger and foul words, filled me with disgust. Not so for many people; such a fight had a laughing, jeering crowd around it in no time. It was the only time I would have been happy to see a copper in our street. One day I asked grandmother Bridget what she thought of women fighting in the street. "It's not a subject for 'dacent' conversation," she silenced me.

I was closer to my sisters than to my brother Dan. He was a real Woodruff, with all the looks of father. Trouble attracted him like a magnet. He was tough and aggressive, and had something of the rebel in him. For all the attention he gave me, I might not have existed. In the house he could be difficult. I never knew whether or not I was going to get a 'lander' to the head from him. But for Brenda who used to take my side, he might have bullied me more.

187

Sometime in the mid-twenties, when he was twelve or thirteen, he'd had brushes with the police. They'd been to the house twice with complaints. Once they flushed him out of the indoor market in town after it had been locked up for the night. Fortunately he had not broken into the premises, nor by the time they got to him, had he had time to eat anything. He was let off with a warning. Next time they picked him up in the railway clearing yard. Again they could not pin anything on him except trespass which wasn't worth pressing.

With his headstrong nature there was no telling what trouble Dan might cause. On an earlier occasion, when he was eight or nine, he had gone on strike against food and school. He had sat in a corner of the house where father left him, his face contorted with rage. Nothing shifted his obstinacy. Mother was out of work at the time. Dan's teacher was gray-headed Miss Grieves who passed our door daily. I don't know how long his hunger strike continued, and under what terms it was settled, but daily bulletins were issued to Miss Grieves as she went by.

"He hasn't eaten his porridge from yesterday," mother called from the front door.

"Give it to him tomorrow," Miss Grieves called back, hardly breaking her stride.

Mother worried about Dan. She worried about him so much that she sometimes burst into tears. He caused her the most sorrow, yet Dan was her favourite.

On leaving school at fourteen, Dan became a tenter (helper) to father in the mill. His destiny was to be a weaver. He had been reared on cotton; cotton was in his blood, but he had no love for it. He hated weaving; he hated the mill; he hated being tied to a machine; he hated being trapped for fifty hours a week; he hated the discipline.

Whenever I ran into the weaving shed with the dinners, father was always on to him.

"That's not the way to put cob on t' shuttle, you gobbin," he scolded.

Dan bristled.

"Look," he went on, "tha's got a mash. That's because tha wasn't watchin'. Tha's goin' to break warp the way tha goin' on. Nah, tha'll have to start afresh. See, pull t' cloth back. Comb it out gently, there's nothing to it. Piece it from t' back and pull it through. Titivate it. All it needs is for thee to use tha gumption."

Dan usually gave as good as he got. "Ah didn't touch cob, it all happened on its own," he bawled back. The last thing he wanted to do was to please father.

I think Dan was right. Perhaps he was wooden-handed and clumsy as a weaver, but sometimes these things happened on their own. Dan got mashes like nobody else; really interesting mashes that caught everybody's attention. They crossed the weaving shed to see them. I've stood with him awestruck before his loom as the threads went wild before our eyes. In no time at all, hidden gremlins had torn them right across the loom. Dan and I were too mesmerized by the growing rent to know what to do. Eventually dad came across to see what we were staring at. Appealing to the Holy Trinity, he leaped to stop the loom.

"Tha goin' to get a prize for this one, Dan, tha are," father shouted, eyeing the damage.

Dan sulked.

"Nobody can weave cotton and hate it at the same time," muttered an old weaver. "Loom won't stand for it."

From what father told mother, I knew that Dan was always being 'fetched up' in the warehouse and fined for bad work by the 'cut looker,' the cloth inspector. As weaving was paid by the piece, it meant a cut in pay. It made Dan sullen and angry.

After my brother had suffered about a year of purgatory, father one day found the weft and warp threads on Dan's loom a tangle of mashes. Dan was nowhere to be seen.

"He's buggered t' job up," father told mother that evening. To mother's growing concern there was no sight or sound of Dan. He didn't come home that night, or the next. Days later we discovered that he had run all the way from the mill to the army recruiting sergeant. Having lied about his age, Dan said that he was sixteen (the minimum recruiting age) whereas he was only fifteen, the sergeant enlisted him and despatched him within hours to a remote part of Scotland. A day or two later Dan entered the barracks of the Argyle and Sutherland Highlanders Regiment in Inverness. It was about as far from

Blackburn as the recruiting sergeant could have sent him. As distances went in those days, he might as well have sent him to the moon.

When I heard about this, I secretly hoped that Dan had found his niche, and that I might never see him again. I hardly knew what to do with a bed to myself. I went searching among his things for the tin soldiers he'd extorted from me over the years.

My hopes were soon dashed. An impassioned, scrawled note we received from Dan told us that he was desperate to come home. However badly written, the note revealed the mind of a confused boy who had been jailed for insubordination. He was too wild to submit to army discipline. He told us how cold his cell was, and that he could see a great loch and empty mud flats from his window.

The more time passed, the colder it got, the more frantic the messages became.

Father's first letters to Inverness, asserting that his son had been recruited under age and under false pretenses, were ignored. But, urged by mother, he kept at it. Eventually he received a reply:

"I have to inform you," the adjutant of the Argyle and Sutherland Highlanders wrote, "that your son, Dan, has willingly undertaken to serve His Majesty for the next twenty years. This is where the matter now stands. It is purposeless to discuss it further." There was a handwritten postscript about Dan having crablice.

Mother became excited when the letter arrived. She kept turning it over in her hand, trying to decipher it. When father came home he sat down to read it. He read it to himself several times.

"Well," said mother, tapping her foot, "for goodness sake, stop dilly-dallying. What does it say?"

"It says, he's got crablice," said father, refusing to be bullied.

Prodded by mother, who seemed to have forgotten all the trouble Dan had given her before he disappeared, father continued to besiege the regiment with letters. There had never been so many letters to and from our house.

Worn down by both father and son, the colonel of the regiment began to have second thoughts about Dan. If father would send thirty pounds, the colonel wrote, he would send Dan home. Thirty pounds was two-thirds of father's annual wage when he was in work.

Shortly afterward another letter came saying that the colonel would settle for twenty pounds. Dan, he said, was giving them a lot of trouble.

"They've bitten off more than they can chew," said father, studying the letter. "If we hang on long enough, Maggie, they'll pay us to take him back." It must have occurred to father that his son had turned out exactly like himself. (His mother, my grandmother Selma, had had to bail him out of the navy because he was underage.)

But mother was not prepared to wait. She took her troubles to Dr. Grieves. Failing Grieves, she intended to approach uncle Eric, or the moneylender. As always, Dr. Grieves helped. He knew what he was doing. The army didn't try any snotty business with him. Mother said the army's reply to Grieves when he sent the twenty pounds was all "please and thank you, and here's your money back."

A week later, Dan came home. It was a Saturday. Mother was busy taking freshly baked bread out of the oven. She stood speechless with emotion when the latch was raised and he entered the house. He'd lost weight; he was thinner; his head was shaven; he looked crushed. With a hoarse cry, mother dropped the loaf on the kitchen floor and ran to Dan. They hugged each other and cried.

Instead of Dan's luck taking a turn for the better, he began to tread an even harder path. A friend of father's at the Bank Top Boiler Works hired Dan as a 'devil.' A 'devil' was a boy who tightened and untightened the bolts inside mill boilers when they were being repaired. Dan was lowered through one of the boiler openings - usually too small for a man - carrying a wrench and a lamp. Except for a loincloth, he went naked. While his mates shouted and pounded on the outside, he struggled with the wrench on the inside. When he emerged, he was covered with soot. The only thing white about him were his teeth and his eyeballs.

Whether he was working locally, or for weeks at a time in other towns, he always came home as black as coal, and dead beat. He came through the back alley to our backyard. Here, wet or fine, he stripped off. With his dirty clothes lying on the cobbles, he stood naked while mother rubbed him with a cloth and scrubbed him with a brush, trying to get him clean. It was as well that water was free, for she poured dozens of warm and cold buckets of water over him. Then she lathered him again and again with soap until all the soot was driven from his rippling body and had settled on his feet. The rubbing and the scrubbing went on until Dan's skin gradually changed from black to gray, gray to pink. Mother never tired. By then the backyard was awash with clothing, soapsuds and soot. Apart from catching his breath when the cold water was thrown over him, Dan never murmured. He was too tired to talk. I felt truly sorry for him and said so.

"Tha gets used to it," he answered me.

Chapter XIII

Bamber Bridge

I spent some of my summers with my mother's kinsfolk, my two maiden aunts, Betsy and Grace, who lived in a rambling old converted farmhouse in a quiet country lane at Bamber Bridge, near Preston. They were Kenyons, and except for heaping love onto my sister Brenda and me, assiduously avoided the Woodruffs. The only link my family had with them, as far as I knew, was through the mail. Brenda, who had spent some time with them recovering from a sickness, was the one who made the arrangements for me to go there. I knew from Brenda that their father had helped grandmother Bridget after the death of grandfather Thomas.

Betsy was the hearty, red-faced, fat one. The folds of flesh on her face almost concealed her small nose and her ever-merry eyes. She was sheer bulk and moved slowly. When she walked across the room the floor creaked. Her feet left an imprint wherever she walked. I was apprehensive that she might step on me. To a child's eye she had a gigantic bosom. When she hugged me, I felt myself smothered between her breasts. She had large powerful hands; the largest I had seen among the Kenyons and the Woodruffs.

Aunt Grace was just the opposite. She was Grace by name and grace by nature. She was shy, pale and slim. Her small, fine head, wispy fair hair, pale blue eyes and tiny hands and feet gave her a delicate look. Whereas Betsy flattened everything that got in her way, Grace seemed to float above it. She was sprightly. She enjoyed life just as much as Betsy, but was restrained. Betsy was forever going into fits of laughter which shook her whole frame; which in turn shook the room. Grace never went beyond a sweet smile. Betsy was what you saw. With aunt Grace you felt she was holding back on you. If a pig, or a hen, or a duck fell sick, Grace was the one who nursed it. Betsy said that Grace had had many suitors when younger, but had neglected her own interests in favour of their widowed father whom, together, they had cared for. When I knew them, I suppose they were both in their forties.

Regardless of their different traits, my aunts loved each other deeply. They were never apart. I came to love them with all my heart.

The third member of the family at Bamber Bridge was Whiskey, a salt and pepper, wire-haired fox terrier. I cannot imagine why they called him Whiskey for my aunts were strict teetotalers. It didn't take me long to realize that Whiskey was the boss of the house. I never knew a dog that took less notice of his mistresses. Regardless of my aunts' cries of 'Oh Whiskey this' and 'oh Whiskey that,' unperturbed, the dog went his own way. He knew exactly how to handle them. Battles of will between the women and the dog always ended up with Whiskey lying fast asleep on their knee. When the four of us came home from our daily walk, ignoring aunt Betsy's loud protests, Whiskey took the big upholstered chair by the fire. They'd long since given up any attempt to dislodge him. Any effort to bother him was answered with a low growl.

Whiskey must have tired of female company. From the moment I arrived at Bamber Bridge he attached himself to me. He took my arrival as sufficient excuse to avoid his weekly bath, which he hated. He slept across the foot of my bed. A large Bible lay on a heavy table in my room. Inside was a steel roller with spikes on it. There also was a tiny key, which when turned caused the book to play 'Faith of our Fathers.' Whiskey and I played it so often that my aunts feared we'd wear it out. He took great interest in the long stories I told him before sleep claimed us both. When he fell asleep before me, I watched my candle flicker and splutter. Moths came through the open window and charged the flame before I had the chance to blow it out. Because of the dog and the kindness of my aunts, I rarely missed my gang once I left Blackburn for Bamber Bridge.

Betsy and Grace Kenyon were well off. Mother told me that their father, a builder, being a shrewd man in all his undertakings, had left them enough money to more than last them the rest of their lives. Mr. John Kenyon's portrait hung in a gilded frame above a marble-encased clock in the parlour. He obviously had dressed up for the occasion. He wore an old-fashioned, black, Prince Albert coat that reached down to his knees. He had a high collar with the corners turned down and a black tie. He didn't look at ease, yet his face and his long white beard exuded kindness and good will. His life had evidently been successful. I suppose he must have been the brother of my grandfather Thomas who had left my grandmother Bridget destitute. His daughters were the only link the Woodruffs had with the Kenyons and that a tenuous one.

He had bequeathed to my aunts the large house, with its flagstone corridors, and its heavy oak furniture, in which they lived. It had several levels with a sharply pitched, red tiled roof, a permanently locked attic at the top of the stairs, and large, bright windows which had recently been added. It must have been an old building because I could scratch out the crumbling mortar from between the bricks with my fingers. At the front - part of which was plastered - was a large white-painted doorway with a roof above it. On the door was a huge, black knocker with a lion's head. One reached the front door by way of a heavy wrought iron gate that gave access to a front garden awash with flowers.

Most exciting of all, the house had a secret door built into the side of one of the steep panelled staircases. The thin, flat piece of wood that served as a door was opened by sliding a piece of the beading on the panelling. This released a bolt and allowed the panel to swing inward. Behind the panel was a hiding place, what was called a Priest's hole, where Catholic priests had taken refuge when fleeing their Protestant persecutors in earlier times. Once I was allowed to hide in the Priest's hole while aunt Betsy, pretending to be an Elizabethan soldier, tried to find me. The hullabaloo she put up when climbing the stairs would have terrified any priest.

Aunt Betsy was funny about religion. She thought that everybody in the world, at least those in their right minds, was Catholic. That's because Bamber Bridge and nearby Preston were chiefly Catholic. But I knew that Blackburn was chiefly Protestant. She refused to listen to me when I tried to put her straight. I don't know what she would have said if I'd called her a 'Cat-licker,' or had repeated the parody: "Catholic, Catholic, quack, quack, quack. Go to the devil and never come back."

Compared with life in Blackburn, my aunts lived in the best of worlds. Whereas in Blackburn we trod on each other's toes, Betsy and Grace had enough room to rattle around. Whereas our house smelt of cotton and fish, my aunts' house was alive with bright, sweet-smelling blooms picked from the garden at the rear of the house. Grace used to spend lots of time each morning cutting and arranging the flowers she placed throughout the house. She also cared for innumerable indoor plants. When she wasn't messing about with the flowers and plants, she was dusting the heavy furniture that shone like a polished apple. Once a week, she changed the lace covers on the backs and arms of the chairs. Because of the large windows, there was light everywhere.

The dark, serious faces staring at me from brown photos hanging on the walls didn't bother me. I presumed they were Kenyons, but I had no interest in finding out. I knew from the flowing dresses, the tight suits, and the hair styles that those Kenyons, like Mr. Kenyon who kept his eyes on everything from above the clock in the parlour, were long since dead.

My aunts were lucky because they didn't have to worry about money. We worried about nothing else. Mill whistles didn't bother them. They ate regularly and well. Biscuits, dates, grapes, oranges, apples, or bananas were kept on the sideboard waiting to be eaten. I was allowed to eat as much as I wanted. Most of what we ate came from an orchard, several hen coops, and a duckpond at the end of a field. I used to throw a stick in the pond in the hope that Whiskey would retrieve it, but he spurned the idea. Some of the produce they grew was given to a middle-aged couple, Jim and Effie Bairns, who came in to help every day. Some of it was sold in Bamber Bridge and Preston. More to keep themselves busy than to earn money, for which they had no real need, my aunts also fattened a pig or two.

In the evenings they read to each other, played their gramophone with its large green horn, sewed, cut out table mats, played Snakes and Ladders with me, or made stockings on a stocking frame, which they sold to a dealer in Preston. If the gramophone became too loud, Betsy would stuff a stocking into the horn. Grace spent a lot of time at night pressing flowers in a large book on the parlour table. She was a collector like her father. As he had collected stuffed birds, she collected flowers. Sometimes my aunts chose to do nothing more than rock in their chairs. Slowly the hush of night deepened. When they were rocking, they avoided talking. Their lives were as regular, secure and stable as my family's life was haphazard, uncertain, threatening. They might have been living in a castle with a drawbridge.

Every afternoon, wet or fine, we all went for a walk. Betsy was in charge and the procedure never varied.

"Grace," aunt Betsy yelled, "have we got the sticks?"

"Yes, sister," Grace answered, unperturbed.

"Billy, you ready?"

"Yes, aunt Betsy."

"Grace, do we have the coats?"

"Yes," Grace responded, her arms full of them.

"Grace! Where's Whiskey?"

Only when everybody had the right stick, the right coat, the right shoes - clogs were not worn - the right umbrella and the right hat did the procession begin. Betsy went first, grasping a heavy cane, moving slowly. She bore herself like some large animal venturing into perilous territory. I walked immediately behind her, carrying the umbrellas, followed by Grace. On these occasions my aunts wore poke bonnets. Wet or fine, I wore a Sou'wester.

Once in the fields, Whiskey streaked off as if he'd seen a rabbit.

"Come back! Come back!" Betsy bawled, raising her stick. "Oh, that dog, he'll be the death of me."

Ignoring Betsy's calls, Whiskey by now had wriggled through the hedgerow. Betsy shouted after him as if he were misbehaving himself for the first time, "You bad dog; you bad dog!" she complained. "We never want to see you again."

Covered with mud, Whiskey always reappeared when we were on the homeward stretch. He fell in line with us as if he hadn't been away. Nothing was said. By then, aunt Betsy only had wind enough to trundle home.

Summer after summer, the walks took the same route. Nothing changed - not even the demonstration that Betsy put on daily by a deep pond where boys sunbathed and swam in the nude. Betsy always got worked up about the nude bathers long before we reached the pond.

"Just look at that, Grace," she shouted in a shocked voice over her shoulder, while pointing with her stick. "Did you ever see such? What are we coming to? That's what I ask you, what are we coming to? There's no shame."

On and on, she went, her moist face becoming scarlet. By the time we reached the pond, her stick was raised like the sword of an avenging angel. By then, the swimmers had slithered down the muddy bank into the water. Betsy marched to the water's edge to deliver her usual sermon about shame and immodesty. She ended on the same note: "You're a bunch of hooligans, that's what you are; you brazen, disgusting ragamuffins. There's no decency in you. You're a disgrace to Bamber Bridge."

All of which sent the swimmers into fits of laughter.

"Silly old bugger!" they shouted back, while splashing water at her. "Why don't you fall in?"

After a summer or two I took all this in my stride. Aunt Betsy didn't mean what she said. It was her way of enjoying herself. She would have been mortified if the hooligans had suddenly worn pants. Quiet, gentle aunt Grace never intervened - she stood at some distance, her face wrapped in smiles. She enjoyed her sister's daily tirade more than the swimmers did.

Aunt Betsy was obviously destined to run into male nudes. She once took me to the Natural History Museum in Preston where she was halted in her tracks at the entrance by a bronze statue of an ancient Greek male. "Well," said Betsy, staring at the metal penis and testicles, "I'll be blessed; if this is what we get at the door, Billy, what will we get inside?"

Each summer, I used to fret until my parents gave me the ten pennies for the train ride to Bamber Bridge. The fare was all I needed. I went just as I stood, wearing a jersey, a thick flannel shirt, corduroy pants, stockings, clogs, coat and cap. Apart from a penknife and some string and one or two other odds and ends in my pockets, I didn't take another thing. I took no underwear, no change of clothes, not even a toothbrush or a handkerchief. Everything awaited me in the heavy wardrobes and drawers in my room at Bamber Bridge.

First time I ever went there, I went alone. I was told where to find and leave the train; I was given an address and ten pence for the fare, and that was that. I had no idea what prior arrangements were made. I'd met my aunts once in Blackburn, and I'm sure my father had sent them a note before I left. Nothing was said about my return. It was all done in such an off-hand way that I was neither confused nor frightened. Nobody at the station thought it odd that I should be travelling alone. I was much too concerned to stick my head out of the carriage window, and drink in all that I could see than to worry whether I should get lost or come to any harm. The journey was only a few miles, but I was as excited as if I were going to the moon. Nobody at Bamber Bridge mentioned Blackburn until the summer was done and it was time to go home.

My aunts were always at home, fussing about in the field, or in one of the out-houses with their livestock. They were never ill, or had gone away. Each time I arrived they were exactly as I had left them the time before. If they were working in the fields they'd be wearing the same funnel-like hats, the same fingerless gloves and the same clogs. Aunt Grace always wore a white lace collar; aunt Betsy a black bow on a white shirt that crackled with starch and was as hard as rock. The aprons and the heavy skirts were always the same. My room, which looked down to the duck pond, was kept ready. As if I'd arrived from an epic journey, on the first night I was expected to give them an account of what I'd seen out of the carriage window. At Bamber Bridge nothing changed.

Whiskey invariably warned everybody. With piercing yelps he flung himself against the back of the door. Then he jumped up to the glass panel to make quite sure it was me. The moment I got the door open he'd be all over me, licking my face and behind my ears. Then he howled his way through the house and across the field announcing my arrival.

Because of an unspoken agreement between us, my aunts ignored my approach. They went on fussing with their ducks and hens as if Whiskey and I did not exist. Meanwhile I crept up silently behind aunt Betsy's enormous figure and suddenly shouted out as loudly as I could, "Auntie, Ah've cum!" Whereupon Betsy dropped whatever she was holding, pretending that she'd had the shock of her life. She slowly swung her immense figure around. Her hands shaking, she stared at me with laughing eyes. "Why, so tha has, luv," she said. "He's cum, he's cum, Grace," she bawled across the field as if Grace didn't already know. Then she took me in a tight embrace, crushing me against her crackling, starched bosom.

Continuing to hug me warmly, Betsy ran her hands over my frame.

"Oh, Grace," she shouted, "Grace, the poor bairn's starving. His bones are sticking out, Grace. Come and feel."

By now, Grace had come running. "Why, so they are," she said, running her fingers over my arms and legs, while clucking her tongue disapprovingly.

At that point Betsy looked at me as if I were a lost cause. "They've let him go too far this time," she said, darkly.

"They've left it too late. He's skinnier than last time, you know. There's nowt we can do."

"We can but try, Betsy," Grace sighed, her fingers running over my spine. "The skeleton's there; we've got the frame to work on."

This talk never bothered me. I knew I wasn't dying. It was my aunts' way of preparing themselves for the challenge that lay ahead. If I looked undernourished when I arrived, they were determined that I would not leave in the same condition. The challenge was to get as much fat on my bones as possible before my summer holiday came to an end. As eating was my possessing passion, I could hardly complain.

For weeks on end, they stuffed me with food. No matter how I protested, 'seconds' and 'thirds' were piled onto my plate. I was encouraged to gobble. I lost count of the many hens and ducks I consumed, or how much fresh milk I drank. I ate so much at noon that I could hardly stand. If I didn't respond to the treatment, I was given a second dinner at night. There were occasions when I found myself almost too taut to totter to bed. The more flesh I put on - and it was impossible not to gain weight with that care - the greater their satisfaction. I was weighed nightly and they beamed at every extra ounce. Even Whiskey seemed to take a delight in it.

When the time came for my departure they weighed me for the last time. By the look on their faces, that last weighing was a life and death matter. If the figure was not to Betsy's liking, the weighing was repeated. "Now, Billy, tha must try a little harder this time, luv," she said, surreptitiously putting her hand on my shoulder.

The weighing having been brought to a satisfactory conclusion, the women ran their hands over me once more to make quite sure they'd done their job. They told the platform man at the railway station what miracles they'd worked on me during my stay. "Billy's still on the skinny side," they said, looking at me critically, "but he'll pass. He might just last the winter. We couldn't do more in the time." At that point they lifted my cap and ruffled my hair.

It was expected of me that I would weep when leaving them at the station, and I did. They wept too. They took turns hugging me till the last moment before letting me go. With my pockets full of apples, and my arms full of food - all of which I was ordered to consume during the half-hour's journey home - and my hot hand clutching a shining half-crown, which was pressed on me at this point, I somehow managed to clamber aboard.

As aunt Betsy was too large to climb into the train after me, she beckoned me down again so that she could give me one last squeeze. She used to squeeze me so long and so hard that it took the platform man, with his neb cap and his shining buttons, to get me back into the carriage. To forestall any further squeezes, he quickly slammed the door behind me. I barely got in before the train began to lurch out of the station. Brushing my tears aside, I waved good-bye until the two bonneted faces, handkerchiefs to noses, passed out of sight. Then I settled down and began to gorge as I had been bidden.

Few summers passed without my spending some time with my aunts at Bamber Bridge. They never came to our house in Blackburn. If I didn't arrive, they sent the whole of my railway fare to mother, so that there could be no excuse for my not coming. Every visit was joyful. Always they were happy and unchanged. I felt that nothing could affect their world. Yet something did.

One summer's day a stranger came to my aunts' house. The stranger had a large cardboard folder under his arm tied with a bow. I met him at the front door talking to Betsy. He was such an odd-looking fellow that I could not help staring at him. He wore a dark-blue suit with faded gray stripes. The garment was threadbare; the arms and legs were far too short. His shirt and tie were equally worn but clean. On his head he had a blue trilby that shone with grease at the sides. He had cracked shoes laced with hooks instead of eyes.

"This is Mr. Simon Gripper, Billy," my aunt said, introducing me. I jerked my head in greeting.

Mr. Gripper put a cold, wet hand around mine, while observing me sharply. Neither of us spoke. I felt an instinctive dislike for him. Whiskey must have felt the same, for he growled. The hair along his back stood up, which was a bad sign.

Mr. Gripper was the nearest thing to a gorilla in a suit that I could imagine. He had wide shoulders, a flat face, fish eyes, a flat nose, a protruding bottom lip, and a wet, steamy brow. When he left, he walked like a gorilla rocking from side to side. I decided to forget all about him.

Imagine my surprise, a week or two later, when running into the living room with Whiskey for tea, I found him sitting on Whiskey's favourite chair talking to my aunts. His suit seemed to have shrunk since the last visit. Apart from a grunt and a wave of the hand, he wasted no time on me. With several cucumber sandwiches and some sticky fruitcake, I chose a chair among Mr. Kenyon's stuffed birds as far away from the visitor as I could. Whiskey sat under my chair with a baleful eye on the stranger. We had never been unhappy at tea before.

While eating as much as he could, Mr. Gripper never stopped talking. As far as I could make out, he was telling my aunts how he had come by his present job; which, of all things, was selling religious pictures from door to door. Hence the large folder he carried.

"It's the Lord's will," he intoned, in what I thought was a slushy voice; then he paused and gave a long sigh. Whiskey growled; I felt like growling too.

Meanwhile Mr. Gripper drew from his folder one vivid picture after another. There was Jesus as a child, Jesus as a man, Jesus crucified. There was the sacrificial lamb. There was the Holy Mother Mary, dressed in silks. Pictures of the Sacred Heart and the Saints followed. Some of the Saints wore halos and floated through the sky, others were covered with blood and gore. There was no end to the pictures. The furniture in the living room was covered with them.

"One cannot make a living this way," Mr. Gripper conceded, "but it gives me the chance to earn my daily bread and spread the gospel of love at the same time. What better task?"

I shall never understand why my aunts allowed Mr. Gripper to cross their threshold. Perhaps he didn't look as ugly to them as he did to me. Perhaps it was downright jealousy on my part that made him seem so greasy and servile. I felt threatened by him. What I found really objectionable was the way aunt Grace had eyes and ears only for Mr. Gripper. Aunt Betsy, Whiskey, and I might never have existed.

One week later, Mr. Gripper was back. The next week he was back again. Once, out of the corner of my eye, I saw him take aunt Grace's hand, which really upset me.

Later that night, when I was on my way to join my aunts in the kitchen, I heard the only cross words that I ever heard between them. They must have been arguing for some time, for they were both worked up.

"Grace," said Betsy, who had been plucking and trussing some ducks for the church, "I don't know what's come over you, luv. We've come this far. Let's go on together. I'm not happy, luv, for your sake."

I was shocked at Grace's reply.

"You're not happy," Grace responded in an unusually hard tone, "the truth is, Betsy, you don't want me to be happy. You'd rather boss me for the rest of my life."

Those words made me catch my breath. How unfair to aunt Betsy! She worshipped her younger sister. I was not surprised to hear aunt Betsy burst into tears. Her sobbing shook the room.

"May you be forgiven, Grace Kenyon," she sobbed. "You know, I don't want anyone to hurt you."

"No one's going to hurt me, Betsy. I'm not marrying Simon. There's nothing going on between Simon and myself if that's what you're hinting at. We're just friends. He's a good man out on his luck who needs help."

The next thing I knew was that aunt Grace had also burst into tears. "Oh Betsy," she cried as she flung herself into her sister's outstretched arms. I crept away with a heavy heart.

The next day I decided to have it out with aunt Betsy about Mr. Gripper. "I don't like him, aunt Betsy," I said. "Nor does Whiskey. We hate him."

"You shouldn't talk like that, Billy. You're jumping to conclusions. You don't know anything about him. As Christians we must love Mr. Gripper, forgive him from our hearts, and pray for him." But her voice betrayed her. She obviously didn't like Mr. Gripper any more than I did.

When I returned the following summer, I was dumbfounded to be met by Mr. Gripper. I ran right into him. Whiskey was nowhere to be seen.

"Oh, it's you again, is it," he said, holding my arm tightly and staring through me.

When I went down the field to give aunt Betsy a surprise she hardly responded to my creeping up on her. She seemed a bit thinner and tired. Her eyes were worried, even haunted-looking. Aunt Grace looked better. She had twice the life she had had previously. Instead of following Betsy's moves as she had done in the past, she seemed to be leading. I hadn't been there several hours before I realized that Grace had transferred her affections from me to Mr. Gripper. On her suggestion, he had moved into the house; worse, he had taken my room. Whiskey now had a kennel at the back of the house. Grace seemed to have lost her head over Mr. Gripper . Nothing was too much trouble. Mr. Gripper was in charge.

That summer was the only unhappy one I spent at Bamber Bridge. With Mr. Gripper giving orders through Grace, the peace and laughter went out of the place. Gripper's shrewd, mottled brown eyes seemed to follow me everywhere. He showed no interest in fattening me up as my aunts had done in the past. He'd given up selling holy pictures. Instead he marketed the stockings my aunts made. Each now had her own stocking frame. When they weren't looking after the livestock and the orchard they knitted stockings; the housekeepers, Jim and Effie no longer came. While Mr. Gripper didn't do any work himself - he had a chest complaint that demanded rest - he was forever on about wasting time. "The Lord never wastes time," was one of his favourite sayings. Even our afternoon walk had been sacrificed to Simon Gripper's need for more stockings.

Yet Mr. Gripper didn't bully them. "I quite understand," he would say when Betsy objected to something. "How foolish of me. You are right and I am wrong. I was only trying to do what is best for us all." I used to watch Betsy's reactions. Her face went from red to scarlet. Then it set on fire. Yet she managed to hold her tongue.

Every evening Mr. Gripper told his rosary. He kept it in an old snuff box which he carried in his waistcoat pocket. It was a poor thing compared to the one aunt Grace had. Hers was made of ivory beads with a silver chain and a golden cross. As my aunts were devout Catholics, they joined him in saying a few Hail Mary's and Our Father's - something they'd never done before. Whenever we could, Whiskey and I fled the house for the fields. We were both heavy-hearted.

Although I attended a Protestant school at that time, my aunts insisted on my going to St. Augustine's Catholic Church with them on Sundays. The church was the center of their life; there was always something being 'got up' by them for the church. Open-handedly, they gave innumerable hens and ducks to the church bazaars.

What I could not stand about Mr. Gripper was his behaviour in church. When he genuflected before the altar, I thought he would never get up. He struck his breast three times during the Confiteor, hitting himself hard enough to break his ribs. "Through my fault," thump. "Through my fault," louder thump. "Through my most grievous fault," crash! The half empty church echoed to the thumps. At the elevation of the Host, he groaned. He relished the words 'miserable sinner,' and beat himself as he repeated them. When he grovelled before the altar rails to receive communion, I wished that the vaulted ceiling would fall on him.

To my aunts' obvious displeasure I couldn't help staring at him. "Aunt Betsy," I whispered, "why does Mr. Gripper have to beat himself like that? You don't."

"Sh-sh. Stop talking, Billy, you can't talk here. What will people think?"

Not only did Mr. Gripper thump himself in church more than anybody else; when the congregation recited the eight Beatitudes - blessed are the poor; blessed are the meek ... Mr. Gripper's voice was louder than the rest. At Benediction one Sunday evening he sang a solo 'The day that Thou gavest, Oh Lord, now is ending' which almost took out the windows. Grace thought it was marvelous. I thought it awful. Only Betsy's shushing stopped me from saying so.

I have reason to remember that particular summer. It was the summer Mr. Gripper robbed me of a tooth. I'd had the misfortune to develop toothache. The pain was awful.

"Simon, take lad beyond t' bridge to Henry's," aunt Betsy had asked Mr. Gripper. "He's a young man just starting out. He'll put it right. They say he's got a new-fangled American drill that does the job in half the time. Tell him to do a good job on t' lad. Mustn't lose tooth at his age. I'll pay when you tell me how much it is."

So off we went to Henry's. Mr. Gripper didn't have to tell me that I and my tooth were a complete nuisance and that he wasn't enjoying the excursion one bit.

Our arrival at Mr. Henry's was announced by a large doorbell. A threateningly, ominously empty chair stood in the middle of the surgery. There were no other patients. Mr. Henry emerged from a back room.

"He's got a bit of a toothache," Mr. Gripper grumped at Mr. Henry. "Can yo put it right?"

I was put in the chair. With a light, Mr. Henry studied the offending tooth. His poking made it worse.

"He needs a small filling," he concluded. "Take a few minutes, that's all. He won't feel a thing. It'll take out all the pain."

I watched Mr. Gripper eye the dentist slyly. "Wot's cost?" he asked.

"Three and sixpence."

There was a pause. "Wot's an extraction cost?"

"Two shillings."

"Take it out," said Mr. Gripper.

"But I can save the tooth," Mr. Henry said. "It's a straightforward job. A perfectly good tooth."

"Take it out," said Mr. Gripper.

"But..." the dentist faltered.

"Young man," said Mr. Gripper, "yo're wasting my time. Dost t' want to earn two shillings or dostn't thee?"

Mr. Henry made a pathetic gesture. "All right," he said. "I've heard yer."

I returned to aunt Betsy without my tooth.

"Had to come out," said Mr. Gripper. "Nothing else for it."

The next time I went to Bamber Bridge, I was surprised to find my aunts' house occupied by strangers. The door was locked and I had to use the knocker. A tall oldish couple came to the door.

"Ah've cum te stay with my aunts," I said. "Ah cum every year."

"Tha won't be staying this year," the man said.

"Why not?"

"Because thi aunts don't live here any more. They sold t' house. It's an old folks' 'ome now. Didn't ye know? Thi aunt Grace has got herself wed."

"To Mr. Gripper?" I asked, my heart sinking.

"The same," the woman said. She was about to go on, but the man gave her a reproachful glance, whereupon she fell silent.

I stood looking vacantly from one to the other. "Where are they now?"

"They're running a general store with Mr. Gripper in Preston." He went back into the house to find the address, which he wrote on a slip of paper for me. He also gave me instructions on how to get there. His eyes told me that I was in for a shock.

An hour later I found a grocer's store in one of the back streets of Preston. The shop faced an ancient aqueduct, the black, greasy stones of which ran with moisture. All around was a bleak industrial area with the railroad and factories only yards away. Dirt and peeling paint were everywhere. If anybody had told me a year earlier that I should find my aunts living in such an awful place, I would have thought them mad.

The shop was empty of customers when I entered. With their backs to the entrance, Betsy and Grace were busy unwrapping and emptying boxes. They got such a surprise when they saw me. They flapped their hands to show their discomfort.

"Oh, Billy," they said, "why did you come here?"

They hugged me, but it was in an absent-minded, apprehensive sort of way. They didn't have the life and strength of earlier times. Betsy moved stiffly. I was startled at aunt

Grace's appearance. She looked crushed. She had great black rings under her eyes. She could hardly breathe from asthma - something she had never had at Bamber Bridge. She told me Whiskey was dead.

While we were talking, Mr. Gripper came up from the cellar. He looked extremely well and prosperous. He'd got himself a better suit. His hair glistened with oil. He wore a gold watch-chain. From the moment he saw me, he was hostile.

"Oh, it's you is it?" he said as he came forward. "Thought we'd got rid of you, we did. Well, you've come to t' wrong place for a free summer this time. Tha'd better go back where tha cum fra. Can't have thee interferin' with our business."

"Simon!" Grace said angrily.

But Simon was not to be put off. He pointed to the door through which I had just entered. The message was clear. He wanted me back in the street. My aunts stared at me with empty eyes. There was time only to squeeze their hands. We didn't speak. We just clung to each other pathetically. None of us cried, but our eyes were wet. I knew in my heart that we all wanted to sob and sob.

I never saw my aunts again. I did write a letter to them when I got home asking them if I could help them in any way, but it was returned to me by Mr. Gripper. Mother came in one day and told me in a sad voice that Grace was dead. The news gave me a lump in my throat. My eyes welled with tears. Betsy had gone to live with friends in Scotland. I thought mother was going to go on about Mr. Gripper - all the Kenyons and Woodruffs knew about Simon Gripper by now - but she didn't. I don't know what became of him. I hope he did ill. He left me with a life-long distrust of unctuous people.

Chapter XIV

Grandmother Bridget

W hen I was about ten, I became closer to grandmother Bridget than to my own family. Hardly a day went by when I was not in her house. With Jenny and Brenda in the mills, it fell to me to help her keep it clean. I chopped the sticks for the fire that heated the washtub standing in an alcove of the downstairs room. I ran errands. When things were especially bad, I'd bring a shilling or a half-crown from mother to buy food. Grandmother didn't take charity easily and was difficult to help.

I cannot remember her sharing our house or our board, yet working-class families were usually close. For whatever reasons, she clung to her privacy. I was the only one - other than mother - who could reach out to her. Father, Dan, Brenda, and even sweet Jenny found grandmother remote. She simply didn't welcome attention. Except from me, she never accepted help gracefully. Apart from my visits, she kept herself to herself. I think she did so because fate had cast her into a society for which she was ill-suited. Maggie was right when she said her mother had 'cum reet down.'

In the mid-twenties grandmother fell on bitterly hard times. Having lost her job in the mills; she tried to survive by doing people's washing, never satisfied until it was whiter than snow. It used to infuriate me the way some of the workers robbed her. "Tell her I'll give her the money next week," they said when I delivered the laundry beautifully wrapped in clean newspaper. I knew they were lying; there were times when I felt like telling them so. I knew how desperately grandmother needed the money; sixpence, ninepence, or a shilling would have kept her going.

"These people don't speak with a plain tongue, Grandma," I complained.

"They're poor too, Billy Boy," she said, clasping her wasted hands, "they don't know which way to turn."

At that time, she was living in a doll-like house at the end of a row of cottages in Astley Street - five minutes walk from Griffin Street. The house was shaped like the tip of a flat iron. It had one tiny room downstairs and an equally small room upstairs. Apart from the street door, two windows (one up, one down), a corner in which to cook and another in which to wash, a broken rocking chair, two stools, a rough, bench-like table, a fireplace and a bed with a wooden chest at its foot, there was little else. Anything of value had long since gone to the pawnshop.

Next door to grandmother's cottage was a high-walled cobbled yard. At one time, grandmother had kept her brooms, tin bath and laundry tub there. When I knew it, the lock grandmother had put on the door had been broken and the yard had become a steaming manure dump used by the town's street cleaning crews as well as by several horse stables in the vicinity. Although the wall hid the manure, there was no mistaking the smell. Because of it, her two windows and her door were kept shut. The final irony was that the police had told grandmother to get rid of the manure.

Desperate, she asked me to go to the police station to get them to stop people dumping manure outside her door. I wasn't happy about going. I'd been raised to fear and avoid the police, but I went.

Having run through the streets, I reached the station and began to lay grandmother's troubles before the sergeant-on-duty. He was a tall, burly man with a clipped mustache. From the word go, he left me in no doubt that my sudden ragged appearance to discuss steaming manure was not to his liking. He had more important things to do.

"The coppers have complained to grandmother about the manure in her yard. But she's not the one who puts it there," I said.

"Who has complained?" His face reddened.

"The coppers."

"And who might the coppers be?"

"You're a copper, aren't you?" I said, my eyes glued to the stick he was holding.

"Bert, Charley," the sergeant called to two policemen who were listening from the other room, "There's a young gentleman here who thinks we're coppers. Not officers, not sergeants, not constables, just plain coppers."

"Well, you are, aren't you?"

From that moment on, the topic of manure was forgotten. Instead, I was given the worst dressing down of my life. I was threatened with a fate worse than that suffered by the Christian martyrs. The sergeant said he would have the whole Blackburn police force down on my head and I believed him. I'd be in the 'clink' for the rest of my life. He put the fear of hell into me. With my eye on the stick, I edged back to the door and fled.

"Well?" asked grandmother, when I returned, breathless from running. "What are they going to do about it?"

"Nothing, Grandma, they didn't want to talk about manure."

Grandmother not only had to tolerate the manure, directly opposite her house lived the town executioner. I was horrified when she told me about the hangman. Not that I ever heard anyone speak against hanging. I spent hours gingerly peeping through her curtains in the hope of catching a glimpse of the hangman hurrying off with his rope to an execution. I tried to draw out of her the fine details of how the poor wretches died. "It's not a subject for 'dacent' conversation," she silenced me. Father knew the hangman; he often met him in the pub. He spoke highly of him. He said he was the happiest of men. The only strange thing about him was his ice-cold hands.

———◄○►———

As grandmother got older she often talked about Ireland; about her birthplace, County Clare, with its ruined castles and the ghosts that haunted its broken walls. She also spoke of her life as a girl before she met grandfather Thomas. She told me about the balls she'd been to. She had had a passion for dancing. No matter how much she tried to conceal it, I detected a wistfulness, if not a downright sadness.

What I know about the feud that has raged between Ireland and England for centuries, I learned from her. "The trouble with the English," she said one day, "is that they can never remember what the Irish can never forget." In a quiet but rich voice, she sang a haunting song about Robert Emmet, the Irish martyr:

> The struggle is over, the boys are defeated,
> Old Ireland's surrounded with sadness and gloom;
> We were betrayed and shamefully treated,
> And I, Robert Emmet, awaiting my doom.

She sang it as a dirge, not as a call to arms. She was never bitter: not against fate, not against the British. Grudges were no part of her.

She also told me about the great famine in Ireland in the 1840's, in which millions had died or fled to America. "It was not a famine, Billy Boy," she said. "It was a great 'starvin'.' And it was to England's shame!"

She taught me to be courageous, loyal and honest. Falseness she couldn't abide. "If you give your word, Billy Boy, keep it." Especially did she teach me to be upstanding. "You must never grovel, Billy Boy. And never beg. Stand on your own feet. And don't whine." Whatever manners and courtesies I learned, I learned from her.

She never mentioned God. The only concession she made to the saints was to wear a large sprig of shamrock on the 17th March, St. Patrick's Day. In her opinion St. Patrick was a "foin

Saint, a very foin Saint," and that was good enough for me.
One of her favourite ballads was about St. Patrick's Day:

> O Paddy, dear, an' did ye hear the news that's goin' round?
> The shamrock is by law forbid to grow on Irish ground!
> No more St. Patrick's Day we'll keep, his colour can't be seen,
> For there's a cruel law agin the wearin' o' the Green!

One night when we were sitting before the embers, she told
me how in 1920, thousands of Irish had gathered outside a
London jail where almost two hundred Irish political prisoners
were fasting unto death. As darkness fell, someone called for
silence. Faintly they heard the sound of voices singing inside
the jail. Then a great thunder rose from the square into the
night sky as the Irish - in and outside the jail - sang 'The Wearin'
o' the Green.' "It stunned everybody who heard it,"
grandmother said. "Papers were full of it. Not long afterward
the prisoners were freed."

Grandmother lived to see southern Ireland become the Irish
Free State.

When my lessons were done, she turned down the glass-
funnelled paraffin lamp and relapse into quiet contentment
before the fire. Often she gently rocked, while humming a tune
or gravely sipping a cup of tea. She didn't touch alcohol.
Although she had few visitors, she tidied herself up at night. By
the time I reached her cottage, she had changed into a long,
dark garment that contrasted with the lace cap which came
down to her shoulders. Sometimes she wore a blouse with big,
shiny buttons. Usually I found her before the fire, her feet on a
stool, her hands on her knees. There was always an open book
- her escape from wretchedness - on the cornice next to her
wire-framed spectacles. I often wondered how she could sit
there by herself for hours on end staring at the flames. I'd catch
her carrying on a conversation with the embers and her
memories.

On occasions, I managed to persuade her to take a short
walk. With her hat and her jacket and her silver-topped cane
and her cracked shoes, all of them relics of her better days, she
looked quite a toff. Even when she had been a slubber in the
mills, she had refused to wear a weaver's shawl and clogs. Poor

or not, she retained her dignified bearing, the Kenyon air of gentility. There were times when her neighbours found her difficult to understand, but they all called her 'royal.'

"And where do you think you're going?" she asked if I walked too fast. "I can't keep up with you."

Only once did I see her truly worried and sad. Regardless of her growing poverty, she was usually happy and cheerful. Shortly before I arrived, a hog of a rent collector had threatened to throw her into the street. I don't know what had happened; father usually helped her with the rent. Tears were rolling silently down her wrinkled face. Her long, thin neck seemed to have contracted. She wasn't crushed - she was too tough for that - just badly wounded. The hardness of her lot never hardened her soul.

By the time she was in her early sixties, about the time of the General Strike in 1926, she was destitute. She had no income at all. I cannot believe that some of the Kenyons did not try to help her, but I saw little evidence of it. Everybody was desperately trying to survive. Also I suspect that grandmother put them off in her own innocent, refined way, as she did the offers of help from her neighbours.

For a period at least, grandmother was eligible for outdoor relief from the town. She could have queued up for one of the Lord Mayor's parcels, which every now and again were distributed in front of the Town Hall. But the idea of queuing with hundreds of others seeking public charity was an anathema to her. She refused to make an exhibition of her need. The churches provided food - in helping to stem the tide of want, Blackburn churches and clergy had a long and honourable tradition - but some churches adhered to the maxim 'support only those that are of the faith.' It grieved mother that grandmother had not applied for the dole. To refuse the dole was refusing good money. Nor did she resort to the Poor Law Guardians. That would have been the final blow to her self-respect. Grandmother preferred to keep her pride and to genteelly starve to death. Pride was all she had left.

Living from hand to mouth ourselves, there was little we could do for her. I couldn't give her anything from what I earned running errands; my people took it. I sometimes brought her a basin of broth from the street kitchens run by the Salvation Army, or the Catholic Sisters of Mercy and Charity. Some of the Protestant churches also handed out free soup or a piece of potato pie. Grandmother wasn't easy. She ate the food I brought her, but she refused to go and get it; that was begging.

The trouble came when she began to lose interest in food altogether; not only in food but in life as well. She became increasingly listless. Etched by a nest of lines, her deep-set blue eyes became deeper still. The light in them was lowered. She didn't seem to care what happened to her. She got so weak that I began to do all her cleaning. That's how, one Saturday evening when grandmother had gone to mother's, I came to open the box that stood at the foot of her bed. I lifted the lid gingerly knowing that I was prying. I was astonished to find a whole lot of fine clothes there. Among them was a beautiful blue ball dress decorated with imitation pearls. There also was a little book headed 'Carmania' with a list of names in it.

As the clothes meant food, I brought up the subject when grandmother returned. I confessed I'd been prying into her trunk.

"You didn't tell me about all the fine clothes you're hiding. That's money. Why don't you pawn them?"

"They're not for pawning, Billy Boy. Not my best feathers," she added with a bright, quick smile. "Not those!"

After a long silence, she spoke up. "Would you like to see me in my best feathers?" There was a note of mischief in her voice.

"Yes," I said, for I knew it would please her.

Before I could stop her, she had jumped up, taken the glass-funnelled lamp from the cornice, and was on her way upstairs. I was left with the firelight.

After a few minutes she called down: "Are you ready, Billy Boy?"

"Yes, I'm ready."

I looked up as I heard her feet on the stairway. What I saw made me catch my breath. Grandmother was wearing the ball dress I'd seen in the trunk. The pearls glowed softly as they caught the firelight. Around her neck she wore a long fluffy boa made of feathers and delicate fabric. On her feet were the elegant slippers. A tiny patch of lace covered her hair. From her wrist hung the little book. Her face was lit by the paraffin lamp she held before her. I noticed that the deep lines and wrinkles had gone. Her face seemed much younger.

"Grandma," I gasped.

As she stepped lightly onto the sanded floor she pretended to consult her little book. "I believe you asked me to dance this one with you," she said as she extended her hand toward me gracefully.

Kicking off my clogs, I hurriedly pushed whatever furniture there was out of the way. Resting her hands on my shoulders, for she was taller than I, we began to turn slowly in the confined space. The lamp on the cornice, which she had replaced, flickered a dim light. It threw our shadows against the wall. Increasing our speed, we danced round and round, grinding the grit with our feet. Grandmother's eyes were almost shut.

In time, I tired. She didn't. She moved effortlessly, like someone possessed; she didn't want to stop.

"Oh, Billy Boy," she scolded when I stumbled, and then we were off again, faster than ever. My head spun.

I don't know how long we danced. The dance ended when I fell over a stool and could go on no more.

I didn't know what to do when I got up off the floor, so I stood there breathless and clapped as I'd seen dancers do. "Grandma, you danced beautifully."

She smiled, made a slight bow, and went upstairs. Shortly afterward, she came down again, coughing harshly. She wore her usual black dress, with her lace cap hanging to her shoulders. The flushed cheeks had paled; the deep lines had returned; dark rings surrounded her reddened eyes; she was strangely cast down; there was a tiredness in her voice - a grating in her throat. She had difficulty breathing. When she stepped into the room I could hear her bare feet on the sand. Her step was halting and unsteady.

I didn't see anything of grandmother the next day. Two nights later I entered her darkened cottage. There was no sign of her. Having struck a light, I saw her empty purse on the table. It lay there wide open as if it had been thrown from the door. My eyes took in the faded pictures on the wall, the setpot, the frayed curtains, the broken rocking chair, the glass-funnelled lamp on the mantelpiece and the gutted candle on the table. I knew something was wrong. I ran upstairs. There was no one there. When I lifted the lid of the trunk at the foot of her bed, it was empty. I ran home and told mother.

Two days later uncle Edward walked into our house to tell us that grandmother Bridget was dead and buried.

Wearing her ball dress, she had stumbled all the way to the workhouse, and had died there a few hours after being admitted. She had declared herself "without next of kin," which had made it all the more difficult for the workhouse authorities to get in touch with us. It was the police who had informed uncle Edward.

A week or so later, Mr. Hetherington, t' bump man who had studied my head years before, told us he'd seen grandmother on the day she was missing. She was sitting on a bench at the edge of town. He'd walked past her and had wondered what she was up to dressed like that. "She was like something on t' parade. Ah've never seen anythin' like it. She was sat straight up, back like a ramrod, head held high, oh, so high, feathers aflutter. She had her silver-topped cane in her outstretched right hand. Her t' other hand lay on her lap. Cheeks were sunken, but t' nose and chin were out there. I could have sworn t' eyes were closed. Well, I didn't know what to say. I felt right bamboozled. I almost stopped and asked her what she was up to. But then I had second thoughts. It was none of my business. It was summer, and t' old lady was known for taking walks. As for t' funny dress and scarf and slippers, who was I to judge? There's no telling what an old woman will get up to. So, I doffed mi cap, held mi tongue, and went mi way."

Several days later, the workhouse returned grandmother Bridget's belongings. There was the silver-tipped cane, the dress, the scarf, the lace cap and the now torn slippers. They also sent a faded photograph of grandfather Thomas, and the little book that contained the list of dancing partners.

Out of it all, came my first great heartbreak. For the first time in my life I knew what it was to be scalded with grief. I was more upset than when I heard aunt Grace was dead. On and off, I wept for days. Several times I cried myself to sleep. I not only wept, I loathed myself for not having done more. I loathed the grown-ups, especially uncle Eric and uncle Edward, when they came together in our house to brood over stewed tea, while they accused and mocked each other for having "driven t' poor owd woman in t' workhouse." Silently, I listened to their mealy-mouthed words. Rage possessed me; they were all to blame. Grandmother had had to die before they recognized her existence. For the first time, the idea of running away from Blackburn and Lancashire entered my head. With all their fine talk they had managed to inflict on grandmother Bridget the two things we all feared most: the workhouse and a pauper's grave.

Between them they'd driven Bridget Gorman Kenyon 'over t' hill.'

Chapter XV

Strike!

Something must have been sadly wrong with Britain when people had to 'genteelly' starve to death as grandmother Bridget had done. Living through the 1920's was like sitting in a boiling pot of broth. There was no peace. By 1926 things had got so bad that the workers began to talk of bringing the country to a standstill through a General Strike. The working class was going to make one last big effort to set everything right. In April 1926 the mine owners posted new wage offers that were so low that they were tantamount to a lockout. When the miners refused the terms offered and stayed out, matters were brought to a head. On 1 May 1926 the government declared a State of Emergency. The fight was on.

I'd almost no idea what was going on, but I was thrilled at the prospect of a decisive fight with the bosses. Not for a moment did I doubt the complete justice of the workers' cause.

Before the strike there was to be a meeting in the Blackburn Trade Hall. Father's trade union had asked him to attend. Everyone talked about it - even at school. I was so excited that I asked father to take me with him to the Trade Hall meeting.

When we entered the crowded hall you could feel the sparks. People were worked up. The place hummed with voices. Delegates from all the major industries: mining, transport, railways, engineering and textiles were present. They all had their banners. To loud applause, the meeting began with one of the miners' delegates taking the platform and appealing to his 'brothers and sisters' to come to the miners' aid. "The hour of decision has struck!" he shouted to wild applause. "Defend us in our fight for a living wage."

What followed came as a surprise. I thought the weavers, the spinners and the twiners would all line up behind the miners, the railway and other transport workers to fight the bosses. Instead, a shouting match began between the textile people in which all order broke down. Nobody seemed to know if we were going to have a General Strike or a National Strike, though I couldn't see the difference. Tall, angular Patrick Murphy - the foreman who had delivered me when I was born - thought that a General Strike would make matters worse, and he advised against joining the miners. He was shouted down as "a capitalist lackey and a running dog." Those who wanted a General Strike were shouted down as "bolshies and 'reds' in the pay of Russia."

"Revolution's out of the question," Mr. Murphy argued, jumping up on his chair. "It's purposeless to talk about a workers' state. The country is not with you. Of course we must continue the struggle, but there is a right way of going about it and a wrong way. Why come out now, when you've already lost so much through strikes and lockouts? I ask you, what can you gain? Nothing. On that you have to agree. Half a loaf is better than none."

While many workers booed Mr. Murphy, half a dozen other speakers stood on their chairs bawling at each other at the top of their voices. One of them shouted, "Half a loaf rubbish. Next thing you'll be telling us that a crumb is better than nothing. What I say is not a penny off the pay, not a second on the day! One out, all out!" By now everybody was clamouring and uneasy.

As far as I could make out, all the speakers were proposing different things. Some were calling for revolution; some were calling for peace; some wanted to support the miners; others wanted to leave the miners to their fate. Everybody was rude to each other. "Hold thi trap," "shut thi gob," and "shut up," were hurled across the room.

Once the meeting got out of hand, the chairman's shouts of "Gentlemen, please! Gentlemen, recognize the chair!" were ignored. So were the appeals of many others who called for "Silence, please. Silence!" The drum beat of the chairman's gavel only added to the din. I'd never been to a workers' meeting as unruly as this. Father's trade union meetings were all solemn affairs, like going to church.

As the noise got worse, father said, "Let's go home. Too many crackpots." Until then he hadn't opened his mouth. Others must have agreed with him, for lots of people were streaming out of the hall. They smelled danger. I looked back as we left: there were more people standing on chairs.

The next day father read from the paper that "Because of the lively differences of opinion expressed at the Trade Hall meeting, a decision to join the other unions calling for a General Strike, has been deferred." Later that week, another meeting was convoked, but that didn't get anywhere either.

Two days after that father came home looking glum. "We're coomin' oot," he said, "a sympathy strike, and a damned lot of good it will do; especially as the TUC (Trade Union Congress) doesn't want us out yet. Anyway, the decision has been made. It is only the timing that's in t' air." Murphy and other moderates had been overruled; the crackpots had won. Father was obviously worried. He began to talk about what was at stake; who would finish up having to give up what. He wanted to get it off his chest. Then he relapsed into silence.

I was with mother in the mill when the strike began. "Where t' going?" mother asked workers who were streaming past her.

"Going? Why, on strike, of course. Didn't you hear the call 'All out?' Why, you must be deaf? Y' either starve outside in t' fresh air with us, luv, or starve in here covered with cotton dust. Which dusta want?"

Mother was bewildered. Reluctantly she threw her shawl round her shoulders, shut down her machine, and walked out. The strike was on. It was 3 May 1926.

"Fight! Fight! Action! Action!" people were shouting in the streets. A river of workers was streaming home. There were bursts of cheering. Mother had a deadly fear of violence. We hurried on.

The whole world fell silent the next day. Even the factory engines stopped. It was the deep, strange silence of the high moors. There was no shouting, no roughness, no disorder, no lawlessness in Blackburn. Soldiers guarded public offices. The newspapers went off the streets. Trains, buses and trams were still. The iron and steel industry was brought to a halt. The mills, mines and engineering shops for miles around were shut down. Some merchants shuttered their stores. For all the work we did, the schools might as well have been closed too.

My family sat in silence in our kitchen in Griffin Street, holding their breath, waiting for the revolution to begin. The streets were full of rumours. In Blackburn, special constables were sworn in; extra police were brought from Burnley and Preston; the mails were censored; the telegraphs were controlled. There was arson at Bank Top Mill. A police spy was taken out of the canal near Whalley Bridge with his throat cut; at Walton-le-Dale, near Preston, the police baton-charged strikers interfering with the buses. In Manchester, demonstrators were fired on. The docks at Liverpool were paralyzed. From John o' Groats to Land's End the workers were answering the call. Troops were in charge of all main roads; there were clashes between them and groups of 'reds.' No tale lost anything in the telling. Uncle Eric was the only one we knew who owned a radio. He could have told us what was going on, but I don't think we asked him.

After eight days the papers were back on the streets with banner headlines: GENERAL STRIKE BROKEN. ENGLAND STANDS FAST. Prime Minister Stanley Baldwin and the bosses had won. There wasn't going to be a revolution after all.

The first general strike in the history of the country had failed. Oh, what a let down! The workers cried. If they had been beaten, it would have been one thing. But they hadn't. The strike had been abandoned. Leaders like Jimmy Thomas of the Railway Workers' Union had betrayed us. Father said the Labour Party had played with fire and then run for cover.

The workers didn't starve after the General Strike, but they were humiliated. Conditions became worse. Despite all the honeyed words, victimization was common. Ringleaders were blackballed. Little pity was shown. The bosses did what they liked. They kept those they wanted and threw out those they didn't. Hours were increased, wages cut. The factory owners had never shared the good times with us. When there was cake, they ate it; when there was sorrow, they lumped it onto us. Under the Trade Disputes and Trade Union Act of 1927, which was passed almost overnight, many rights that the workers had fought for over long periods were abolished. General strikes and sympathetic strikes were outlawed. New laws were introduced against picketing. Using any excuse, workers were jailed: 'The accused was lurking in a doorway.' 'The accused had his foot over the factory threshold' during a lockout. Labour Party finances - and hence the strength of the Labour Party - were deliberately undermined. Political activity of the trade unions was curtailed. The policy of fining workers also became harsher. In 1928, Nelson (it was called 'Red Nelson') was brought to a standstill for seven weeks because of what the workers felt was an unjust weaver's fine. In Nelson a lot of families went hungry. Henceforth, you toed the employers' line or you were for it.

What the textile workers suffered was nothing compared to the miners who had started the row. The miners stayed out on strike for seven more bitter months. "We'll starve before going back," they said. By the time they went back they were starving. They took a heavy beating: hours, wages, the lot. Over one million mineworkers, together with their womenfolk and children, were abandoned to the mercy of the mine-owners. It was soulless capitalism at its worst. Mother's only comment, when father told her of the miners' plight was, "Why do people have to be so cruel to each other?" She never realized that her God of mercy was not widely known; it was the God of wrath, the vindictive God that ruled.

So bad did conditions become that a proposed visit of the king to Lancashire was cancelled.

231

The ever-darkening scene in Lancashire after the General Strike of 1926 prompted a shift in the labour movement from trade union to political action. There was a new interest in winning seats on the town council and in parliament. If the workers could replace the toffs in parliament a new day might dawn.

Blackburn began at the local level. We tried to get Patrick Murphy onto the town council. His sunken, snub-nosed face was well-known in town politics. His fairness and candour made him well liked. The workers trusted him. His honesty was apparent. His opponent was an absentee conservative factory owner, Henry Hen, whose slogan was: "Vote for Hen, the man who lays the golden eggs."

I was ten at the time. With Harold Watkins, Rosie Gill, Annie Morgan and others, I gladly helped Mr. Murphy by distributing handbills in the streets and at the factory gates. I got cross at workers who called him an Irish mongrel. Murphy had been kind to me since I was born. What did being Irish matter? Grandmother Bridget was Irish.

Anyway, as was to happen time and again, Labour lost the election. Despite all our shouts of "Vote, vote, vote for Mr. Murphy, Murphy's sure to win the day...," most workers preferred to vote for the Tory bosses, who, with the Anglican Church, were all-powerful in our town. The very people Labour wanted to help proved to be their worst enemies. Too many of the workers didn't want change. They had a mental block that prevented them from putting their own people in charge. Like father, they were not radical at heart. Also, the mill bosses were generous in doling out free beer in a round about way.

All Patrick Murphy could afford to give his election helpers - when his predicted defeat was announced - was twopenny worth of fish and chips in a white paper bag with as much vinegar as we wanted. Mr. Murphy stood at the fish and chip counter - the strain of the election showing on his face - doling out twopence for each of us. When we'd finished eating we all sang "For he's a jolly good fellow!" It must have touched him for he had difficulty holding back his tears.

As the contraction of the cotton industry continued and wage levels fell, industrial action came to the fore again. Strikes and lockouts became endemic. There was no stopping them. From the General Strike of 1926 until the mid-thirties, two-thirds of all working days lost in strikes in Britain were in textiles. Things got so bad that agitators worked on people's feelings to bring about a clash between the workers and the police at the factory gates. For boys of my age, the prospect of such clashes offered excitement. Mother told me to stay away from these meetings. "They're dangerous," she warned, gently rubbing the sides of my head with her hands.

I ignored her warning. Riotous meetings before factory gates drew Harold Watkins and me like a magnet. The more dangerous, the more we were drawn. I'd never heard such fiery speakers. Harold said they'd been brought in specially. One day we were in the middle of such a crowd when somebody shouted "Coppers!" Panic-stricken, Harold and I fled with the rest. Suddenly, I tripped and fell. A tidal wave of workers passed over me. I caught a glimpse of the horses and the raised batons. I struggled to my feet. The horses were almost on top of me when I felt a stunning blow to the head. There was no "In the name of the law, I order you to disperse," just a crack on the skull. Stars jumped before my eyes. I suddenly felt dizzy and weak. I nearly fell again. Somehow we got away. Despite my thick woolen cap, I had an egg on my head, which I tried to conceal for weeks.

Father didn't turn up at these factory gate meetings. He was suspicious of anybody letting off steam. It embarrassed him. Yet he was ever loyal to his union. When the union said 'Strike!' he struck; when they said 'March!' he marched - though like a lot of factory folk he didn't enjoy it - if they asked him to carry a banner, he carried it. When his fellow unionists sang: "You should rally round our banner in a true and loyal manner, And be eager in the fight that's being waged..."he sang as loud as the rest. He had his reservations about strikes, which he shared with the family, but he never let the union down. The trade union was the only thing my father ever joined and he remained loyal to it.

Father's staunch loyalty to his trade union almost proved to be his undoing. The occasion was a strike meeting before the Town Hall. The time was the late 1920's. Almost everybody in town was on strike. There were to be a number of speakers including Patrick Murphy. There wasn't a 'red' on the programme. Like many others, just for the fun of it, Harold Watkins and I decided to go with father to hear what the speakers had to say. The rest of the family showed no interest.

It all began peacefully enough. Handfuls of people on their way to the meeting became a stream; the stream became a river. No one expected the crowd to become as large as it did. Drums, flags and banners came from nowhere. Some said we were going to the Town Hall, others said the meeting had been changed to the Trade Hall, and that's where we should go. Still others didn't care; they'd seen a crowd and joined it; they loved a parade. Some even brought their children and dogs.

Drawn along by the drumbeats, the procession wound its way toward the center of town. Caps pulled down, most of the men were buttoned up to the neck. Here and there, the women had thrown their shawls back onto their shoulders. Some wore woolen hats and scarves. There was mist in the air; the leaden sky had not yet turned into rain. With the factories stopped, the air was free of soot. Odd shouts and snatches of song echoed in the street. Children skipped in and out of the crowd.

The farther we got, the more people joined in. When we got to The Royal there was a crowd standing in the doorway trying to find out what was up. There were lights inside and glints of glassware. They didn't respond to our shouts to join in. They stood there wordless, looking on.

It was just beyond The Royal, that a column of mounted police slowly emerged from a side street and blocked our path. A silence fell upon the crowd; there was a confused murmur; the dogs at the front began to bark. Harold and I thought it was just another group of police going about their business. They'd nothing to do with us. Ours was an entirely peaceful demonstration.

I was impressed by the horses. I'd never seen so many police horses in Blackburn before. They must have been brought in from outside. They were spotlessly clean and groomed as on parade. The silver pieces on the harness glinted.

I continued to be fascinated as the horses jingled toward us in a slow canter, their hoofs ringing on the stones. There were shouts: "Get out of our bloody way! It's our bloody street!" Boos followed. Everyone began to talk at once. For a moment the column slowed down, but people pushed from behind causing the procession to sway forward again.

Only when the canter changed to a gallop, and the police drew their long batons, did I become afraid. The terror I'd felt once before, when I'd fallen in the middle of a mob, returned.

As the crowd turned to flee, a shot rang out. Pop! it went. It sounded like a firework. Somebody shouted "They're firing on us! It's bloody murder!" Panic seized the crowd, which now tried to fall back, screaming in fear. People ran in all directions to get out of the horses' way.

Running along the sidewalk, father, Harold and I clashed with a group running the other way. They were led by a man who was still carrying a banner UNITED WE STAND. DIVIDED WE FALL. A group of us was swept into a furniture shop doorway. The door was locked. With the battle going on all around, we huddled there.

Baton-swinging riders repeatedly swept past our shelter. Lashed now by cold gusts of rain, the horses galloped, turned, reformed and galloped again. They were led by an officer who rode at great speed, shouting commands. The street was full of cries for help. The windows of the bakery across the street were smashed. The sound of batons on flesh - a dull whack - made me wince. Flags, clothing, food were scattered all over the cobbles.

A few feet from where we were crouching, Patrick Murphy lay on the ground. One of the horses pranced all around him. Telling us to stay where we were, father and another man ran out and, with blows raining down on their backs, dragged Mr. Murphy from under the horses' hooves into the doorway. Mr. Murphy had blood on his bald head. His eyes were glassy and unseeing, his face pallid. "They've cracked his skull like an eggshell," father said. He was calm, as firm as a rock, Harold and I were shaking.

Once the police had moved farther down the street, the shopkeeper opened the door and offered us an escape through the back alley. He was obviously on the workers' side. "Bloody murderers," he called the police. He refused to have Mr. Murphy carried into his store, but promised to call an ambulance. We'd be sure to be arrested if we tried to carry him through the streets.

Leaving Mr. Murphy on the step, the shopkeeper led us through several rooms piled high with merchandise. As he'd turned off the lights, we bumped into each other. From the rear entrance we hurriedly made our way home. Father had a nasty welt across his back. "What a gobbin you are," mother scolded. "Might have got the child killed." The experience left me shaken.

The town was in an uproar after the police attack. No one had the right to drive law-abiding people off the streets. It was a disgrace. Some preachers made sermons about it.

"It will all die down," father grumped. "Nothing will come of it. You'll see."

Which is what would have happened had Mr. Murphy's condition not deteriorated. Vigils were held outside the hospital. Carrying lanterns, church choirs sang hymns. Murphy became a symbol of the town's troubled conscience.

I came home one day to find mother crying. "Patrick has gone," she said. We were all stunned.

There followed one of the greatest funeral processions our town had known. Mother and I joined in; we felt we owed it to him. We got to the church service at St. Michael's too late. It was crowded out. Willie Gill, with his cocked hat and his long robe, was up front with the Knights of Columbus. The coffin was carried on a horse-drawn hearse. The horses wore black velvet capes and black waving plumed headdresses. There were several bands. Everybody tightened up when they played Handel's Dead March. The dirge mingled with the grinding of the carriage wheels, the clink of the horses' hoofs, and the shuffling of the crowd. There were so many flowers that they had to be carried on carts. The whole route to the cemetery was lined with sad faces. Not all were hushed. "It's a fine funeral," someone said. "He deserves it," said another. "Pity he can't see it. Upright in 'eart he was. Ah well, pray for his soul."

Mother and I couldn't get near the grave. Father Prendergast said a few words. He used the text "Blessed are they which do hunger and thirst for righteousness." He said that Patrick had led a blameless life and had gone to his reward. We saw the flowers and the piles of sods. We saw Father Prendergast reach down and scatter earth over the coffin.

"Ashes to ashes, and dust to dust, to the consummation of the world."

Then Mrs. Murphy bent down, her white hair blowing in the wind, her face marked with grief. We heard the click of spades. We waited until the solemn crowd dispersed along the cemetery paths. As their voices died away, we went forward to pay our last respects and to see the mountain of flowers. In time, except for the harsh note of the raven, the graveyard fell silent again.

Chapter XVI

Parents

My parents couldn't have been more unlike each other. One was dull and gray, the other was brightly flashing. Whereas father was placid, mother was mercurial; he was a plodder, she was a romantic.

I learned early in life that my father was a man of routine. He was a man you could count on. Whatever hour of the day, we all knew where he was and roughly what he was doing. He was the first up in the house. When there was work, he was the first to reach the mills. I think he loved the mills; he loved the humming, clattering machinery, the oil and the dirt. He started each week with a clean,collarless cotton shirt, buttoned at the neck, and cheap, blue overalls. The sleeves of his shirt were rolled up to the elbow. When he was a tackler, he wore a natty red neckerchief and a fustian waistcoat, which we thought dandy. When he went drinking, he exchanged his red neckerchief for a white criss-crossed scarf. He scorned English braces for his American belt. He would threaten us children with his belt, but never used it. There were no brutal beatings in our house.

241

I was proud of my father when he was a tackler. I felt it important to take his dinner every day. The way he set up a loom fascinated me. He first brought the heavy beam holding the warp threads on a two-wheeled sled to the back of the loom. Alone, he then manhandled the beam into the loom, threading hundreds, if not thousands, of warp ends through the eyes of a heald board, which was as wide as the loom. From the heald board he passed the warp ends through the teeth of a fine comb called a reed, after which he came to the front of the loom and tied all the new warp ends to the ends of the previous warp. Then he made various adjustments, which tacklers called tuning. Sometimes the warp threads were arranged by a 'drawer-in;' usually he plodded on thread after thread, by himself. I never saw him get rattled. I suppose that's where I learned about patience long before I knew what the word meant.

Day done, he'd come home, fifteen minutes after the five o'clock whistle, and put his empty basin in the same place on the sink. He also brought the *The Blackburn Telegraph*, which he read to mother. He had no interest in books, but borrowed one now and again to read to her. He read it as if he was reading a funeral notice. One night a week he'd give a hand with the heavier washing. Another night he'd get down on his knees to pummel a large bowl of dough in preparation for mother's baking. I marvelled at the way in which, with one blow, he could bury his arm up to the elbow. Plop! plop! went his fists. It sounded like something heavy being dropped into water.

When the mood took him he shaved at the kitchen sink before a small looking-glass. One day he broke the mirror. "Mm...mm," the grown-ups said in a dark way, "seven years bad luck!" Father didn't speak, and he didn't look happy either. I think my people feared the breaking of mirrors. They knew that their spirit was reflected in the glass as well as their face. Sometimes father forgot his beard. Among the workers, nobody took any notice of an unshaved face.

Each Friday night father came through the door and placed his pay packet on the table in the front room. Quietly, mother picked it up; money matters were left to her. Other than to pay his trade union fees and shop for groceries with mother, he never handled cash. Even his cheap Woodbine cigarettes - which he called coffin nails - were bought by mother. She stacked them on the mantelpiece above the kitchen fire. Day by day, the stack was reduced until it was renewed the following Friday night. Despite all the trouble he had had with his lungs as a result of being gassed, he never stopped smoking.

The only time he showed an interest in his pay was when a co-worker cheated him. The joint earnings of father and two other men had been placed on the kitchen table awaiting division. The three of them had been working together in the factory on a special job, for which they'd been paid a handful of silver. With my head the height of the table, I saw Mr. Lamp flick half-a-crown under a fold of the newspaper that covered the board. He did it so quickly that father and Mr. Clay didn't see it happen, but I did.

Why would Mr. Lamp want to do that, I wondered? I was doubly puzzled when I watched Mr. Lamp secretly retrieve the coin before he left the house. His eyes met mine; he looked troubled. Later that night I asked father why Mr. Lamp had played such a game. He paled. "Are you sure, he did that, Billy?"

"Oh, yes, Dadda, I'm quite sure."

Father put on his cap and went out and came back clutching ten pennies.

Sunday was a day of rest. It was the only day when the factory clocks could be ignored. Sport and entertainment were forbidden inside the town. Woe to those who disregarded this unwritten code!

One Sunday morning I and other heathens were playing football behind St. Philip's Church hall when a group of black-clad women, wielding umbrellas attacked us. Until I received a whack across the head, I thought they were making fun. Far from it, the wrath of God was in their eyes. We'd fouled the Holy Day and they were after blood. We never played football on a Sunday morning in town again. Outside the town, in the hills, we could play to our heart's content.

Father and the other grown-ups had long since learned this unwritten code. When he went wrestling on a Sunday, he did so on the moors. Men and boys met at a site 'up top.' My brother and I rarely missed a match. We knew the jargon of wrestling, and could talk about chips and backheels, hanks, clicks, hypes and hitches just like anybody else. With us it was wrestling for its own sake. Kicking, gouging, biting and tripping were all forbidden. The procedure was always the same: a ring was formed, small bets were placed. Father and his opponent stripped to the waist, rolled up their trouser legs, took off their clogs and stockings, squared up to each other, gave a touch of the hands, and the fight was on. The fight ended when both shoulders of one of the wrestlers touched the ground, or when one of the men conceded defeat.

Father was an outstanding wrestler. He knew all the holds and falls. He was all muscle. For a man in his thirties he stripped well. His arms were tattooed with a mermaid on one and an anchor on the other. On the moors I saw him as a man rather than my father. He was about medium height, had a barrel chest covered with hair, a massive ox-like neck, wide-spread shoulders, a well-muscled body and hairy legs like the trunk of trees. He had a large head covered with straight, brown hair, a Roman nose, a firm mouth, the strongest teeth, the dark blue eyes of his mother, and a healthy-looking skin. I was proud of him because physical strength was admired by us. For his age, having recovered from his wartime wounds, he must have been one of the fittest men about. He could lift, push, or pound anything. Few wrestlers managed to floor him. I never understood how anyone who could fight for hours on end could be as gentle with flowers and birds as he was.

Usually the wrestling contests went on until the smell of Sunday dinner wafted across the moor. At that point the fighting stopped, bets were settled, and everybody hurried off for the best meal of the week. Often father was congratulated by the other workers. It made no difference to him; he was neither elated nor downhearted. He'd had a good 'punch-up' and that's all that he cared about. It must have been a wonderful escape from what seemed to me a monotonous life. Having struggled into his shirt and jacket, he left the field as calmly as he had entered it.

Father's quiet ways didn't deceive me. I learned early in life when to keep out of his way; lurking beneath that still, quiet nature was what we called his Viking temper. It was that same Viking temper that had sent his mother Selma to jail. When aroused it was an anger that would stop at nothing. One Sunday morning on the moors I saw it almost kill two men.

It happened like this. Father had wrestled and beaten one of the Calvert brothers fairly and squarely. It was the brother who always boasted about his strength and prowess. He was then challenged by the other brother, an equally solid man. In this match father was tripped from behind by the first Calvert, and was sent sprawling. The movement had been so quick that most of the onlookers didn't catch it. As father got up the first Calvert called him a half-breed Yank. At that, dad suddenly went wild - this time with his fists. I heard the click as he struck his opponents' jaws. Suddenly there were three men rolling on the ground.

I'm convinced that father would have killed the two Calverts had the crowd not rushed in to separate them. The three men were dragged to their feet: gasping for breath, heads down, wet foreheads almost touching, pale with anger, they glowered at each other through bloodshot eyes. His arms gripped firmly from behind, father made several efforts to break free. In a display of self-destructive fury, he twisted and turned, reeled and staggered, dragging the three men who were hanging on to him across the turf. Everybody was shouting at the top of their voices and falling over each other.

With a superhuman effort, father shook off those who held him. Hitching up his pants, he walked away. I knew from the way he walked that he was in a fearful rage, and that the brawl might be renewed. With the crowd in uproar, the Calverts followed him, but then had second thoughts. Father may not have had many brains, but when it came to fearlessness and brawn he was up front.

Except for the intensity, a fight like this was normal. People used their fists to settle disputes all the time. There was nothing wrong in punching someone on the nose, or threatening to 'knock yer bloody 'ead off.' Other workers intervened only when there was danger of someone being killed. That would complicate matters.

———◇———

Oftentimes, supper over and the light still good, my brother and I accompanied father to the cindered wasteland outside the walls of Dougdale's factory where he had a small plot. He grew flowers there and kept a cabin with a score of homing pigeons. It was five minutes walk from our house. Ritual-like, Dan and I trudged behind father who carried a bucket of water in each hand. The allotments, of which there were many, were rented from the mill for a minimal sum. They were used for growing vegetables.

Usually Dan and I released the pigeons. We undid a catch and raised a wooden screen. With a frantic, noisy flapping of wings, the birds were gone. Occasionally, as a special treat, we were allowed to hold one. They pecked each other, but never pecked us. Having scraped the hut clean of muck, we sat on the upturned buckets to watch the birds in flight. Father didn't sit on a bucket; he could squat on his haunches for hours on end.

Cooped up all day, the pigeons expressed great joy at being free. Endlessly, they banked and turned, wheeled and whirled. The wonder is they never collided. They watched us from neighbouring roofs, but mostly they stayed aloft, dancing in the evening sky. They had an uncanny way of knowing when their food was ready. The moment the grain was put in their trough they returned with the same eagerness they'd shown on departure. Supper done, they fluttered up noisily to the rooftops. Father seemed to fly with them.

Mother said that father talked to the pigeons more than to us. So he did. He talked to them the whole time he was there. When the time came for the birds to be fastened up for the night - not he but they decided when that was - they glided down from the roofs. He used to lure those nodding and strutting about on the cabin roof by rattling the food can or calling their names from inside the cote. He went on muttering at the birds until the last one was in and the safety hatches had been dropped into place.

He also talked to his flowers, which he grew behind protective wire against the pigeon-shed. Bending over his blooms, he was deaf to whatever was said to him. Mother would have preferred 'greens' to flowers, but 'greens' to father meant 'rabbit food.' He had no interest in growing them.

How he grew anything at all was a miracle. Every ounce of soil had to be carried in and enriched with diluted pigeon droppings. The climate with its flooding and its heavy frosts presented a constant challenge. One vicious hailstorm could devastate his garden. In thirty minutes magnificent blooms became broken stalks. Yet for years he had the best chrysanthemums for miles around. Some years they were ridiculously large and reminded me of Jack and the Beanstalk.

Time and again, I watched him rebuild his garden after it had been washed away. On his hands and knees, with a trowel, he'd replant everything that had been lost. As the light faded, he'd go on tilling, mulching and watering until his garden was restored.

Father was not alone in clinging to nature and a bit of earth. All across the wasteland, workers struggled to grow potatoes, cabbages, carrots, radishes, beets, turnips, peas and beans. They needed the vegetables; even more, they needed to be out of doors, close to the earth, growing things. A cinder tip could not have been the healthiest soil in which to grow vegetables, but nobody died of it.

With the light almost gone, father banged the empty buckets together to signal that it was time to go home. No words. He marched off, with a bunch of flowers in his hand and several pigeon eggs in his overall pockets. We followed, carrying the empty buckets. On arrival home, he put the eggs into a basin on the sink. Awkwardly, almost abruptly, he handed the flowers to mother. No words, no glances, just a muffled grunt that seemed to say all that needed saying.

———◦———

The only occasion when father threw all routine to the winds was at the time of the annual pigeon race from France to Britain. Every year the family lived on the edge of a precipice until the race was over. Madness would reign. The chosen birds, as many as six, were placed in a special box, which was taken to the railway station and, with dozens of other such boxes, sent to France. I used to go with father to see the birds onto the train and to wish them farewell and good luck. He never stopped talking to the pigeons.

"Tha mustn't loiter this year, Harry," he told one of his favourites, as we went along. And to another: "Bernie, if tha finishes up in t' wrong cote this time, tha goes in t' pot."

Silently, with other somber bird fanciers, we stood together on the platform until the train departed.

Because of his war service, father knew every station the train stopped at in France until the birds reached their destination. He kept a list of the stations on the cupboard door at home.

Once it was time for the birds to be released in France, the tension in the house became unbearable. A great excitement swallowed up all other activities. So that the whole family could be free to search the sky, meals were forgotten, baking was postponed, clothes stayed dirty. Everybody went onto the tip to watch.

The moment a tiny dot was spotted darting in and out of the low clouds, a cry went up from the crowd occupying the hilly ground. Then came the sweating: was it our pigeon or somebody else's? Only father could recognize a pigeon at that distance. With everybody frozen to the spot, the pigeon fell out of the sky onto one of the cabin roofs. A sigh of relief went up. In a race like this seconds counted.

One year father's favourite bird, Charlie, had raced from France to the north of England leaving the other pigeons behind. Father saw him long before he was visible to the rest of us. In time, we spotted the bird swooping through the clouds, tacking this way then that; breaking his heart to get home first. There wasn't another pigeon in the sky. Blessedly, the wind had died down. We all knew Charlie and we swelled with pride. Father was inside the hut waiting to clock in the winner. Everybody in the surrounding pens and on the hillside kept so still they might have been carved of stone. We were certain that, for the first time in the history of the race, Charlie and Blackburn had won the coveted prize.

Hypnotized, we watched as a flapping, fluttering Charlie came in low over the house tops toward the cabin roof. He flared, braked and was down.

To our horror, instead of hurrying inside as he had been trained, Charlie strutted about on the roof. The more he bowed and cooed, the louder the oaths coming from father inside the hut. While we resorted to prayer, father swore, whistled and rattled the feed can. All to no avail.

The reason for Charlie's delinquency was not long in finding. Against all rules, a female bird was strutting about on Mr. Pindle's cabin roof next door. In a moment, Charlie had hopped across and joined her. With everybody holding their breath, Charlie began to make little pretended dashes at Mr. Pindle's pigeon. He hopped and bowed and cooed and puffed up his chest and spread his tail. What on earth was Charlie thinking about? Didn't he realize he was on the edge of fame? Obviously, he had forgotten the race.

When father realized what was going on, he came roaring out of the cabin like a mad bull. "What the bloody hell," he shouted. He was so infuriated that he ran to Mr. Pindle's fence shaking his fist. Seizing the fence, he almost wrenched it out of the ground. Mr. Pindle and father began to hurl insults at each other. "Tha's dun it on purpose," father accused Mr. Pindle. From Mr. Pindle came a cry of outraged innocence. "Ah've never heard sich." Father must have said something dreadful, for the next thing I knew Mr. Pindle had climbed the fence and was aiming blows at father's head. "Take that! And that!" Father exploded with anger. Before anyone could stop him, he had grabbed Mr. Pindle by the scruff of the neck and the seat of his pants and hurled him back over the fence. Mr. Pindle sailed through the air, arms and legs outstretched, an astonished look on his face, to fall with a great bone-shattering bump at the other side. The wonder is he wasn't killed.

I saw a great deal of my father when I was a child, but I rarely got close to him. Other than mother, nobody did. But when he did talk to me, he had strange tales to tell. As a sailor, he'd visited lands where there were lions and tigers and giraffes and elephants. He'd seen a volcano erupting; he'd seen whales and seals and many creatures of the sea. In far-eastern waters he'd seen ships scattered by a typhoon. The effect upon me when he told me that we go to bed when the Chinese are waking up was electrifying. The Chinese intrigued me. It pleased me when people pointed at him and said: "Will Woodruff's been to China and to America."

As the years passed, he became ever more silent and heavy of mood. I've trudged miles with him through the streets of Blackburn without exchanging a word. I always wished it would happen, but I can't remember him holding my hand or carrying me on his back or patting my head. Although he kissed mother good night before going to sleep, he never kissed me or anyone else in public. Kissing was not a Woodruff trait. Even when he stood me on a box in front of one of his looms to show my how to weave, he didn't say much.

I was five or six when I first took father's hot-pot to him in the weaving shed. It was a long, low, stone-flagged, glass-roofed building. Getting through the great metal-plated door that gave access to his workplace was a nightmare. To keep the humidity in the shed, and render the cotton soft and pliable, the door had to be kept shut. To open it you had to haul great weights on chains. It was too heavy for me, and I had to wait until somebody came to my help. Once through the door, the weights came crashing down behind me as the door slammed to. I thought I was about to be crushed.

Inside, I was overwhelmed by the steam, the heat, the clatter, the smell of gas and the shattering din of the machines. Too frightened to move, I froze where I was. Hundreds of looms stretched as far as I could see - all of them crashing frantically. Most of the workers were women and young girls. I was mesmerized by the army of picking sticks jerking backward and forward, ready to give me a crack on the head. The sticks hit the shuttles across the loom faster than I could watch: Lat ti tat. Lat ti tat. Lat ti tat. A forest of black driving belts hummed up and down between the overhead shaft and the looms. I would have stayed frozen on the spot had father not caught sight of me. Sleeves rolled up, he came across the sanded floor and took his hot-pot from me. He didn't thank me, or make fun. "Don't stand theer, gawkin'," was all he said. Yet his fellow workers thought well of him. "Yo dad's aw reet," they shouted as I tried to get away. I could hardly hear them above the racket.

I couldn't get through the door fast enough. I was quite deaf when I got outside.

———◦———

Mother was the youngest of Bridget Gorman Kenyon's four children. She had grandmother's fine features: the lovely blue eyes, the long eyelashes, the fine hands, the lovely, thick, dark-brown hair, the soft, sensuous oval face, the warm unaffected gaze. Of medium height, she was neither thickset nor slim; she was in between.

The early death of her father, and her being orphaned off as a child to foster parents, explained her life-long feeling of insecurity. 'No' and 'yes' were followed by 'but-er-I...' Although Bridget had assumed that the farmer, who had 'adopted' Maggie, while rough-mannered, was kind and honourable, there is a mystery about what happened. I suspect that she was brutalized. She definitely was neglected. She does not seem to have been sent to school. Eventually, in desperation, she fled back to her mother. The farmer didn't come after her. Bridget said he would not have dared.

Her childhood experience left mother with a fear of not being wanted. She must have been glad to marry the strong and resolute young man that by all accounts father was before the war. The marriage gave her a feeling of security, which she so badly needed. My sister Jenny told me that mother had once said that only after her marriage did she recover the sense of belonging she had known before her father's death. That's why father's running off to war in 1914 came as such a shock to her. She felt vulnerable again.

I was at a loss to understand Maggie's relations with her mother. For someone who had been orphaned off and neglected at an early age, it is a wonder that Maggie had any relations with Bridget at all. How could Maggie be so illiterate when Bridget was so schooled? Why did Bridget spend all the time educating me, when she had neglected her own child? Mother was ever tight-lipped about it. Bridget was equally silent. In all the time I knew grandmother Bridget, I cannot remember a single occasion when she talked about her daughter's early life. The only comment that Bridget ever made about mother's life-long illiteracy was that "Maggie was not one for 'larnin'." Mother never did overcome her lack of schooling.

With mother you didn't know what she would get up to next. Father was concerned with each day; with getting by, with the immediate and the present; mother was concerned with change, with eternity. She was a stargazer; she not only knew there was life after death, she looked forward to it. Father didn't give a thought to the unknown; she never stopped thinking about it. He didn't expect much of life; mother knew that sooner or later it would be glorious. She had visions and hopes. "No 'arm in 'opin'," she would say.

Her God was a merciful God. She was a firm believer in the 'Kingdom come' idea, 'of the glory there's to be'; of a world where everybody would be judged and punished or rewarded. She never mentioned the punishments; she stressed the rewards, and the peace and rest there was to be. She expressed herself with such conviction that you got carried away.

Mother was forever vibrant and passionate. She was spontaneous, expansive, impulsive. She needed to touch, to pat, to kiss. Nobody ever doubted her warmness of heart or generosity of spirit. Her talk was 'up in t' air,' but she was never dull. On the contrary, she crackled with life, living each moment intensely; laughter and tears were never far apart. Sad or glad, she was always singing. She had a fine, melodious voice. I never heard father sing, except at his trade union meetings. She was forever doing something different; she had to; she was easily bored. She tired when father read the newspaper to her at night. Although she couldn't read or write (the only time she had written her name was on her wedding certificate, and that with father's help), whatever father read to her, she wanted to jump to the end. He droned on monotonously reading every single word, with no sign of tiring; or for that matter, of interest either, unless perchance he came across some news from America.

When the newspaper bored her, she stopped listening and told us children a story. In one story a bird came to our rescue at the last moment. She really believed in luck. I liked best the story in which she was the queen and I the king. She had lots of coloured ribbons and dressed herself up with elaborate care. Halfway through the story I ceased to be the king and, much to my delight, became the villain. A dab or two of soot on my face from the back of the chimney, and a hat, which mother quickly made out of a newspaper, turned me into a marvelous-looking scoundrel.

Mother thought and spoke in terms of imagery. With her it was a gift. She could create magic with scissors and paper; she could snip people or animals into existence in no time. With a clay pipe filled with soap and water she did even more astonishing things. With her, we sailed away inside a bubble to a shining new world in the sky. One of my earliest memories was blowing bubbles with her, while she sang:

> I'm forever blowing bubbles, pretty bubbles in the air;
> Oh they fly so high, nearly reach the sky,
> Then, like my dreams, they fade and die.
> Fortune's always hiding. I've looked everywhere.
> I'm forever blowing bubbles, pretty bubbles in the air.

She sang the words lightly, skipping about. She would suddenly grab my hands and dance me off my feet. When she played 'Ring-a-ring-o'-roses, all fall down,' she didn't pretend to fall, she fell as a child does: 'all fall down' - bump. She fell among the daisies and the bluebells, her lovely, dark hair streaming in the wind.

Mother was deaf, dumb and blind to details. To talk about ends and means to her was to take an unfair advantage. I remember the look of dismay on father's face one day when mother threw money into a beggar's cup. While father was worrying how to find enough money to feed the family, mother was chucking it away. One day, with little money to spare, she went and bought a new hat for which she could have had no use. "Why did you buy it?" father asked incredulously. "Because I laked it," she answered innocently. Father almost had a fit. Usually, she didn't respond to his anger.

Money baffled her. On one occasion I stood at her knee while she emptied her purse on her lap. She made several little heaps of coins to meet her bills. I watched while she moved the piles from one knee to the other. It was like moving pawns on a chessboard. Except that the more she moved her coins, the more bewildered she became. Fear entered her eyes. Then she broke down and cried. The sobs were heartfelt; they conceded total defeat. There was no way that she could manage.

She did not have any idea of the nature of the industrial changes going on around her. Strikes and lockouts frightened her. They not only introduced violence into her life, the outcome was always the same: less to eat. "What's the use of fighting?" she would ask. At heart she was a pacifist.

The Kenyon pacifism almost cost her her life. One afternoon she and I were coming home from the market. We'd almost reached our door when our path was suddenly blocked by a giant of a woman who wore a black shawl fastened tightly at the neck. Neither of us had noticed her approach. Although I assumed that the woman was an acquaintance of mother's, I was repelled by the pockmarked face, the bloodshot eyes and the strong smell of drink.

Before anyone could stop her, the woman had seized mother by the throat and had begun to shake the life out of her. Mother's screams were stifled by one of the woman's hands; my shouts were ignored. Mother's shawl and parcels were on the ground; her long, dark hair had come undone and was hanging down her back. Deep, bloody scratches marked her face. She didn't strike back or struggle. She was too terrified. "Oh my God," was all she said. I stood there paralyzed. All I managed to do was to drag the woman's shawl off her head.

Having struck mother in the face several times, the woman picked her up and tossed her onto the cobbles as if she were a rag doll. Mother lay there groaning. With every kick from the woman's steel-capped clogs her groans grew. "Oh, my God," she kept saying. By now bright red blood was on the stones. Every time mother tried to get to her feet, the woman knocked her down again with a vicious kick. Screaming with pain, mother recoiled from each blow, twisting and turning like an eel trying to escape.

Panic-stricken, I ran into the house. Brenda was the only one at home. "Mother's being murdered!" I screamed. "She's being kicked to death in the street!"

Brenda's response was to grab the long broom and dash out. I ran after her.

A jeering, shouting ring of passersby had formed. The woman was on top of mother pummelling her for all she was worth.

Brenda dashed through the spectators' legs dragging the broom. I followed. Before anybody could stop her, she had swung the broom head into the air and brought it down on the woman's head with a sickening thud. The blow was so hard that it broke the broom handle. Squealing like a stuck pig, the woman slid off mother's chest onto the cobbles where she lay unconscious.

With the help of a neighbour, we got mother to her feet. Head down, face covered with blood, she tottered toward our door. I picked up her shawl and the torn packages. Nobody interfered. Had they done so, they would have been impaled on the splintered shaft that Brenda held spear-like before her.

I never discovered why mother was attacked.

———◄◦►———

Maggie seemed to attract trouble. Her simple, unaffected, credulous outlook was just not up to life. It landed her in one pickle after another. The gold coin episode was one of them.

It began with a knock on the door. There was just mother and I in the house. She was ironing. She had just clicked the iron's trap door shut when there was a rap on the door. As it was unusual for people to knock, we peeped through the curtains to see who it was. We couldn't see anyone. When we opened the door, a small, dark-eyed stranger stood there, grinning. He had long, black, curly hair that fell down the sides of his face. I could not help noticing the gold rings on his fingers. He also had several gold teeth. In a twinkling he had his foot in the door. Mother thought him a Gypsy. There were always Gypsies about. My people feared them. From missing children to missing washing, it was the Gypsies who got the blame.

"We want no Gypsies here," mother said, as she struggled to get the door shut.

"Do Gypsies come as well dressed as I?" the man asked in a hurt tone. He was wearing a dark suit - a little worn and greasy, but still a suit. He also wore a collar and tie, a black trilby and shoes. Whatever he was, he didn't look like a Gypsy.

"What do you want?" mother asked.

"I want to make you rich."

"And how do you think you're going to do that?"

"It's easy, you give me your gold and I'll give you more money than you've ever had." At this point the man produced a role of bank notes such as neither of us had seen before. Holding the bundle before our eyes, he flipped his thumb through the notes several times. It was enough to make our eyes pop.

"We don't have any gold," mother said, making to shut the door again.

"You know that's not true," the man said in an oily voice. "There's always a ring somewhere, or a trinket, or a coin that you're hanging on to. Now I ask you, what good are you doing locking them away in the house, gathering dust? Use your gumption, woman, get rid of your dust catchers and get some real money. You can't buy food with dust catchers, but you can buy food with these." He flipped through the bundle of banknotes again. The notes made a comforting, swishing sound. "This is your one and only chance. For your gold I will give you enough money to pay all your debts. Think what your husband will say when he comes home: enough money to pay all the bills, and some to spare!"

I could tell that mother was dithering. She started her 'but-er-I...' business.

"Well, that's it." He stuffed the money in his jacket pocket and took his foot out of the door. "You don't know a good thing when you see it. Ta, Ta!" He touched his trilby. His gold teeth flashed a smile.

I knew that, in addition to mother's wedding ring, there was one piece of gold in the house. It was a gold coin, an heirloom from father's side. Mother said it had belonged to great-grandfather Arne. Thus far, it had survived all the ups and downs of the family fortune. It was hidden in a crack of the wall upstairs.

"Hang on a tick," said mother, as she ran from the door, through the house and up the stairs.

In seconds she had returned with father's heirloom.

The moment the gold coin was in the man's hand he was all business. There was no more laughter, no more chatter about making mother rich. Ignoring mother's 'but-er-I,' remarks that she had decided against selling the coin, after all, he popped a piece of glass over one of his eyes and studied the gold piece carefully.

"Oh well," he said, "if this is all you've got, I suppose it will have to do. It's inferior, that's what it is. I'm in two minds to take it."

He then counted out some paper money, placed it in mother's palm and was gone. Before mother could shut the door, the man was half-way down the street. "But-er-I," said mother, "Ah do hope Ah've dun t' reet thing."

I shall never forget the look on father's face when he came home and mother told him what she had done. He stood and grasped the back of a chair, his face inflamed with anger. His knuckles were white. "Tha's done what?" he murmured. "Tha's done what?" He couldn't grasp it. Then, flinging the chair aside, he exploded. "Tha's a gobbin! A damned fool gobbin, that's what thi are!" That was as close as father ever came to striking mother. We children stood there, helpless, wide-eyed.

Mother having stammered out a description of the man, father put on his cap and went in search of him. "Ah'll kill him! Ah'll kill him!" he yelled, as he banged the front door behind him with enough force to shake the house. I silently hoped he wouldn't find him. I knew that in a temper like that father would beat him to a pulp.

Father was gone for hours. We sat around waiting, imagining all kinds of horrible things. Eventually he came home still looking like black thunder.

It was a long time before we learned what had happened. He'd traced the fellow across town as far as the station. By the time he'd got there and made inquiries, the man had been and gone. Just left to catch the Manchester train, they told him. Dad had rushed off to the Manchester platform only to see the peddler leap into the last coach of the already moving train. In a towering rage he'd watched as the train whistled its way into the dark tunnel, its tail lights glowing.

He never saw his coin again.

———◦———

Father was never sure what surprise mother would spring on him next. As mother handled the money, the only thing about which he could be fairly certain was that she would pay the rent. Rent was sacred. If you didn't pay it, you finshed up in the street. Every Friday night, before any other spending was done, three shining half-crowns (seven shillings and sixpence) were placed in a little coffin-shaped box that hung on a nail behind the front door. There had to be three coins - it made it easier for the collector. You didn't argue. You paid the lot in three half-crowns. I'd reach up and shake the box to make quite sure the money was there. It made me feel better when I heard the coins clinking.

The rent was collected every Saturday afternoon by a burly, red-faced chap who burst into the house from the street. He never knocked, he never took off his cap, he rarely spoke. When he did, he was surly and abrupt. If you said that the roof leaked, and would he please ask the landlord to fix it, he'd give a grunt and leave. Complaints got us nowhere. Most times he simply pocketed the three coins, made an entry in the blue, penny rent-book that stuck out of the box and left. We feared the rent collector; we also despised him. The dislike we felt for our landlord, who was unknown to us, we turned on to him.

There were occasions when mother's romantic nature caused her to violate the all-important rent-rule. The danger signals were a penitent look on her face or new hats on my sisters' heads. When she had money, she spent her last penny on dressing up her children. I knew from the growing tension in the house as the time for the rent collector's visit approached, that the rent had gone.

The first occasion when the coins didn't roll into the collector's hand, he stood on the doormat, clutching the empty box, an incredulous look on his face. I was hypnotized.

Mother, who believed in miracles, kept her eyes glued to the box. She wouldn't have been the least surprised to see a little bird fly in and three shining coins roll out.

Alas, the little bird that saved her in her fairy stories didn't arrive. The collector began to shake the box like a terrier shakes a rat. Finally, he threw it and the rent-book down. "Well, tha knows what it means," he said, scowling, "three times and ye're oot." Then he slammed the door behind him so hard that mother's punch bowl tinkled.

My parents feared the rent collector because of the power he wielded. He could not only put us in the street, he could ruin our credit. We bought 'on tick' at Tom Tat's grocery store round the corner. I ran for different things during the week, mother and Tom Tat made a reckoning every Friday night. What she couldn't pay she would 'carry over' until the following week. What the bank-book was to the toffs, the rent-book was to the working class. Uncle Eric actually showed us his bank-book to impress us. A rent-book without any red entries meant that you could get a loan from a moneylender, or do business with the pawnbroker. It gave the poor respectability as nothing else did. A 'clean' rent-book without delinquencies could be the difference between eating and going hungry. No wonder my parents put the rent in the box behind the door on a Friday night before they bought food or went drinking.

Mother's protest about living conditions came from the heart rather than the head. Because her sensitivity and her imagination were so strong, the ugly surroundings in which we lived hurt her more than the rest of us. The saying "where there's muck, there's brass," made no impression on her. She simply hungered for the decent life she'd known while her father was alive. Like her mother, she didn't blame anybody for the way things had turned out. She just wanted to live decently. She vowed that she would find a better place to live.

"And how will you do that, pray?" father asked.

"I'll follow a rainbow," mother answered. Which is precisely what she did.

One night, father came home, tired out, to learn that we were moving.

"Will," she announced, her face alight, "I've taken a house on Livingston Road close to Eric. It's where the toffs live. We're going to leave the grime behind. We've lived too long in a house in which you can't swing a cat. The rent collector can keep it."

Father was dumbfounded. He stood there and blew out his cheeks as if recovering from a blow. He had difficulty breathing. Mother didn't give him a chance to recover. "It's a champion house. There's room for everybody, four bedrooms." Ignoring father's 'but' and 'in heaven's name' and 'have you taken leave of your senses, woman?' she raced on.

Mother suddenly became wonderfully eloquent. The dykes burst. There was no stuttering, no 'but-er-I,' no hesitation about what she wanted to say. She described the new house better than any rental agent could have done. "There's an indoor petty," she said, "one that flushes, and a bathroom; a bathroom; now think of that, Will - a whole room to wash in with a sky-light and a gas water heater. There's a proper kitchen, a proper dining room and a proper sitting room. A real sitting room, Will, with places to sit and no smoke or drafts. And it's all lit by electricity. That makes us as good as Eric. Can you imagine it?" She went faster still. I suspected that she was adding rooms that were not there.

With father waving his arms like a drowning man, and the rest of us standing around gaping, mother described the garden. "Just think, Will, a proper garden. Not a pen on a cinder tip." She pummelled him with the garden. "Think what you could do with a garden like that, Will - front and back! Have you ever thought of the difference a hot-house would make to your plants? Have you ever thought what it would be like to go out of your front door and for the first time in your life step into a garden instead of into the street?"

Father just stood there. "I want you to see the changing colours of the hills against the sky, Will. I want you to look up..." here she paused about to cry, "instead of looking at this sanded floor and these greasy stone flags."

She'd got it all worked out: my sister Jenny, who was about to marry Gordon Weall, would rent the front rooms overlooking the hills. Gordon, a painter, would paint and repaper the rooms. On and on she went. Then half-way through a sentence, tears rolling down her cheeks, she faltered. "Well?" she said, brushing the tears aside and looking at father.

We all held our breath. Surely, he couldn't say no to all that. But he did.

"Tha off thi 'ead, woman," he shouted. "How can we afford to live with toffs? We're 'and to mouth as 'tis."

"That's war ye're wrang," she sobbed, hiding her face in her hands. "That's war ye're wrang. Don't you understand? We've got to do summat or we're goin' te dee in this dirt."

Then Jenny joined in. "We can do it dad, we can do it. Mother wants to move up, and you've got to help her. Your trouble is that you're not listening. You've got to listen to what she's saying. She's worn her feet off looking for a better place and all the thanks she gets from you is to say it's madness."

By now the three women were crying; the kitchen echoed to their sobs. I'd never heard the three of them at it together. Father stared at them with glazed eyes, slowly wiping the sweat off his brow.

My sisters needn't have cried so hard. Mother had no intention of being done out of the house. She knew that father didn't want to change houses. He didn't want to change anything. There was no ambition in him. But the new house was mother's rainbow and she wasn't going to let anybody take it away. Producing all kinds of papers from her blouse, she delivered the final blow. "Look at these," she said.

Father looked at the papers. "Oh Maggie, tha's really done it this time, lass."

Of course, he could have repudiated the estate agent's contract. Mother could not read and had signed with a cross. But he didn't.

It took father some minutes to recover from shock. "Hmm... hmm..." he kept saying to himself while staring at the floor.

"Well, hasta made up thi mind?" mother prodded him.

"Aw reet," he answered, with a nod. "Aw reet, provided tha'll promise no more shocks and no more fancy houses. A promise, mind?"

Maggie nodded, as she danced around the room, her eyes streaming.

"Aw reet" took us to Livingston Road.

We all became excited about the move. We kept going up to Livingston Road and sitting on the floor of our new house to see what it felt like. It was a substantial two-story brick and stone house next to the last in a row. It was surrounded by duck and hen farms and open pastures. Its great bay windows looked out across the valley to Pendle Hill. It must have been several times the size of our Griffin Street cottage. The first night we went there, we were standing at the door of the tall, narrow bathroom wondering what it would be like to have a whole room in which to wash, when father joined us.

"Too much washin' isn't good for you," he muttered.

We loved the wrought iron gate and railings, the front garden and the stone steps that led up to the front door. In Griffin Street we could stand at the front door and touch the horses and carts going by. We also loved the surrounding fields and farms. What a treat it was to breathe fresh air.

Everybody agreed that the house was "Champion!"

"Oh," said mother, striking further fear into father's heart, "wouldn't it be luvly if this was really ours." After which she gave a long sigh.

Chapter XVII

Livingston Road

W e moved from Griffin Street to Livingston Road one Friday after midnight. We used a flat-topped hand cart with iron-shod wheels, which father had hired overnight for one shilling. Onto the cart we piled three beds and bedding, pisspots, four broken rocking chairs, four stools, a stand chair, a bench for sitting, a rough table and several orange boxes. We also loaded the peg rugs, pots and pans and cutlery. Personal belongings and clothing were packed in straw valises. All was tied down.

We took the rent-book with us. We also took the seven-and-sixpence. All we left in the little box behind the door was the key. Late as it was, Gordon Weall gave us fits pretending to be the rent collector taking down the empty box the next day. He took off the collector to a T: the cap and the turned-up collar, the shaking of the box, the sudden freezing, the dreadful frown, the terrier and the rat bit, the throwing down of the box and the book. His antics missed nothing. He glared at us and threatened us with the box, but then he broke down and laughed as much as everybody else.

Despite Gordon's clowning, it took little more than an hour in which to load the cart and make ready to leave. Other than turning off the gas, and taking the penny asbestos gas mantle from the kitchen, there was not much else to bother about. Anyway, gas came at a penny a time and our penny's worth was almost done.

Father was the last out. He didn't look back. Having spat on his hands, he got between the shafts and began to push the cart along the cobbled street. I ran behind to ensure that nothing fell off the cart and was lost. My brother Dan was not there to help; for several months now he had been travelling northern Britain with his work crew cleaning and repairing mill boilers.

Despite the clatter, no neighbours' curtains moved. They knew perfectly well what was going on and deliberately kept out of the way. Without blinking, they could tell the rent collector the next day that they had no idea that the Woodruffs had gone. As for the police, they didn't interfere with moonlight flits.

This was the first move in my life. It was a cold starlit night. I was ten at the time. It gave me a glorious feeling. With our belongings piled high, and the chair legs pointing to the stars like masts, I saw the cart as a tall ship in which we were setting out on a voyage around the world.

It took less than an hour to get the cart up the hills to Livingston Road. At the worst points, Gordon, and I had to put our shoulders to the wheels to get the cart out of the ruts and to keep it moving. Father held on to the shafts. The only sign of strain he showed was to wipe his forehead, adjust his cap, and spit on his hands.

We drew up outside the house on Livingston Road. It looked to me - accustomed as I was to a tiny cottage - like a glorious castle standing against the stars. We'd reached the shores of another land.

Mother and my sisters awaited us. They had lit the fires and were quick to give us a hand. Everybody worked with a will. To celebrate, we had hot tea on arrival. We hugged each other at our triumph, all talking at once. "We've done it!" we laughed. Our hearts were grateful. By four or five in the morning we were all in bed and fast asleep. By then the first pale streaks of light coming through the uncurtained windows were probing our unopened bundles lying about on the floor.

I woke the next morning for the first time in a room of my own. It smelled of fresh paint. I couldn't get used to the space and the amount of light. Going downstairs was like entering a ballroom. I was amazed at the distance between things - like how long it took to walk down a corridor from one room to another. I found mother making breakfast and singing. She was in high spirits. "You see," she said, "it can be done." She'd won. She wasn't going back to squalor anymore.

With breakfast burning on the stove, she dragged everyone into Jenny's part of the house to look at the distant, sun-lit hills. "Look, look," she cried, pointing through the large bay windows: "Did you ever see anything so beautiful?" The sun was streaming in. With her hands under her breasts, her eyes soared across the valley, over the mills, the smoking chimneys, the mud and decay, until they came to rest on the coloured fells and the long straight line of Pendle's back standing stark against the sky. A dark tide of heather lapped the summit. The surge of emotion she felt when a rainbow lit the distant hills brought her to the edge of tears. "Well," she said to father, who was standing by her, "do you still want to go back to Fall River?" Having drunk it all in, she gave a great sigh and went back to the kitchen. She couldn't have enough of it. For days she kept running through the house to see the hills, looking at them as if she were seeing them for the first time.

There was no stopping mother now. Unknown to us, and despite her promise to father, she was planning further shocks. We came home one night to find the house transformed into a palace. There were rugs on the floors. They were not new - later we noticed holes in them - but they were our very first rugs. We took off our clogs and stockings, and danced about in our bare feet. It tickled our toes. There were curtains instead of newspapers on the windows. There was furniture in every room. Dining room furniture, living room furniture, kitchen furniture, bedroom furniture. There were great upholstered couches and chairs such as none of us, except mother, had ever dreamt of having. I found it an extraordinary experience to lie on a couch. I felt I ought to be ill. None of the furniture was new, but it looked new. Forgetting money, mother had tastefully furnished the whole house. This was Maggie on the grand scale. If ever she had a moment of glory, this was it.

Father nearly fell down when he limped in from work. He was tired out. For a moment he thought he was in the wrong house. He couldn't believe it. With a stunned look on his face, he went from room to room, his eyes getting larger and larger. In a state of shock, he gingerly sat down on the edge of one of the chairs in the sitting room, but on second thoughts he got up and covered it with a sheet of newspaper.

Mother just stood there silently, avoiding his gaze. With her hands across her apron, she looked a picture of abject guilt.

"Maggie, lass," father asked in a funny quaking voice, "where did you get all this stuff?"

Gradually the awful truth came out. She'd gone shopping for one or two little items of furniture, in the course of which she'd met such a nice man. He'd persuaded her that it was cheaper to hire furniture than to buy it. Buying furniture was out of date. For just a few shillings a week they could live as they ought to live. After all, they were living on Livingston Road. He had delivered the furniture the same day, and had worked hard putting it exactly where mother wanted it to give the family a great surprise. He had done that all right.

"But you promised...," father stammered.

"Ah didn't promise I wouldn't get a chair to sit on," mother shot back. "Ah promised I wouldn't get any more fancy houses. And Ah 'aven't."

Money aside, as mother would say, the next three years were the best years we would ever know together. We lived in splendor. "Better than America," she said. She joked that we'd joined the middle class because she now stayed at home to look after the family instead of toiling in the mill. The pity that grandmother Bridget could not have seen us - such a sight would have pleased her.

With Jenny and Brenda, mother transformed the house into a comfortable home. This is where Jenny showed her talents. She sat in a corner, giving a little chirp now and again, while stitching the most marvellous curtains and cushion covers. Her needle flew as swiftly as the shuttle in the loom. Jenny could do wonders with needle and thread.

Outside, both around the house and at the back, father created an oasis of flowers. They grew so high and so thick that you had to hunt for him. I think there were moments when even he thought mother had done the right thing. He began to talk about building a hot-house. He came up with such wild ideas about growing red currents, gooseberries and raspberries in the back garden - ideas that would have cost a mint of money - that even Maggie became alarmed. I think she felt he was appropriating her role as the squanderer of the family.

------◦------

We knew that in joining the toffs we'd jumped the class barrier, but that didn't bother us. The rest of the working class would have jumped it too if they had had the chance. Father was mentally confined to a class; he was loyal to it. Mother wouldn't have known what to say about classes. She knew, as we all did, that there were classes within classes. 'Loyalty to class,' 'Standing firm,' or 'Closing the ranks,' meant nothing to her. She didn't use the terms 'them' and 'they' as other workers did. She knew that some people were rich and others were poor. If the working class meant dirt and poverty, she was glad to be out of it.

It was our new neighbours, the Peeks, who did the worrying about class. They were hoity-toity. They had feared for their lives when we arrived. Wakened by the din, Mr. Peek had seen us approaching the house in the moonlight with the flatcart. "Agnes, my dear," he had said to his wife, as he peeped through the bedroom curtains, "we are not only condemned to live in a slum, we are about to be overrun by savages." Clogs and shawls had not been seen on Livingston Road before. It took a year for Mrs. Peek to tell me this, but eventually she did. Mr. Peek had been a factory owner who had gone broke. As we'd gone up in the world, the Peeks had come down.

Our new neighbours were quite different from those on Griffin Street. They dressed differently, talked differently, and were standoffish - but decent just the same. The Peeks talked to us, as if we were inferior. There was a gulf between them and us; you could see it in their eyes. Brenda asked me if I'd noticed it. I said I had. It was a long time before we 'savages' were accepted. Thanks to Roger Peek, who became my close friend, I led the way. Gradually, the barriers fell.

The Peeks influenced me greatly in the three years that I knew them. There were five of them: Terence Peek, his wife Agnes, their sons Roger and John, and their daughter Millicent. Roger told me how well off they'd been before his father went bankrupt. They had lived in a large house set in spacious grounds, with servants, ponies, everything. Then it had all gone.

Roger's only drawback was that every time he had a fall, he broke a bone. I became quite expert at handling these emergencies. The brittleness of his bones, however, did not stop him from having the most dreadful fights with his younger brother John. Fortunately, when the fighting was over, it was all love and sunshine again.

Millicent, sixteen, was the eldest. She was just out of school. Like her mother, she was pretty in a doll-like way. She went in for flowery dresses and big frothy hats. I think she found our presence jarring. It didn't help when my parents told her they'd been to America. We thought she was stuck-up. She was always putting on airs; being 'Lah-de-dah' we called it.

Our relations with Millicent were marred from the start. One bright moonlit night shortly after we had moved into Livingston Road there was the most frantic knocking on the Peek's front door. Something was dreadfully wrong for anyone to knock like that; there was a note of panic about it. Putting on the outside light, all the Woodruffs, including Jenny and Gordon, rushed to the front door to see what was going on. Imagine our surprise to find Millicent pissing in the bushes, hiding underneath her frothy hat. The poor girl must have made a desperate dash up Livingston Road only to fail at the last moment. When Agnes Peek put on the light and opened the door, Millicent was still squatting among the shrubs.

"Milli!" Mrs. Peek shrieked in a shocked tone, before quickly switching off the light.

"I don't believe it," said mother, who was as stunned as Agnes, "not in Livingston Road;" after which she quietly switched off our own light, gently pushed us all back inside, and shut the door. We left Millicent out there, trying her best to merge into the shrubbery.

Once inside, we looked at each other for a moment. "Milli!" mimicked Gordon, and we all exploded. He made us rock with laughter. We laughed so hard that we could no longer speak. That night we laughed our way to bed.

We never met Millicent after that without her blushing like a peony.

Agnes Peek was my favourite. I thought of her as plump, warm and friendly. It may have been more as a result of sickness than of good health, but she had the loveliest round face. There was a haunting beauty about it. She was never without her pearls and elegant shoes. Her fine fingers were covered with jewels. I used to look at them and think what Mr. Levy at t' pop shop would give for them. Other than her wedding ring, mother had no jewelry. Grandmother Bridget's jewelry had long since been pawned. Strange, I thought, that the Peeks should call themselves poor.

Agnes had such a toff's way of talking that there were times when I couldn't tell what she was saying. But I knew her heart was good. Roger said she'd had tuberculosis, and had been treated in Switzerland. She gave me the impression of being lonely, of being cut off from former friends. She just couldn't adjust to her changed condition. It showed in her eyes and at the corners of her mouth. There were times when she looked non-plussed. She had a delightful way of fluttering her soft, white hands at problems that became too much for her. Mr. Peek could escape from his troubles into books. There was no escape for Agnes. Little wonder that she had fits of moodiness.

If Agnes Peek was my favourite, Terence Peek was the man who changed the course of my life. He was as kind as any man I had met; as kind as Willie Gill but in a different way; I never saw tears in Mr. Peek's eyes as I had seen them in Willie Gill's. To me he was all brain. He had a large forehead, yellowish skin, gray eyes, a little nose out of proportion to his face and the largest ears. His hands fascinated me. They were nothing like father's hands. The palms were soft, the fingers long and delicate with broadish tips. I used to watch them as they drummed the table or the arms of his chair when he was talking to me. He wore an odd-looking pince-nez, and had his hair parted down the middle. He was forever shaking hands. We only shook hands after playing football or wrestling. He never worked - not as we understood the word. He spent most of his day either in his study or walking to and from the library in town.

I was astonished when, having won entrance to the house, I discovered that he had a whole library to himself. It was a darkish room with a long table, cluttered with books, papers, maps and prints. It smelled of stale tobacco. He smoked with an elegant cigarette holder. He had a framed picture on the wall of the factory he had owned. It looked an enormous place, bigger than Hornby's. In a corner of the room stood a silent grandfather clock that he was always going to fix.

After several months, Mr. Peek began to take a deep interest in me; even though he continued to call me 'the young savage.' I think he talked to me more than he did to his own children. I knew I'd won his confidence when he allowed me to borrow books. I think he looked upon me as a young disciple.

One day Mr. Peek explained to me how it was possible for a man to be rich one day and poor the next. I thought that, outside America, where according to grandmother Bridget anything could happen, to be rich or poor was something you couldn't change; at least not as quickly as Mr. Peek had done. I thought you were born poor and you died poor, or you were born rich and you died rich. Uncle Eric was the only man I knew who had started poor and had become rich. No matter what reason Mr. Peek gave for his coming down in the world, most of which I failed to understand, his talk about being poor baffled me. By our standards, he was well-off.

I learned early on that Mr. Peek shared uncle Eric's belief in science. Like uncle Eric, he was a leading member of the local Mechanics Institute. He was convinced that science was going to improve the workers' lot. He was writing it all down in a book upon which he worked every day. He never stopped talking about it; it would change the world; at least it was the only hope for Lancashire. I didn't understand half of what he said, but I had no difficulty following him when he argued that what the world needed was more money. Every cotton weaver knew that. Money was the one thing we lacked. Mr. Peek had worked out a scheme whereby we could have all the money we needed. He was so sure of this that even I thought him a little mad.

When I told him that I intended to follow my father as a weaver, he warned me to look elsewhere. He was the first to convince me that there was something irretrievably wrong with the Lancashire cotton industry. He knew that it had been dealt a fatal blow.

"Thank God," he said to me, "that I'm not younger. I couldn't stand to see a great industry die again."

"Rubbish," said father when I told him. "Cotton isn't dying. Peek is tapped, that's what he is. There will always be cotton."

Mr. Peek taught me much of what I came to know about the cotton industry. "It's one of the greatest accidents in history that it's here at all. At one time Blackburn was just a village in the Ribble valley. Nobody predicted that a pastoral backwater would become the workshop of the world."

As the weeks and months passed, I began to learn how cotton had come to Lancashire in the 1600's, and how great textile inventions, such as the Spinning Jenny and the Spinning Mule had fostered its growth. "The older weaving traditions in linens and woolens helped it. We had all the land, coal, stone, clay, slate, iron and other building materials that we needed. Canals and railways were built. English and Irish workers came here in their thousands. In Liverpool we had an ideal port; in Manchester an ideal market place. There was a time," he went on, his voice ringing with pride, "when Manchester challenged London. In 1913 Lancashire exported seven billion yards of cloth. Imagine that, Billy, seven billion yards! We clothed England before breakfast, and the world after breakfast."

"But the people of the world must have had clothes before we sold them cottons, Mr. Peek."

"Of course they did. Most of the fine cottons came from India and China. But the weavers of those countries, who used handlooms, were no match for the masters and men of

Lancashire. Despite Asia's cheaper labour, our steam-driven machines and our inventions beat them every time. Profits were ploughed back; we took the long-term view. Absentee ownership was unheard of. Factory owners and their sons were known to every worker in the mill. This way we got bigger and bigger. Countries like America, India and Egypt couldn't keep up with our demands for raw cotton. In the United States the growing of cotton with slave labour led to a terrible civil war.

"But then came the Great War, which gave the other people the chance to industrialize and take Lancashire's markets away. By the 1920's, India, China and Japan were taking our trade. We sold them the textile machinery to do it. The machinery is still out there, Billy, working 24 hours a day to take our bread away. We only have ourselves to blame."

On still another occasion, he explained how, since 1921, the course of the Lancashire cotton industry had been all downhill. "Since then many parts of the world have shut out our goods, especially the low-count products upon which Blackburn depends. When the Indians can't compete they find a political reason to boycott our goods, Billy. Gandhi was in Darwen yesterday. That fellow is costing England half a million jobs. For the cloth upon which we depend, we simply can't match the Japanese, Indian and Chinese prices. I know, because I've tried. America is hitting us from the other side. She's miles ahead of us now. Foreigners are killing us, Billy."

At this point, tracing a line with his cigarette holder, he showed me on his globe where most of our raw cotton came from in America, 4,000 miles away, and where Blackburn sent most of its woven cloth, to India, 12,000 miles away. "Any industry that gets all its cotton from abroad and sells four-fifths of its cloth to foreigners, as we've been doing, is asking for trouble."

One day Mr. Peek was particularly down-hearted. "Nobody recognizes what is happening to cotton. Nobody cares. Everybody tries to make a killing and get out. Those who plough their profits back into the industry and hang on get wiped out. There's no loyalty to the industry anymore. Those who run it are either daft or greedy. They still cling to the idea that Lancashire will go on leading the world. Yet they know as well as I do that our markets are disappearing and our factories are being shipped to Japan." I watched his fingers restlessly drumming the desk. "Something is missing," he went on, "we're not pioneers any more; we're hangers-on. Smugness and self-satisfaction rule. The money-spinners do the rest, they make a quick profit and get out. For us, Billy, the glory is over."

"Sounds serious, Mr. Peek."

"It is. There's only one thing the industry understands," he went on, tapping the surface of his desk. "Dog eat dog. Soon there will be no dogs to eat."

"What about the workers? Where do they come in?"

"They're just as blind as the bosses. They're sheep led by the nose."

"That's not fair, Mr. Peek, it was not the workers but the bosses that caused the General Strike."

"Nonsense," he replied puffing on a cigarette, "the General Strike was labour gone mad. There wasn't a chance of the strike succeeding. English workers aren't revolutionaries; they like to tinker, not to smash. They don't believe in tidal waves and big ideas like a General Strike; they believe in muddling through. They prefer to be haphazard. They're happier when they're arguing over price lists and pay lists. As a boss, I know. In 1926 they squabbled among themselves and got what they deserved. They fought for a share of a cake that is fast disappearing. Without recognizing it, what they're squabbling over is the death of the Lancashire cotton industry. "

My family's only comment when I told them what Mr. Peek had been saying was "Poor devil's barmey. If he goes on like that they'll lock him up."

In some things, I think, Mr. Peek probably was a little barmey. In other things he was practical and down to earth. I have to thank him for clearing up one great problem about which I had been complaining to my parents for years. To pass water had become agonizing for me; instead of flowing, it leaked out drop by painful drop. It was a crippling defect. Roger told his father of my plight.

Mr. Peek was appalled, even horrified at my parents' primitive view of medicine, and their refusal to resort to surgery. He told them so. He came bouncing into our house one night determined to change their point of view. He became as committed to having them take me to a doctor as he was in providing the world with money. For him, it became another cause and he kept at my parents until they gave in. They took me to Dr. Grieves who decided upon immediate surgery.

Getting rid of the problem was as simple as Mr. Peek had predicted. Two mornings later, Dr. Grieves arrived with an assistant. Fearful, I climbed onto the kitchen table, over which mother had spread a clean sheet. The table had been carried into my sister Jenny's room at the front of the house where there was more light. I could see the hills. A gauze cup was placed over my nose and mouth. "Give him a whiff," said Grieves to his aide. "All over in a tick," he said to me reassuringly. I can only remember a sickly smell. When I came to I was on the couch still facing the hills. I was dazed from the chloroform. Dr. Grieves and his helper had gone. Mother was at my side hushing me. Mr. Peek came every day, sometimes with a book. Apart from a week or two of agony, the cure was complete. It confirmed my confidence in Dr. Grieves; also that Mr. Peek was an ally worth having.

———◁◇▷———

The reluctance to call in Dr. Grieves stemmed more from father than from mother. Although father had recovered from gassing in France during the war, he had no faith in either doctors or hospitals. Unless he was forced to, he avoided them. Once he had collapsed at work with what Dr. Grieves diagnosed as acute appendicitis requiring immediate surgery. Mother had been warning father for years that the peanuts, which he ate by the pound, would land him in hospital with appendicitis. The ambulance was sent for. Against father's protests, he was bundled into the ambulance and despatched to the Royal Infirmary. But he never arrived. Somewhere en route he managed to persuade the ambulance driver, who was a mate of his, to take him home. His mate had great difficulty explaining the empty ambulance when he got to the infirmary. Meanwhile father had put himself to bed. He resorted to folk medicine: fistfuls of steam-heated bread placed between sheets of brown

Livingston Road

paper and applied to the inflamed area. Mother continued the
treatment when she came home from the mill.

All that can be said is that father survived.

Dr. Grieves was not informed about his patient's escape.
Meeting father later on, he asked him how he felt after the
operation.

"Couldn't be better."

"You're a lucky man, you are. It was touch and go with you,
you know. A few hours later and you would have been a goner."

"I can believe that."

Father believed that if he ever entered a hospital he would
die. It was a deep superstition he held. Many years later his
fears were fulfilled precisely as he had foretold.

Father may not have appreciated Dr. Grieves' skills, but there
were many others who did. He was a legend in the community.
Everybody knew him and his spaniel Joy. Joy always jumped
into the gig and sat on guard while the doctor made housecalls.
The housecall ended, the dog happily took to the street again.
Everybody admired Dr. Grieves. Not least because he
sometimes forgot to send bills. House visits, when he
remembered to charge, were two shillings and sixpence. His
stock soared after it got about that he had risked his life in a
collapsed mine gallery tending injured miners.

While any kind of illness was considered shameful by my
people, there were occasions when we were persuaded to take a
bottle of his cure. Invariably, it was I who was sent to the
surgery to pick up the medicine for sixpence a bottle. I knew if
I'd got the right bottle by the colour. Coughs and chest
problems were treated with a blue liquid. (If goose grease and a
home-made concoction of lemon, glycerin and cod-liver oil had
failed.) Aches in the head, eyes, ears and nose were dosed with
yellow; joint troubles with red; troubles in the belly - there
being no response to the usual doses of prune and fig juice -
with a black, tar-like substance. I wondered what would
happen if somebody confused the colours.

The only reservation I ever heard about Dr. Grieves was that
he dabbled in veterinary medicine. There was the catch. People
swore that there had been occasions when Dr. Grieves got his

medicines mixed up and that he gave to humans what was meant for horses. Nobody in his right mind ever followed his instructions to the letter and swallowed a tablespoon at one go. They first wet their tongue or took a small sip to make sure they were not going to be knocked flat.

———◄○►———

Soon after we moved to Livingston Road, Jenny married Gordon Weall. That was when I got my first pair of long pants. Father took me to a shop called Weaver to Wearer where I was measured for a suit of dark brown worsted wool. Weaver to Wearer was the cheapest tailor in town. Their cloth was thought to be better than that sold by the workers' Cooperative Store. Also, Weaver to Wearer gave me two fittings, at the Co-op I'd have got only one.

When I took the suit home in a big cardboard box, I felt like a millionaire. At last, I had stopped being a boy and had become a man. I explored all the pockets and found the sixpence, which the tailor always hid in a boy's first suit. That night I put the suit on and paraded before the family. There were many 'ooohs' and 'aaaahs.' It was the first time in my life that I had ever worn anything over my knees. It made them itch.

The wedding itself was the most elaborate affair in the family's history. Mother was not prepared to settle for second best, not in Livingston Road. It was one of the high points of her life. That's how she thought life should be.

At great expense, we went the whole way. Everybody had new clothes. Mother was in her seventh heaven deciding what everyone should wear. Jenny wore white. Her dress had a low neck with a tight waist and sleeves all puffed up. She had a veil and carried lilies of the valley. Beautiful she looked. She also had two little girls as train bearers. Gordon wore a hired frock coat, pin striped trousers and a special gray waistcoat with a watch chain. He looked like the Lord Mayor. Nobody would have guessed he was a painter's apprentice. Like the rest of us, he got a new suit and new shoes for the wedding but kept them for going away on his honeymoon.

As it was a June wedding and the weather was kind, family and friends stood outside the church for a moment to say hello and wave greetings before going in. It's amazing what clothes will do to people when they are wearing their best. Everybody held themselves stiffly and spoke in funny voices. I never saw such a change; they weren't the same folk at all.

When we went in, the organ was playing quietly. We had organ, choir and soloist. There were six little flower girls. Gordon and a fellow-painter were waiting near the altar rail - white gardenias in their buttonholes. There were a lot of people there whom I'd never seen before. All the Wealls were present, Mrs. Weall constantly wiping her eyes. Mr. Weall, a little red-nosed man, who looked as if he had just stepped out of a hot bath, steadily supplied his wife with clean handkerchiefs. Mother put our neighbours, the Peeks, including Millicent, well up front. "Savages, are we!" I could hardly recognize mother and Brenda in their flowing pink dresses and enormous wide-brimmed hats.

Then father arrived with Jenny and the train-bearers in a shining limousine. What agony father must have suffered having to pay for that car with its chauffeur and its white ribbons and orange blossom! Jenny looked an angel; she glided down the aisle with her tiny toes peeping out of her white slippers. She had the easy motions of a good dancer. Mother had seen to it that Jenny wore "Something old, something new, something borrowed, something blue." Father walked at her side as if he had just fallen off a wall. It was one of the few times I ever saw him wearing a tie. If the organ hadn't been thundering," Here comes the bride," we could have heard his new suit creaking.

Then Jenny joined Gordon. We all stood and sang: "Rejoice and be glad." Then we sat down while a young woman sang, "Love divine, all love excelling." Then the preacher came forward and talked about matrimony, and what a serious business it was. He went on and on about loving and being faithful to each other, and bringing up children. "The fear of the Lord," he stressed, "is the beginning of all wisdom."

Then they got on with the marriage, with Bertha Weall crying so hard that she could be heard throughout the church.

Then the preacher asked Gordon if he would marry Jenny, and Jenny if she would marry Gordon - which is what I thought we'd come for. You could hardly hear Jenny's reply, but Gordon's "I do" was strong. Then the preacher gave them his blessing. "What God hath joined together, let no man put asunder."

While Jenny and Gordon were in the vestry, the choir sang, "Blessed be the tie that binds." Then everybody together, including the married couple and the choir, sang, "God the creator, God the good."

After pictures had been taken outside the church, Jenny and Gordon and the parents of both sides went off in the limousine. The rest of us - relatives, friends, and those who hung on in the hope of a free meal - walked down town to Harper's where the reception was to be held. It wasn't far, the weather was good, and we made fun all the way.

Jenny told me later that both mothers cried in the limousine. Mrs. Weall blubbered most. She kept saying, "I've lost my only son, Maggie, I've lost my only child."

In response to which mother sobbingly replied, "Aye, but tha's got a good daughter, Bertha."

"Hisht, women," father had scolded.

At Harper's we first had family pictures taken and then sat down to a proper ham and tongue wedding breakfast. Trifle followed, and there was lots to drink. Gordon made a speech in which he couldn't help being a clown.

While everyone was stuffing themselves and having a good time, Jenny and Gordon changed to go away. Then we all got up in our best clothes and trooped off behind the married couple, who went hand in hand, across town to the railway station. Gordon had already dropped off a suitcase there. We were a happy, laughing throng of about twenty or thirty people. Several excited children brought up the tail end.

"God bless you," passers-by called to the bride and groom.

"All the best."

"Never grow old."

"Here's to your health and wealth."

On reaching the platform we rained confetti and streamers upon the happy couple. The women hugged and kissed the bride. The men were more restrained. They patted the bridegroom on the shoulder as if he was going to war. Father stood stiffly to one side, preoccupied with his thoughts. I'm sure he was still worrying about the cost of the ribbon-bedecked limousine that awaited him in the street.

It must have taken father a long time to pay for that wedding. He must have spent the family's savings on it, and gone into debt. It will always remain a mystery to me how a man who resented paying a penny on the tram, and who was not known for giving his children anything, could suddenly spend like a profligate. The money for all the clothes must have come out of his pocket, for none of us belonged to a clothing club in which garments were bought by payments made over time.

I can only think that marrying off a daughter was something special. Of course, mother was the driving force. She didn't let price interfere. Besides the Wealls were a cut above the Woodruffs and it was up to us not to let the side down. Pride demanded that we should impress them. Also, we lived in Livingston Road. A threadbare marriage from such an address would have been unthinkable.

In any event, money was never better spent. We had a wonderful time, we all got stuffed with food and drink; and everybody finished up with new clothes. Father's suit lasted him the rest of his life. We'd never spent like that before, and we never did again. "Everybody is entitled to go mad once," mother said. Mother saw to it that the wedding got into the paper. She kept asking father to read it to her over and over again. I think she often relived Jenny's wedding in her dreams.

---◦---

Several months after Jenny's wedding, Brenda became engaged to Harry Entwistle. They were both members of the Salvation Army. The Army thought the world of them. Harry was a Derbyshire man. Twice the size of Brenda, he had a ruddy, well-weathered face, a mass of blond hair combed back, hands like shovels, and a body like an ox. He was one of the boilermen at Dougdale's mill. He'd been in Blackburn about a year. Not much was known about him. He didn't seem to have any family. When I first met him, he had two passions: Brenda and the Salvation Army. Brenda at this time was about twenty.

With all the tenderness of possession, Brenda brought him home one night to show him off to the family. Harry's big, bright eyes and his infectious, happy laugh exuded warmth. We took to him at once. He was so open, friendly and genuine that we were drawn to him instinctively. In an ox-like way he was also good-looking; handsome would be the right word. There were not many young men in town with as rich a blond beard as Harry's; his eyebrows were equally splendid.

Mother thought them a good match. Harry was four years older than Brenda. He had a job, and he obviously loved her. Brenda couldn't have enough of him. Without a dissenting word, the family came down on Harry's side.

Henceforth, Harry became a member of the Woodruff household. He was always coming up to Livingston Road; always eating with us, always engaging us in jolly laughter. Brenda and he often went off to Salvation Army meetings, their faces glowing.

One night they came back and announced to the family that they were going to get married. Harry didn't formally ask father for Brenda's hand, but then members of the working class rarely did. The couple just said they'd made up their mind.

Everybody was delighted. The date was set. According to Salvation Army tradition, they were to be married under the flag, which meant that the Army took responsibility for the service and the reception. The wedding breakfast had all been arranged; two bands had agreed to play. Brenda and Harry were to lead a short demonstration march, to be followed by prayers and massed singing. Nothing was going to be left out for the couple who had won everybody's heart.

None of us will ever forget the wedding day. There was such hustle and bustle in the house on Livingston Road. Other than Brenda, who wore her Salvation Army uniform, we all put on the new clothes we'd obtained for Jenny's wedding and hurried down to the Salvation Army headquarters where the marriage was to take place. We took umbrellas because the weather looked bad. Father and Brenda were to follow in a taxi. The Army captain received us and made us all real welcome.

Scrubbed, glowing faces, black hats and red bands were everywhere. Resting against the wall in the hall were the flags to be used in the march. Harry stood waiting with a Soldier of Christ as best man.

While one of the bands was playing, Brenda and father arrived. They were just walking up to Harry when a young woman hurried toward them from one of the side doors and blocked their path. Her face was gray and drawn. Brenda stopped. She looked flummoxed. Everybody stared at the intruder.

"What can I do for you?" Brenda asked the stranger who seemed distraught.

"It's more what can I do for you," the intruder gasped.

"Who are you?" said Brenda, her face darkening.

"Mrs. Harry Entwistle," the woman sobbed. "Thank God I got here in time."

Brenda's face became distorted; her lips quivered and throbbed. She looked at the woman with stony eyes.

Mother pushed past me and threw her arms around Brenda. "Come home child," she pleaded. Everybody in the hall was so still, they might have been struck by lightning.

Brenda turned on Harry. "Harry Entwistle," she asked, "is this your wife?"

Harry shifted his feet uneasily; he was trembling; his face was flushed; he was staring at the floor. After a moment or two he looked up. "Yis," he stammered.

Snatching the umbrella from father's hand, Brenda struck Harry across the face. A red weal appeared. "You scum!" she screamed, as she delivered blow after blow. Harry didn't move. Didn't flinch. Nor did anybody else. The crowd just stared. "You rotten devil!" Brenda went on hitting him until the umbrella broke. So did her spirit. With a sob she collapsed onto a chair. With all the women weeping, the family somehow managed to get her home.

For days, Brenda didn't speak to anyone. When she did come downstairs her face was a frightful sight. She looked twenty years older. A vague sadness had replaced her distress.

She never wore the Salvation Army uniform again.

In time the wounds healed. She married a good man called Richard Paden. He was a clerk at a store in town with little money and fewer prospects. In contrast to Jenny's wedding - it was an in-and-out-of-church affair with no trimmings. Nobody said it, but I think everybody felt that the ghost of Harry Entwistle was there, mocking us with his hearty laughter. Somehow Brenda and Richard weathered the hard times. Like my sister Jenny and most other workers who had little to eat, they only had one child. Brenda remained with her spouse until death intervened.

———◦———

It was shortly after Brenda's wedding that Agnes Peek was struck down with tetanus. She cut her finger on a piece of glass that was lying on her kitchen floor. I was standing next to her at the time. It was only a prick, which she sucked clean. That night there was a commotion next door. The ambulance came and carried her off. Mrs. Peek lay at death's door in the infirmary for weeks. I often went with Roger to see her. She was never the same when she came home.

Chapter XVIII

Earning my Keep

While we were living at Livingston Road I really began to earn my keep. I took pride in doing so. I started delivering morning and evening newspapers for George and Madge Latham, a young, childless couple in their thirties, who ran a sweets, tobacco and newspaper business on Revidge Road. The Lathams were an honest, hard-working couple. They were Lancashire folk: active, tough, resourceful. They were always cheerful. I was a year below the minimum age, but they took me on just the same; no one enforced the law. They paid me the princely sum of two shillings and sixpence per week, of which I kept a dodger. Mother took the rest. That was my contribution to help pay for the house.

I came to love the Lathams and looked upon their home as my own. They treated me as their son, which meant that Madge periodically put my head over the kitchen sink to scrub my neck. She also insisted on my taking a weekly bath in their bathroom. For the first time I started wearing woolen underclothing, which she bought. It made me feel hot. I loved Madge because she was so kind, but when she asked me to part my hair on the other side, I pretended not to hear. When I left the shop to go to school she always tucked a bag of shortbread into my jacket pocket.

Several times the Lathams tried to adopt me. My father was agreeable; my mother, conscious of her own childhood, refused. I would have been happy to join them. In George Latham I found the companionship of a father I had never really had.

I came to spend so much time with the Lathams that home and school fell into the background. Winter and summer, wet or fine, I got myself up at five to meet George at the newspaper depot in the center of town about a mile and a half away. I had to run through the dark, hushed streets for half an hour or so. I'd find him waiting for me with his bicycle. On cold mornings his teeth were chattering. Together, we then fought our way in and out of an ill-lit warehouse that served as the newspaper depot. It was a daily hand-to-hand battle with other men to get our newspapers. It was bedlam there.

Once we'd got the warm, damp bundles under our arms, we loaded them and George's bike onto the first tram to Revidge Road at six o'clock. Kneeling on the ribbed floor, we sorted the papers as the tram lurched along. When the floor was wet with melted snow off people's clogs, we used the seats. At Revidge Road, George helped me off the tram. With a bag of newspapers on either shoulder, I began my round. Depending on the weather, I'd be running through the streets for the next hour, or hour and a half. I found it wonderful to have the world to myself.

I had no difficulty knowing which paper went where. Labour people took the *Herald* or *News Chronicle*, conservatives the *Mail or the Telegraph*, liberals the *Guardian*, the toffs took *The Times*. A switch in newspaper usually meant a switch in political allegiance. I knew how my customers would vote.

Delivering newspapers taught me a lot about human nature. I learned to recognize the news addicts and the insomniacs. In summer, these chaps paced up and down their lawns awaiting my arrival. The way they snatched the paper out of my hand, made me feel important. I knew by the way they rushed to the financial pages that, like most of the rich, they were fearful of losing their money. I'd nothing to lose so the financial crashes left me unmoved. I decided it must be worrying to be rich.

In bad weather, the kind-hearted awaited my arrival with a cup of tea and a bun. The not so kind angrily waved the paper in my face as if I were responsible for the success of Labour at the polls, or the assassination of the head of a foreign state. I felt like saying: "Look, Mister, I don't write these papers, I just deliver them." Usually, I kept my mouth shut. One thing I did learn was never to give a man the wrong paper. You've no idea how touchy some people can be. They'd bawl me out as if I'd permanently committed them to the wrong religion.

In time I came to have a large family of newspaper readers. I knew them more closely than they realized. I knew them by the way their houses stared, sat and slept. I closely followed my customers' births, weddings, divorces and deaths. I knew who had gone broke, and who was doing very nicely. I knew when a move was underway. I delivered Dr. Michael's paper. He was the great ear, nose and throat specialist who was unable to save his own daughter from a fatal ear infection. "And how is the Michael child?" some customers asked me as if I were a consulting physician.

With a passion for the printed word, I not only delivered newspapers, I read them too. I started every day eager to see what the world was up to. One morning in 1927 I was thrilled to read about Lindbergh's solo flight from the United States to France. My friends and I didn't stop talking about Lucky Lindy. The only airplanes we had seen were three single-engine aircraft flown by a group of American rough riders who came for three days to barnstorm from a field on the edge of town. They charged five shillings for a ten minute ordeal. My mates and I saw the whole show and were awestruck. The planes were thumped and banged about so much that we expected them to fall apart. When we saw people getting out and throwing up, we concluded that it was just as well that nobody was pressing a free ride on us.

The newspapers were full of politics. That's how I first heard about Mussolini in Italy and Stalin in Russia. I cut their pictures out of the paper and lined them up like a rogue's gallery on my bedroom wall. With the world depression in trade and industry at its height, the papers also had a lot to say about commercial crises, strikes and lockouts.

Sometimes the news was so arresting that I stopped under a street light to read it. Banner headlines greeted the formation of a second Labour government in 1929. We believed that Labour would put things right this time. Ramsay MacDonald was to be Prime Minister.

With the further collapse of trade and industry, equally large headlines announced the fall of the Labour government in 1931. The man upon whom all our hopes had been pinned - Ramsay MacDonald - then deserted the Labour Party to work with the Conservatives and the Liberals. My family couldn't believe that the Labour government had gone to pot.

One thing I did learn, was the way newspapers contradicted each other - that truth is not as straight-forward as I thought it was. A disaster in politics in one paper was a victory in another. I asked myself how could that be? I also learned to be suspicious of the writers who had a simple answer for everything. Every day I read the column by Hannan Swaffer in the *Daily Herald*. Why, if they'd have put Mr. Swaffer in charge, the country and the world would have been on its feet again in seven days. I found it confusing.

I asked George Latham what he made of it; after all, he had newsprint all over his hands as I did, and he was much older.

"I'd never deliver the news, Billy, if I tried to make head or tail of it," he answered. "We're businessmen, Billy. We have our work cut out delivering papers without worrying about what it all means."

Being a businessman did not deter me from reading the news as I ran through the streets. By the time I reached the Lathams, where a wash, and a hearty breakfast awaited me, I knew pretty well where the world was going. After school I read the evening paper as avidly as I had read the morning edition. At the end of the day, after George, Madge and I had eaten together, I was allowed to plunder the magazines and books from the Lathams small two-penny lending library. I must have read them all. I read Edgar Wallace's detective stories one after the other as they came off the press. In Latham's lending library I continued the education that grandmother Bridget had begun. When I got tired of reading, I'd play table tennis either with Madge or with George. Before I went home, I had tea and cake with them.

------◦►------

Each Christmas the Lathams raffled a box of chocolates - the largest and most extravagant box available. It contained several pounds of the finest confectionery. A ticket cost a dodger. Everybody who visited the shop bought one. People came from miles away to join in the raffle. As it was my first Christmas with the Lathams, I decided to have a go.

Two days before Christmas, with hundreds of tickets sold, I stood in a packed shop waiting for George to draw the winning ticket. The crowd was so large that it spilled out onto the street. With a lot of shouting going on, "Cum on now, lad, don't keep us in suspense," George dipped his hand into the box of tickets held by Madge. In a loud voice he called out: "283!"

I couldn't believe my ears. "A've got it!" I shouted. I was speechless with excitement; it was the first thing I had ever won. I hurriedly pushed my way through the crowd to claim my prize.

"Oh, not you, Billy," George said. He gave me a sickly smile. "Billy," he leant over and whispered, "would you like to sell your ticket? I'll make it right with you. We could raffle the chocolates again. It would look better." There was a desperate look in his eye.

"No!" I shouted; I was aghast at the thought of being robbed of my trophy.

An embarrassed George had to declare me the winner. Reluctantly he placed the box in my outstretched arms. After making one or two veiled comments about shops winning their own prizes - some of them good-humoured, some not so good - the crowd dispersed. I expected the customers to slap me on the back and congratulate me; nobody did.

The box of chocolates caused a sensation in my family. They'd never seen anything like it. Nor had I. The colourful lid depicted a scene from St. Mark's Square, Venice. The wrapper said so. It was all ancient buildings and lots of gondolas and glistening water. There was gold ribbon round every corner of the box. It was an adventure to raise the lid. There was a box within the box. There were several layers, drawers and hidden corners. There was even a secret drawer at the bottom, so that when you thought the feast was ended, you could start all over again. Neighbours came and admired and fingered the box. It was left to me to decide who could have a chocolate and who couldn't. And what chocolates they were! Great delicious, hand-made things wrapped in bright tinsel. Some of them actually contained liqueur, which disturbed my sister Brenda who had become a rabid drink hater.

When the next Christmas came round, I had my three pennies ready. But I was not to be given the chance to repeat my victory. "Billy," George begged, "do me a favour and don't buy any more of my raffle tickets. It would ruin me, if you won it again! You are, after all, part of the business." I put my three pennies away.

———<o>———

Some months after I had joined the Lathams I found a collie dog. Well, really, she found me. She came from nowhere one day when I was delivering evening papers, and adopted me on the spot. In a transport of joy, she suddenly leapt all over me, licking and fussing me. She made real loving sounds at me. She was black and white, with bright eyes and the most beautifully shaped head. She bestowed herself upon me there and then, as if she'd been looking for me all her life. We became inseparable companions. I called her Bess.

After Rosie Gill, Bess was the second great love affair of my life. Morning till night, we were never apart. Although she was allowed in the house, she was not allowed to go upstairs. Every morning she greeted me by the kitchen fire writhing and leaping around as if I'd been absent for months. She ran through the streets delivering papers with me in the dark every morning. She slunk onto the first tram with us. With her cold nose, she supervised the sorting of the papers on the ribbed floor. She knew where I had to get off, and where we had to deliver. She only got mixed up - as I did - when people stopped and started their papers. When I had to go to school or inside

292

the mills, she waited for me outside. She was always there, lashing her tail with affection. She gave me a little bump with the side of her head to tell me that she had missed me; other times she rubbed her head against my knees. No one could have had a more good-natured or more loving companion. I paid no attention to my family's complaints that she smelled - she did, beautifully. Nor did I listen when they said that there was no room or food for her. Together, Bess and I overcame all opposition, solved all problems. We lived our own lives; the rest of the world did not exist.

One day when we reached home, a big red-faced farmer with black leggings and a check cap was waiting for us. He had a collar and a leash in his hand. His angry mottled brown eyes spelled trouble.

"Tha cumin' with me," the farmer said to the dog.

I was horrified. I got as far away from the man as I could and clung to Bess in a corner.

"Doesn't ta know that stealin's a sin?" he asked me with an unblinking stare. "Tha'll finish up in jail, th' will. And then, by gum, tha'll go t' 'ell."

Bess and I trembled. Her head was down, her tail tucked in.

"'As t' told boy this?" he turned on father.

"Dust ta expect me t' look after all t' bloody stray dogs in town?" father grumped.

"Wot dus t' think a dog like this costs?" the man said, turning to me. "Well wot dust t' think? Ah'm waitin' fur an answer."

"Ah don't know." I said. I was shaking. Bess and I clung closer still. I could feel her heart thumping; she was as terrified as I was.

"Well, if Ah'd got nothin' better to do, Ah'd tell thee. As it is, Ah'll just take me dog and go."

The farmer reached across and grabbed Bess by the neck. With Bess squirming to be free, he put the collar on her. He then attached the leash and began to drag the dog across the floor to the door. I didn't know what to do. Father just sat there as if nothing was happening. So I burst into tears. I sobbed as if my heart would break.

"You can't take Bess away from me," I spluttered. "She's the only thing Ah've got." Over her shoulder, Bess pleaded for my help. I cried harder. Much harder.

The man stopped at the door and looked back. Shifting his weight from one foot to the other, he seemed embarrassed and uncertain what to do. "Tha needn't bawl thi 'ead off," he threw at me. "Anybody'd think Ah'd murdered thee."

Bess began to whine. In tears, I threw myself on the floor.

"Now, tha should stop that at once. It sounds as if tha being murdered. Ah've never seen sich. Tha could make thiself ill."

While father looked on in a disinterested sort of way, Bess and I kept it up.

"A fine pickle," the farmer said, "Ah've not only had me dog robbed, Ah'm goin' t' lose me 'earin' as well." After that he stood there bewildered, opening and shutting his mouth. "Ah'll tell thi what Ah'll do: rather than 'avin' thee caterwaulin' like that, Ah'll give thee t' dog." He bent down to remove the collar.

Bess was with me in a flash. I put my arms around her and together we went on crying and shaking.

"'Tis been a bad day," the big man muttered as he left the house. "A very bad day," he said, still shuffling his feet. "Yo two have just wasted mah time."

The moment the door was closed, Bess ceased whining and licked my face and hands. She declared our victory by thumping her tail on the floor.

The man never returned, and Bess and I lived happily ever after. Well, almost. One winter's day an angry neighbour entered our house:

"Would ya remove yor dog from my kennel!" he demanded. "My own dog's in t' snow." Early in the morning, Bess had wandered down the street, found a warm kennel, tossed out its occupant, and taken possession.

Chapter XIX

A Grocer's Lad

At fourteen I'd come of age and felt I ought to make my own decisions. It was tacitly agreed with the Lathams that if I couldn't find a full-time job I'd continue to work for them.

Had times been better, I'd have had no difficulty in finding a job. I'd have joined father in the mills. There had always been a place in cotton textiles for cheap child labour. A child could easily be thrown out later on. But the depression was at its height and most of the mills were shut. Nor was there hope of becoming an apprentice to a plumber, or a carpenter, or a machinist, or a glazier, or a boilermaker, or a painter. They were all looking for work themselves. People were fighting over pick and shovel jobs.

The best thing I could find was to become a shop assistant to Charles Grimshaw.

Mr. Grimshaw owned a large grocery store in the wealthier part of town. He lived above the shop. Everything about the building was pretentious: it had pseudo-Tudor beams across the front; the entrance was flanked by hollow wooden pillars. Apart from himself, his wife and his daughter, there were two other assistants, Cyril and Arthur. The shop had a bakery, and was licensed to sell wines, beer and spirits. It also sold fresh fruit and vegetables. Its doors opened precisely at eight and closed at six - later on Saturdays. It catered only for the rich.

I was interviewed by Mr. Grimshaw at six one evening as the store was closing. I don't think I'd ever seen anybody who looked more like an eagle. Tall, gray, with closely clipped hair and mustache, Mr. Grimshaw had the eagle's ever-watchful, baleful eyes, and its strongly carved, beak-like nose. I waited at the shop door for at least thirty minutes until he had finished struggling with a large ham. Having wiped his hands thoroughly on a towel, he recognized my existence and came over to question me.

"What's your name?"

"William Woodruff."

"Where do you live?"

"Livingston Road."

Mr. Grimshaw paused. "What does your father do?"

"He's a weaver, but he's out of work."

"How many of you in the family?"

The questions went on and on. They were sharp and precise. There was no end to what he asked. After I had finally assured him that I was a God-fearing boy, he took me on at ten shillings a week. Of the sum, I received tenpence from my parents. The rest was needed at home. Mr. Grimshaw's last words before dismissing me were: "Watch thi P's and Q's and tha'll be aw reet. Don't sing in t' shop and don't whistle. Give me trouble, and tha're out on thi ear. Remember," he warned, "jobs these days are not two-a-penny."

The next day I stood with the other two assistants Cyril and Arthur waiting for Mr. Grimshaw. On the dot of eight, which he checked with his watch, Mr. Grimshaw emerged from the house and entered the store. He looked as sharp as a razor. He wore a stiff, stand-up collar, a well-pressed gray suit, a gold watch chain across his ample chest, and highly polished shoes. We assistants froze into place holding out our hands, palm up, for inspection. Nobody talked until the inspection was done. For a moment or two, watch still in hand, he looked around,

298

taking everything in.   After which he repeated his Five
Commandments, which I soon knew by heart: work hard; be
humble; don't waste; be punctual; be clean. Then he snapped
the watch lid to with an air of finality.

The snapping of the lid was the signal for everyone to start
work. Until the shop shut at six in the evening, Mr. Grimshaw
didn't spare himself or others. I never saw him waste a moment.
I never knew anyone as hard-working or as efficient as he.

It didn't take me long to realize that there was nothing
anyone could teach Grimshaw about groceries; nothing anyone
could do, as far as I could see, to improve the Grimshaw
business. He had spent his working life getting everything
right. He had built his business up from nothing. He knew
every nook and cranny of the store. Better still, he had a first-
class mind for figures. He could trace every penny that came
and went. No wholesaler dared to take advantage of him. He
could smell a rotten basket of fruit at ten yards. No one
embroidered accounts when he was about.

As a salesman, he had no match. Ticklish customers were his
specialty. He'd have them eating out of his hand in no time.
He was a marvel on the telephone. People had to be sharp or
he'd sell them the shop. He never lost a sale. I think he felt an
obligation to succeed. I once heard him sell a number of chests
of tea to a customer who came into the store looking for
something for his poor relatives for Christmas. Grimshaw was
poetic. "Why sir," he said, "in the circumstances, I can think of
no better Christmas present than a chest of tea. Think of the
cheer it will bring. Think with what gratitude they will
remember you daily..." He was as good at selling tea as anything
else. I learned later that there was a high profit on tea.

One day I heard him sounding off to one of his customers
about the strikes going on in cottons. "They're spoiled, that's
what they are. Yes, sir, downright spoiled. It's not good for the
likes of them to be molly-coddled. Only makes them lazy and
ungrateful. They'll ruin any business. They'll ruin the country
with their demands. Having got a penny, they want a pound.
If you don't keep them down, you won't get a thing done. I
know them - they have to be threatened: hunger in this world,
hellfire in the next. Strikes can't take the place of hard work and

the certainty of the Lord. Shoot 'em," was Mr. Grimshaw's final word on the matter. He said these things with such heat that I expected flames to shoot out of his mouth. "Any man who strikes on me goes through the door."

It was taken for granted from the day I arrived that the other assistants, and members of the family, would be free to take their frustrations out on me. "Billy, give a hand!" "Billy, why are you standing there?" "Billy, you're loafing." "Billy, look what a mess you've made!" "Billy, you'll never learn." "Billy, it's a wonder we pay you." Every crisis was solved, every problem explained, by somebody bawling at me.

Mildred, Grimshaw's daughter - a large woman who lacked all the aggressive traits of her father - was the exception. She didn't bully me. Often she defended me from her parents. She taught me to be silent. In the early days when I was just about to get my blood up at Grimshaw and answer him back, I'd catch sight of her face. "No!" she'd warn me with her lips and eyes and a slight shake of the head. She later told me that I'd got the job because I came from Livingston Road.

Mildred was in love with the Reverend Black who lived a street away. For such a young man, Mr. Black had unusually gaunt eyes. He used to carry a tin round with him in which he collected donations for foreign missions. "Don't forget the poor souls of the West Indies," he'd say, shaking the can vigorously under someone's nose. I'm sure there was no connection between his name and his avidity to save black souls. The look he used to give me suggested that white souls were boring and beyond redemption anyway. Mildred put one of his collection cans on the counter, but her father removed it. "Nay, nay, mustn't mix religion and business."

I think Mildred's love affair made her brood. I'd catch her, elbows on the till, lost in thought. On occasions, I had to cough to make my presence known. The only odd thing about Mildred was the way she paid us from the till on a Friday night. It was like receiving communion. She raised the money before our eyes before placing it in our eager hands. When everybody else had left, she slipped me a package of bacon ends and other scraps for my family. "Faith, hope and charity," she said, emphasizing the charity. "Hide it under your jacket, Billy," she cautioned, with an eye out for her father.

Mildred was kind to Bess, who followed our movements from across the road. Occasionally she slipped out with a bone. They were conspirators together. I cannot imagine how these things escaped her father's notice, especially as he was always going on about how businesses failed because people didn't watch the little things.

"Take care of the pence," he kept saying to anybody who would listen, "and the pounds will take care of themselves." He was always shooting off remarks such as "A stitch in time saves nine," or "Penny-wise and pound-foolish..."

"Oh father," Mildred would respond, "you are a one. You'll wear yourself out."

Mildred had a sister, Nancy, who was married to the Reverend Spick, a bright-eyed, vigorous young curate, with a scrubbed face, who seemed to be running a race. Nancy was not like Mildred, loving and warm. Despite her shapeless dress and footwear, she was imperious. Whenever she visited the shop she threw me a stiff, "And how do you do?" to which I replied, "Quite nicely, thank you." Her husband didn't waste time on me. A half nod or an oblique glance was the best I ever got out of him. The shop assistants never called the Reverend Spick anything else but 'Spick and Span.'

It was while I was at Grimshaw's that the notorious Rector of Stiffkey in East Anglia, the Reverend H.F. Davidson, was defrocked. There had been a sexual scandal, following which the rector, with an apparent disregard for doctrinal orthodoxy or the interests of the Church of England, proceeded to air his differences with the church in public. His case was heard before the Privy Council. The press wrote editorials about him under the heading "The Stiffkey Scandal." Questions were asked in the House of Commons, his picture was in all the papers, his church was inundated by a multitude of sightseers who came by special buses from neighbouring towns. When he climbed into the pulpit the church was packed to the nave, and hundreds of men and women stood outside.

Once defrocked, the rector fell on hard times. To make ends meet, he finished up sitting in a barrel on the fairground at

Blackpool, side by side with an exhibition of performing fleas, where people peeped at him through a hole at twopence a go. It was all in the papers and it didn't do the Church of England any good. Mildred, her sister Nancy and the reverends Spick and Black were appalled at the rector's conduct. Mildred shook her head sadly when the unhappy details of the rector's broken life were related to her - not without certain relish - by a customer in the shop. "Oh dear," Mildred said, "those who test the Lord's patience do so at their peril." (The peril proved to be more serious than Mildred realized. In 1937 the ex-rector appeared as a modern Daniel in a lion's cage at Skegness Amusement Park, where he was mauled to death.)

I didn't like Mrs. Grimshaw. She was a small woman with a hard face, deep gray eyes and a prominent nose. There was a crushed look about her. She usually wore a black blouse with a white lace collar, a string of coloured beads, and a thick black skirt. She had an unpleasant high-pitched voice, and croaked and wheezed all the time. A large pair of scissors dangled from her waist. I never saw her use them. Except when customers entered the store, when she suddenly became all smiles and friendliness, Mrs. Grimshaw sat on her stool like a molting hen. She was stiff with me and the other shop assistants.

Of the other two assistants, Arthur and Cyril, I liked Arthur best. Several years my senior, Arthur was a handsome fellow with roguish gray eyes and thick, wavy black hair parted down the middle. He had the best teeth in the shop when he laughed. He was a born mimic, and loved to impersonate the Reverend Black shaking his collection can for the foreign missions.

Nobody got the better of Arthur, he had an answer for everything. Nobody guarded his flanks like he did. Nobody could handle the butter paddles or cut bacon like him. He'd get through a job in no time. "I gave it a lick and a promise," he'd say. It amazed me the way he made excuses for jobs not done.

Like his boss, Arthur could mold the customers like clay. Difficult customers who were forever tasting the cheese, or saying that the bacon had been cut too thick, were his speciality. He had them smiling in no time. No trouble at all. Only Mrs. Grimshaw saw through him. She was cool toward him. Yet women customers preferred him to anybody else. Grimshaw would have sacked him long ago had Arthur not been useful.

I ate my lunch with Arthur in the dimly-lit, dank cellar under the shop floor. It was the only room in the building where Mr. Grimshaw did not have a peep-hole. For the thirty minutes lunch break we sat on soap boxes down there. We had to sit, the ceiling was too low to stand. Throughout lunch, Arthur was always laughing. He took nothing and nobody seriously.

What astonished me was how well he ate. After cheese sandwiches, he ate chocolate, fresh fruit and cake, which he fished out of a giant pocket at the front of his black apron. He'd then lie back and blow rings from an expensive cigarette. While he smoked, I ate what was left.

One day I asked him how he could afford to eat as he did. For a moment or two he looked at me quizzically. Then he beckoned me over and placed his lips against my ear. "Ye 'elps yerself, that's 'ow," he whispered, giving me a sly wink.

"But that's ..." I began.

"Tommyrot!" He laughed uproariously at the effect his words had had upon me.

I was too shocked to know what to say, especially as for weeks now I'd been sharing the spoils. Good God, I'd been eating stolen goods! My mouth went dry.

"Cut yer throat if ya tell," Arthur warned in a low voice, while he held me with his eyes.

Not knowing what to say, I laughed nervously. I suddenly realized that I was in danger of losing my job. I was scared.

I came to the conclusion that Arthur's philosophy was simple: it was for the poor to rob the rich.

"Not 'alf," was his only comment when I asked him.

Mr. Grimshaw's chief assistant, Cyril, was a different fish. I couldn't stick him. He seemed to me to be full of malice and calculation. He had a funny little face, which he hid behind large spectacles. He had black eyes and black hair. At first I feared him as much as I feared Mr. Grimshaw. He pushed and shoved me about as if I were a piece of merchandise. He hated Bess. He would have stopped Mildred feeding her if he could. What put me off more than anything else, were his damp, fishy hands.

Cyril had no real skills, other than monumental servility. I think Grimshaw had bullied him for so long that there was nothing left. He must have been paid a pittance. One day, when Cyril was away at a relative's funeral, I was sent by Mr. Grimshaw to deliver a message to Cyril's father who lived in the woods on the outskirts of town. I was astonished how poorly they lived. I lived in a substantial house in Livingston Road, all Cyril had was a leaking wooden hut and a bicycle.

His father was terrified that his son might lose what little income they had. A white-haired, bent old man, he clutched my hand on parting. "Look after my Cyril," he begged. "Tell Mr. Grimshaw that Cyril's a hard worker." He said much more about the merits of his Cyril, while moving bowls around to catch the rain coming through the roof.

Instead of fearing him, I came to pity Cyril. I knew from her eyes that Mildred felt the same. When he was not calling out: "Yes, Mr. Grimshaw. No, Mr. Grimshaw. Right away, Mr. Grimshaw," he was worrying himself to death what on earth he would do if Grimshaw fired him. There were simply no other jobs to be had. Terrified at the thought, he clung to Grimshaw as a drowning man clings to a raft. His wildest dream was to marry Mildred and inherit the business.

Arthur roared with laughter when I told him of Cyril's hallucination. He kept slapping his thighs as if it was the funniest thing he'd ever heard.

I happened to enter the shop one day at the moment that Grimshaw was sacking Arthur. He must have caught him helping himself. Or perhaps Cyril, who looked oilier than ever, had betrayed him. The only thing that surprised me was that Grimshaw had not got on to Arthur's pilfering sooner. "There's a week's wages," Grimshaw snapped. "Now get out!" Arthur was his usual cool self. He didn't seem rattled, not even when he was being fired. He knew from the shocked look on my face that I'd had nothing to do with it. "Ta, Ta! Woody," he said as he sauntered off, hands in pockets, trying to look casual. He whistled as he left. That takes some doing when you've just been sacked. I never saw or heard of him again.

Most of the time while I was working for Mr. Grimshaw, I was too busy to worry about other people's troubles. My day began when Mildred let me into the store at seven-forty-five. My first job was to carry out the trash and ashes from the house and the store from the day before. I then carried innumerable buckets of coal from the cellar up several flights of stairs to the rooms above. I also lit the fire in the living room behind the shop. The room was richly carpeted. Almost covering a wall was a glass cupboard containing fine china and silverware. There were double curtains on the windows and a clock on the mantelpiece faced with black marble.

In winter my progress was speeded up by shouts from the rooms above. When the grates were cleaned and the fires lighted - the so-called house cleaning woman-cum-cook arrived later - I carried wood, coal and flour to the bakery. I learned not to stand about in the bakery talking to the cook. One morning when we were chattering away, a small wooden door slid back and Mr. Grimshaw's eagle head appeared. "I'm not paying you two to stand there gassing," he threw at us.

Having finished the house chores, I swept the shop, first sprinkling the splintery floor with used tea leaves. Then I washed the shop windows and the pavement in front of the store. That done, I turned to my day's work, which was to deliver groceries. Cyril and Arthur had been round the district on bicycles earlier taking orders. I was never allowed to serve behind the counter.

I delivered Mr. Grimshaw's groceries from a two-wheeled hand-cart - a large tray on enormous iron-clad wheels - which I pushed and pulled through the streets. On both sides of the cart were advertisements of Mr. Grimshaw's merchandise. The cart had a tarpaulin cover in case of rain. My only cover was a fustian cap pulled well down and a muffler wrapped round my neck. I could get wet, the groceries never. I also had an oil lamp, which I used at night.

On the outward journeys, in order to keep my eye on the stacked boxes before me, I pushed the cart. Returning to the shop, I ran in front between the shafts like a donkey. Some passers-by asked me if I was a donkey. I doubt if a donkey could have handled some of the heavy loads. There were times when

Cyril and Arthur had to help me make a wobbly start down the cobbled street. The pushing and pulling left me stiff and sore, but there was nothing like it for developing the back and shoulder muscles.

Wet or fine, I went out. Once on the road, Bess joined me. Rain, it seemed, was an almost permanent condition. I became accustomed to all kinds: dreary rain, slanting rain, driving rain; viciously cold rain that beat against my face, blinding me until I yielded; rain that soaked me to the skin, and oozed in my clogs; rain that on occasions I found exhilarating and sang to.

Often the wind held me up, trying to drive me back. I became expert at waiting until the gust had passed and then pushed on. When sleet and snow hit me, I held my head to one side. Bess was smarter; she ran along underneath the cart. Sometimes in winter a lighted tram would pull alongside us and the passengers would look lazily down at the strange apparition on the road. Bess and I were careful to yield to all other vehicles. We were at the bottom of the heap; nobody gave way to us.

It didn't take me long to realize that Mr. Grimshaw's customers were living off the fat of the land. It was the same with their houses and their gardens. Everything they had was solid and prosperous. It puzzled me that while my family were fighting to make ends meet, others were eating sides of bacon, legs of lamb, whole hams, quantities of fish, eggs, milk, fruit including fresh grapes, vegetables, drink, fresh bread, pies, confectionery and whole tins of Peak Frean biscuits. It didn't seem fair. The bad times meant self-denial for the workers, self-indulgence for the rich.

I was not alone in thinking thus. One day a gang of locked-out weavers stopped me and, despite my protests, began to rummage through my boxes. Bess barked at them and ran between their legs, threatening to bite. I had trouble keeping her down.

"Just look at this," they shouted as they uncovered one choice item after another. "Pigs at trough! Greedy buggers!" Then they turned on me. "What kind of a lackey are you? Pandering to the gluttony of the rich. Tha working class and tha ought to be shamed."

Fortunately the demonstrators confined their anger to words. They didn't steal anything. After being pushed and shoved I was allowed to go my way. One of them shouted after me: "Tha'll get nowt but crumbs from t' rich man's table."

True, I thought as I went along. At ten shillings a week that's all I was getting. But to anyone who was hungry, the crumbs from Mr. Grimshaw's table were worth having. For my family they were indispensable. It was the crumbs from the rich men's tables that kept Bess and me going. There was hardly a house where the servants didn't feed us. They were working-class people speaking my dialect. They knew that there were a lot of hungry people about. I wouldn't be pushing a cart through the streets in the pouring rain if I wasn't poor. Besides, I was only fourteen and I think they felt for me.

"Tha must sit thiself down, lad," they said, "and have a bite; tha looks clemmed." Servants and maids came cheap and were everywhere. There were maids dressed in starched white, black, or brown; maids with fine aprons and pretty caps perched on their heads; maids with a rich Irish brogue.

And so, with a roaring fire in the grate and the pots spitting, Bess and I sat among the maids in the kitchens, and tasted the food we'd just delivered before the rich could get to it. Many's the piece of hot pie or tart I had; many's the scrap that Bess got. There were so many of us eating the food downstairs that I wondered if there'd be any left to go upstairs.

During the year I worked at Grimshaw's the servants of the rich were my guardian angels. I couldn't have survived without them. They not only fed me and my dog, and dried my wet clothes before the great kitchen fires - they even provided me with cast-off clothing - they also covered up for me if I accidentally damaged some of Grimshaw's goods. They were so kind to me that I would stay in the kitchens too long. Realizing that I was late, I raced back to the shop like a mad horse, dragging the empty, bouncing, clattering cart over the cobble stones after me. Bess led, barking. Sure enough, as we approached the shop, I caught sight of Grimshaw waiting for me on the sidewalk, red in the face, watch in hand. "Wher's ta bin?" he snapped.

THE ROAD TO NAB END

One of my special guardian angels was a sweet old lady called Mrs. Sand who lived in a large, gabled house surrounded by trees. She was a tiny, gray creature, with gray eyes, and a long gray dress. I sometimes thought she was a ghost. The only other occupant was her sick husband who lay upstairs, making all kinds of choking noises. When he needed something he rang a bell. The moment the bell rang, Mrs. Sand dropped what she was doing and rushed upstairs, calling out to her husband as she went. I couldn't understand why she had to keep running upstairs when there were so many empty rooms downstairs.

Mrs. Sand's loneliness was so great that I could touch it. She welcomed our arrival by feeding Bess. Then she sat and drank tea with me while telling me all the family business. The way the words came pouring out, I wondered if she had anyone else to talk to. In all my visits, I saw no one else entering or leaving the house, not even a gardener, or a maid, or a physician. Mrs. Sand told me how her son's wild life had caused her husband to have a stroke. Somehow the boy had got hold of their money and spent it on gambling and women and drink. They hadn't seen or heard of him since her husband's collapse. He had dropped out of their lives.

"Wouldn't it be awful," she said to me one day, talking more to herself than to me, "if he were to die in some God-forsaken place with no one to comfort him?"

"Yes," I said, "it would."

"He is our only child, you know."

She must have said this a dozen times.

Her troubles did not seem to have undermined Mrs. Sand's faith in God's goodness.

The tears rising freshly in her eyes, she vowed not to leave the bell-ringer as long as he lived. She said it as if I'd made the suggestion, or she was beating back a wrong thought. Staring through her window at the garden, she wistfully talked of the coming of spring.

In return, I told her all about the worlds I intended to conquer. I told her that I was thinking about getting a big job in Manchester or London. I also told her that grandmother Bridget had once urged me to go to America.

"Yes, yes, you must," Mrs. Sand encouraged me. "You must go at once. How exciting," she exclaimed, jumping up. "How I envy you."

And then, suddenly realizing that Grimshaw was waiting, I drank my tea, swallowed my cake, and rushed off.

When Christmas came she asked me in a faltering voice to drink a toast with her. There was a miniature fir tree on the table. The two small glasses were ready. She insisted on pouring the drink, though I noticed how badly her hand shook.

"Merry Christmas," I said, raising my glass and bowing slightly.

"Merry Christmas," she answered smiling, "and may all your dreams come true."

I stood in silence, not knowing what to say.

———◇———

It was while I was working for Grimshaw that I fell in love with Betty Weatherby, the daughter of one of Grimshaw's customers. Of course, it was ridiculous. One can't have a fourteen year-old errand boy running off with a manufacturer's daughter. But nobody intended it that way. It was as much of a surprise to me as it was to everybody else, including Bess, who sat and stared at me as if I'd gone out of my mind.

It began one night at the town's indoor swimming pool where all the schools were competing. I'd learned to swim in that pool. The first time I let go of one side of the pool in the deep end and struggled to the other side, I nearly drowned. After that swimming became an obsession.

The meeting was packed and noisy. The shouting in the confined space was deafening. I was swimming for St. Philip's. I'd taken up my job at Grimshaw's a couple of weeks earlier but I was still officially allowed to compete. I was pitted against the best in the town. Luck had brought me through several heats to the finals for my age group. Now I faced the ultimate test.

"Come on Woody," my supporters yelled. "You can do it."

As I stood poised, waiting for the starter's gun, I suddenly made up my mind to win. I felt a sudden urge to come out on top. It was a funny feeling that came from inside like a flash of anger. It said: "You've got to win."

At the crack of the gun, I and five others dived in. Dimly, I heard the thunder of voices. In the green, shimmering water I saw the black line on the bottom snaking away in front of me. To my left was another boy; at first I was level with his thighs, then he drew ahead and I caught glimpses of his feet. Gasping for breath, I chased after him.

He was still leading when we turned for the eighth and last lap; the other swimmers had fallen behind. With my lungs bursting, I ordered my arms and legs to go faster. I strained until I was level with the other fellow's head. I heard the constant thump of his arms and legs. I wondered if I had strayed out of my lane. With one last frantic effort I hit the wall. When one of the judges touched me on the shoulder, I knew I'd won. I was more exhausted than elated.

The girl's final heat for my age group followed immediately. A short, small-waisted, dark-haired girl was the winner. I had no idea who she was. Together we stood in our dripping swimsuits before the judges to receive our silver medals. Real silver. The town's poverty was forgotten. Amid all the shouting, she and I stole side-long glances. I noticed the full cheeks, the well-shaped mouth and the rounded chin. She gave me the warmest smile. I smiled back. She smiled again. It was enough to make my face burn - enough to make me forget all about the judges and the medal around my neck.

While I wouldn't have dreamt of talking to her, I tried to follow her with my eyes after we left the dais. She was soon lost in the crowd. My friends pressed around me to see my medal; I dressed in a daze.

I slept badly that night. I didn't know what had come over me. I felt pierced from top to bottom. Rosie Gill, or Annie Morgan, or any of the other girls I'd met had never affected me like that. The next day I got up without any appetite.

Several days later, while delivering Grimshaw's groceries, I was amazed to see the same girl in a blue school uniform entering the Weatherby's driveway. Ahead of us lay the Weatherby mansion, standing among wide lawns and park-like shrubs. I was too flabbergasted to know what to do. I didn't want to bump into her; not pushing a handcart.

Instead of yielding to my immediate reaction, which was to flee, I slowed down and entered the driveway well behind her. As she walked ahead of me, crunching the gravel beneath her feet, her doe-like body looked lovelier than ever. I hoped she wouldn't turn round. I think Bess knew what was going on, for she ran to the girl, wagging her tail, whining. The girl petted the dog but ignored me. Then she skipped through the front door. Shamefaced, Bess and I went round the back.

In a round-about way I asked Mrs. Pegg, the head cook at Weatherby's, who the girl was.

She stopped what she was doing and looked at me curiously. "Tha not gettin' any fancy ideas in thi 'ead, ar' ta?" she asked jovially.

"Oh no, Mrs. Pegg," I protested, blushing.

"Tha'd better not, lad. That's Betty, the apple of Mr. Weatherby's eye. Mustn't throw thi cap at 'er."

"Oh no, Mrs. Pegg," I said. "Ah've got some gumption."

All the kitchen hands laughed.

A week later, when Bess and I were leaving the Weatherby's drive, the same girl stepped out from behind the small, open pavilion that stood at the edge of the tennis court. She was wearing her school uniform, but was without hat. Her silky black hair was blowing in the wind. I reddened, she smiled. Bess ran to her, wagging her tail.

"I just wanted to congratulate you on your win at the swim meet," she said in a delightful voice. "I thought you were pretty good."

"Well, thanks," I stammered. I felt my face redden. "You were pretty good yourself."

She gave the gayest laugh and petted Bess. I saw the first blush on her face. How could anyone have such pretty, bright brown eyes," I wondered.

Every week after that, wet or fine, I met Betty Weatherby in the pavilion by the tennis court. For me, the whole week was simply the prelude to our meeting. I couldn't get her out of my head. My feelings went from utter joy, to utter sorrow, to utter joy again. It's a wonder my nerves stood up to it. I could not conceal my delight each time we met. Nor could she. She always ran toward me, arms outstretched, her face shining with delight and happiness.

With the handcart parked next to the pavilion out of sight of the house, Betty and I entered an imaginary world. It was a world without past or future, containing only the two of us. Holding each other's hands, we were deaf, blind and dumb to everything except ourselves. Instead of talking about my job, or about Grimshaw, or about her family or mine, we teased each other light-heartedly. We lived only to be together.

The time came when I told Betty that I loved her. I followed this declaration by giving her an ill-contrived peck on the cheek. To my astonishment, she responded not by pecking me back again, but by nibbling my ear. For some odd reason, she became obsessed with my ears. But surely, ears are a small price to pay for boundless delight. As the weeks passed, we began to love each other without reservation. We would have loved each other with even greater abandon had we known what was coming.

The Weatherby's housekeeper, Mrs. Shaw, was our undoing. I'd seen her in the kitchen once. She had cold, rebuking eyes and a tight mouth. She had talked as if she was a cut above the rest. Her tall, thin body, with its funny little head sitting ill on her neck, suddenly appeared at the entrance of the pavilion where Betty and I were rolling about on the tennis nets. She was scowling. Bess had not warned us of her approach.

"Betty!" Mrs. Shaw shrieked, as if Betty's delirious eating of my ears was the work of the devil. "Betty! I am surprised at you."

She was not half as surprised as we were. Suddenly, Bess came bounding up, growling.

"Young man," Mrs. Shaw pierced me, "you will take yourself and your dog off Mr. Weatherby's property." She looked grim enough to throw me, my cart and my dog through the gate.

Betty and I squeezed hands. Then, head down, lips trembling, red-faced, she went with Mrs. Shaw up the drive. Dazed, I made my way back to Grimshaw's. Bess ran alongside, wearing a contrite look.

"Tha some use," I scolded her. "Tha's got us into real trouble, tha 'as." She knew she'd let us down, she ambled along, her tail tucked in.

Mrs. Shaw must have telephoned Grimshaw. He was waiting for me outside the shop. Even though there were customers about, he didn't hesitate to have it out with me.

"Tha 'ere to deliver groceries," he told me in a biting tone, "not to go courtin'. Tha deserves to be sacked." He really got himself worked up. The veins on his forehead protruded. I stood there between the shafts, with Bess cowering at my feet. He went on and on. "If tha must go courtin'," he stamped his foot, "go in thi own time, not at my expense."

I was too dazed to make any response. For all the impact his ranting and raving had upon me, he might as well have blown smoke. I was more fascinated with the globule of sweat hanging from the tip of his nose. Had he run me through with a sword, I wouldn't have cared. My thoughts were still with Betty, romping on the tennis nets. All I cared about was seeing her again.

The next week, when I pushed my cart up the Weatherby's drive, Betty was not there. I thought I'd die. I tried to pump Mrs. Pegg in the kitchen, but she kept a tight tongue. She'd obviously had orders. A week or so later, while watching the other servants closely, she whispered that Betty had been sent to a boarding school outside London. No one seemed to know where the school was. The news made me sick for days. I became convinced that I was going to die. Bess seemed to sense my feeling of complete hopelessness. She rubbed her nose against my hand, trying to gain attention.

Mrs. Pegg shared my sorrow. Every time I entered the kitchen she looked at me and sighed. "Tha just too young to 'ave anything in t' 'ead," she said to me one day. "Tha'll 'ave to learn that life can be very troublesome." She then relieved her frustration by pounding a lump of dough. Later, in great secrecy, she undertook to get a note from me to Betty. "They'd have me 'ead if they knew."

I returned the same day with my letter. I told Betty that I was dying without her; that I loved her; and that I'd wait for her for ever. I also gave her my address. For weeks after that, Bess and

I used to trail the postman through the streets to see if he had a letter for me. Nothing came. "Tha're out of luck, they've taken thi letter out of t' post at t' other end," Mrs. Pegg concluded after some reflection. "Tha'll have to wait," she counselled. "Others do. Tha not t' only one round 'ere with a broken 'eart."

———◄◊►———

It was about the time of Betty's departure that tragedy overtook the Grimshaws. I arrived one morning to find the shop in darkness. Grimshaw had had a stroke in the night, and was paralyzed down his left side. His speech and hearing had been affected. Although I continued to carry coal for the fires upstairs, he never spoke to me again. He lay on his bed, his face twisted beyond recognition, his ugly, shrunken body like half a sack of flour on the counterpane. To catch his saliva a towel lay under his chin. One morning while I was sweeping the hearth, the sack-like figure flapped its hands at me and grunted. I dropped the hand brush and fled in horror.

For the business, hard times followed. The family did their best, but, without Grimshaw, the shop was a ship without a rudder. Wrong accounts were sent out. Some wholesalers took advantage of Mildred and her mother. The women were just not as sharp. Cyril used the occasion to worm his way into the family business, but he didn't have the brains to help. Without Grimshaw on his back, he was at a loss to know what to do.

Grimshaw knew that his business was dying. He made heroic, if futile, efforts to get out of bed. One day he managed it. Mrs. Grimshaw, Mildred and Cyril dressed him and dragged him downstairs as far as the shop floor. Held upright, he managed to get across the threshold. After each step he paused to gain strength for the next. For a few moments he stood in the shop shaking, his hands fluttering, his wild, bloodshot eyes taking everything in. What he saw must not have pleased him, for his twisted face underwent further contortion. Gasping for breath, he began to make unfriendly, unintelligible noises. Then he wobbled around and turned his back on the store. With Cyril and Mildred lifting his stricken leg at every step, he was slowly dragged back up the stairs.

The final straw for Grimshaw was to fall into the hands of a charlatan couple from Manchester who pretended to be physicians. There had been some difference of opinion between Mrs. Grimshaw and the family doctor, as a result of which he was passed over. Alas, in the care of the Manchester couple, Grimshaw's condition became worse. Mrs. Grimshaw suspected nothing until the police came to the shop. By the time a warrant had been issued for their arrest, the birds had flown. Everyone was dumbfounded when the story got around. Imagine Grimshaw being hoodwinked like that! It put Mrs. Grimshaw in a towering rage.

The shock of being diddled was too much for the old man. I heard Mrs. Grimshaw tell a customer how he'd sighed deep enough to break his heart. Mercifully, three days later, he had a second stroke and died. We put black ribbons on the shop door and on my cart. Two days later he was buried. Wearing black armbands, Cyril and I went to the funeral. It was a bitter day. The wholesalers and most of the customers had sent flowers. There was a mountain of them. I was too busy pushing cartloads of wreaths from the shop to the cemetery to attend the church service. I carried the flowers through a great crowd to the edge of the grave.

In deepest mourning, Mildred, Nancy, Mrs. Grimshaw and the Reverend Black, stood by the graveside. The Reverend Spick read the funeral service for his father-in-law. It was the usual one about 'the resurrection and the life.' I was at the back of the crowd and heard only snatches. He spoke of my boss as a father, as a merchant, as a citizen and as a God-fearing, church-going man. He said he was convinced that Mr. Grimshaw was already enjoying his heavenly reward. We were all the poorer for his passing.

I must confess that despite the Reverend Spick's moving oration, my thoughts were not so much concerned with the whereabouts of Mr. Grimshaw's soul as with the whereabouts of Betty Weatherby.

My stay at Grimshaw's did not long outlast the death of my employer. One day, on turning a corner with a heavily laden cart, Bess and I ran slap-bang into another workers' demonstration. There were more of them this time. They were led by a man beating a drum. It struck a sinister note. A sea of hungry faces approached me, some of which I remembered from my earlier encounter. Inwardly, I groaned. They marched straight at me with their banner emblazoned with the words: WORKERS OF THE WORLD UNITE! No one else was about. The policeman who occasionally trudged along at the side of demonstrators was absent.

"Would you believe it," somebody bawled, "he's still serving the bloody rich."

"Bloody lackey."

"Disgrace to his class, that's wot 'e is."

Barking loudly, Bess ran from me to the men.

In panic, I tried to turn the cart round, but someone grabbed one of the wheels. Several of my boxes fell over. As I reached down to secure them, a demonstrator wearing a long, black coat seized me by the collar in a violent manner. Bess attacked him; someone kicked her off. Another worker made a menace of striking me with the back of his hand.

The crowd shouted encouragement. "Why should he help them to eat while we go hungry?"

Shaking off the man who held me by the collar, I tried to stop the pillaging of the groceries.

"Leave bloody stuff alone," I bawled. I was hotted up by now and ready for a fight; so was Bess. Realizing that if I didn't escape there would not be a thing left, I clutched the shafts, put down my head and charged. "Fetch them, Bess!" I shouted.

The cart hit several bodies as I fought to break the encircling ring. My clogs stomping the cobbles, I hurled myself forward again and again. With Bess nipping their heels, the line began to give way. To my great relief, I broke through the crowd and began to run down a steep hill. Several of the men came after me. I heard their footsteps behind me.

Panting and crying, with Bess at my side, I rattled away faster and faster. I ran so fast that I could neither guide nor stop the cart. I knew that if I didn't let go, it would drag me along the ground. With a cry of despair, I let go.

Transfixed, I watched the cart lurch away from me, stand on its end and then flip over, wheels spinning in the air. Groceries flew in all directions. Trickles of vinegar, wine, milk, flour, eggs and hot rhubarb pie began to ooze into the gutter. My heart sank into my clogs.

With several of the demonstrators, I ran to see what might be salvaged. Together, we got the cart back onto its wheels. Helpless, I looked at the pile of food lying on the ground. It was a terrible, chilling sight. There were pickles and jam and broken glass everywhere. With Bess barking furiously, I stood there staring at the mess, not knowing what to say or do.

By the time I recovered my wits, the men were already helping themselves. They were like locusts. Hungrily, they rummaged through the packages. Whatever could be eaten, was eaten on the spot; the rest was carried off. In no time, all that was worth taking had gone. I was too bruised and shaken to intervene.

Distraught, I watched the crowd line up again in a quiet and orderly manner, raise their banner against the wind, beat their drum, and march off up the hill eating as they went. Boom ! Boom ! went the drum. With my heart thumping, I sat in the gutter wondering what to do next. Bess sat beside me, whining and licking her wounds. Without really intending to, I broke into a passion of crying. I wished that the earth might open at my feet. "Oh Bess," I sobbed, throwing my arms around her neck, "what are we going to do?"

Eventually I got as much of the broken glass off the road as I could. Then I threw the empty boxes back into the cart and, with a silent, downcast Bess, slowly made my way back to the shop where, with Cyril listening to every word, I told Mrs. Grimshaw what had happened. Clutching at the beads around her neck, she nearly choked. Her face became contorted. In her croaking voice, she sacked me on the spot. Not far from tears, I went home and announced to the family that my ten shillings had just been stopped. Ten shillings was a small sum, but it was the only earnings coming into our house. The rest of the family had been sitting about waiting for work for ages. My ten shillings and Mildred's bacon scraps had been an indispensable part of our welfare. The loss of that money, and those scraps, worsened an already desperate situation.

A few days later I had a note from Mildred Grimshaw, which made me feel better. She was sorry for what had happened. She asked me to go to Lady Fielden's estate on the edge of town where I might get a job as an assistant gardener. She had spoken for me. Lady Fielden, I knew, was one of the town's richest widows. I wasted no time in getting there. I arrived breathless. I simply had to get this job.

The house itself was a beautiful place surrounded with wrought-iron railings. Lilac trees and beds of peonies faced the street. I made my way through archways of roses, past an artificial rock garden and bright borders of flowers, to the back of the house. From there I was sent to the front.

To my surprise, it was not the head gardener but Lady Fielden herself who awaited me. Having been admitted to the house by a maid in starched white apron and pretty cap, I was ushered into a side room rich with tapestries and curious figurines. There I found a short, hard-faced woman in her seventies sitting perfectly upright on a high-backed chair. She was dressed in lace from head to foot. A skein of pearls was around her neck. She smelled faintly of lavender. She had an unusual amount of hair on both sides of her face and almost a beard on her chin. I put on my best smile, "I'm William Woodruff," I said.

"I know, child," she said stiffly. She then smoothed her dress while looking over her wire spectacles; her searching look went right through me.

"Sit there," she commanded, pointing to a chair opposite her. I did so quickly, but with a sinking feeling. I was intimidated by Lady Fielden. I felt that if I moved I might break one of her treasures.

Lady Fielden proceeded to question me. The way she pursed her lips told me that I was giving all the wrong answers.

"Which church does your family attend?" she asked finally.

"My people don't go to church," I said, attempting to smile.

She shook her head deprecatingly, while fingering her pearls. I shifted uncomfortably inside my clothes. I began to revolve my cap in my hands. From the stern look she gave me, I knew I'd said the wrong thing.

Curtly Lady Fielden made a dismissive gesture. "That will be all," she said. "I will write to you." I gave a stiff little nod. She never did write. Another gardener there told me later that I had failed the 'religious test.' I should have boasted membership of the Church of England, he said. Instead, I'd given her the impression that my family were heathens, which they were. She wasn't going to have any heathen touch her flowers.

The last thing I heard about Grimshaw's came from Mrs. Sand, whom I visited one day. She was delighted to see me again. I heard the bell still ringing upstairs. She told me that the errand boy who had replaced me had told her that Cyril had also left Grimshaw's. There'd been a storm between Mildred and Cyril and he'd been thrown out.

Weeks later, I saw a notice in the paper saying that Grimshaw's was up for sale.

Chapter XX

To Nab End

While I'd been earning my living, our neighbour, Mr. Peek, had been working at his book that would save the world. He was always on about it. The more talk in the papers about a world depression, the more time he spent in his study. "The workers don't know what's coming," he muttered darkly one day when we were talking about the growing problems of the cotton industry. My family didn't thank Mr. Peek for his warnings. Things were bad enough without listening to him.

Alas, Mr. Peek's gloomy predictions gradually came true. In the summer of 1929 the cotton industry took another nose dive. The spinners were locked out to enforce wage reductions. In 1930 the weavers were locked out to enforce the increase in the number of looms from two to six, or even eight. But that only affected father and the lockout was lifted. We breathed freely again for several weeks. One way or another, my family got along. We hung on for our dear lives to the house in Livingston Road.

In 1931, when stoppages and wage reductions became general, Mr. Peek's dire warnings could no longer be denied. By then there were three million people without a job, and perhaps a similar number under-employed. Most of my family were now out of work, working part time, or double shifts, or working for less. In late 1931 the industry reached a state of collapse. By 1932 Britain slipped into the depths of a world depression. At the workers' expense everything was done to keep the industry alive: wages were cut, the hours of work increased. For the same pay workers were forced to man six, even eight, instead of two or four looms. The fight against six and eight looms went on mill by mill, Todmorden and Burnley weavers leading the way. The workers could do nothing but surrender or fight back - and go hungry.

At the beginning of 1932 my family was surviving on little more than Gordon's dole and my ten shillings from Grimshaw's. When I got the sack that left us with Gordon's money only.

One week when Gordon went to pick up his dole, the lines outside the Labour Exchange were longer than ever. There were so many people standing about, it was like after a football match. It took him ages to push his way through the shabby, hungry-looking crowd and join one of the queues shuffling toward the counter. When he got there he was faced by an unfamiliar clerk.

"How t' be?" the clerk said.

"Nicely," Gordon lied, expecting to sign his name, take his money and push his way out again.

"I've got a job for thee," the clerk went on, shuffling some papers.

"Tha 'as?"

"Yes."

"Wher' is 't?"

"Cornwall."

"Where's Cornwall?" asked Gordon. "It sounds a long way."

"That it is. A very long way."

"What kind of painting is it?"

"It isn't painting."

"It isn't?"

"No."

"What is't then?"

"It's digging tin down a mine."

"Ah'm not a tin miner, Ah'm a painter."

"Does t' refuse to go to Cornwall?"

"Ah do."

"Then tha's just lost thee dole."

"Tha can't mean it." Gordon didn't just need the money; he needed it desperately.

"Aye, but I do. If tha not 'genuinely seeking work,' and obviously tha not, benefits have to be stopped."

Gordon returned to Livingston Road dumbfounded. He couldn't understand how anyone could be so mean. The fellow didn't even say he was sorry; he just stopped Gordon's dole and that was that. We wanted him to go and fight it out, but his pride wouldn't let him. For Gordon and Jenny it wasn't love on the dole, it was love without the dole.

Somehow or other, by pinching and scraping, by using up our joint savings, and by pawning whatever was left, we continued to pay for the furniture, and hang on to the house in Livingston Road. Mother was prepared to fight to the death to stay there. We went on living day by day, watching our resources dwindle, knowing that disaster threatened. As winter gave way to the spring of 1932, and spring to summer, we sat around for hours trying to come up with schemes to make a few shillings, or discover ways to spend less.

Armed with a sledgehammer, father earned a few pounds smashing looms that earlier he had tuned with all the skill of a piano-tuner. I watched him destroy his idols - some of them a hundred years old, and thanks to people like him, still in first-class condition. I cannot imagine what went through his head as he tossed the broken pieces through the open window. I think it took a lot of meaning out of his life. A hundred years earlier in Lancashire they'd hung people for smashing the first power looms. Now they paid them to do it.

Mother and my sisters did odd jobs like washing up and peeling potatoes for club dinners in town, and for the hotels. Gordon - now that his dole was stopped - for the shame of it, put on a false nose and mustache and carried a sandwich board on his shoulders through the streets advertising Harper's lunches and dinners. Harper's was the restaurant where Gordon and Jenny had had their wedding breakfast. He kept his eyes on the pavement as he walked along and he didn't try to make anybody laugh. I think they paid him twenty-five or thirty pennies a day, plus a bowl of soup. And that job didn't last long either. I added little to the kitty. I did some ditch-digging for the Town Council, but after several weeks that fell through.

So much for our income. As for our outgoings, after I'd been fired from Grimshaw's and my indispensable ten shillings had been lost, we fell behind on rent and furniture payments. We spent less and less on food. We got charity bread where we could; for the rest we went hungry. Stealing was never considered. The local Public Assistance Committee refused help on the grounds that we were 'living on a scale disproportionate to [our] position.' It was their way of saying that poor people do not live on Livingston Road. Bess and I didn't do badly because the Lathams fed us, as they would continue to do as long as I had need. Also, many were the parcels of food they sent home with me at night. For the shame of it, we revealed none of these things to our neighbours, the Peeks, or for that matter, to anybody else. Certainly not to old friends such as the Watkins, the Gills and the Morgans. They had troubles of their own.

With almost no money coming in, and everything going out, our resources continued to vanish before our eyes. Hanging on to Livingston Road was like trying to bale out a boat with an egg cup. As each member of my family was thrown off the dole, and we struggled to hang on to a house and a way of life that was obviously beyond our means, we found ourselves with no resources at all. No amount of paring and scheming could help us. Whatever funds we still had were sacrificed in the struggle. Even father's war medals and Jenny's wedding dress were pawned for food. We would have given up earlier had we not been used to a roller-coaster existence. We were hardened to it. But now our resources and wits were finally used up.

Meanwhile mother continued to postpone the inevitable. Time and again she'd find a way to get by. She was brilliant in fending off creditors. She had no trouble at all with the thin, insignificant men who came with fly-marked paper-files from the rental agency and the furniture store. She gave them a cup of tea and charmed them out through the door again. But they were the decent types who didn't want to hurt anybody. They were followed by the muscle men who knew exactly what was needed. They were impervious to mother's charms.

"Have you read your contract, Mrs. Woodruff?" the muscle men asked, knowing full well that she couldn't read. "It states clearly..."

"But we've nowhere to go," mother countered, fear in her eyes.

"That doesn't give you the right to occupy a large house rent free. The contract is quite clear and must be upheld."

"Even if it throws my family in the street?"

"The truth is harsh, Mrs. Woodruff, but it must be stated and upheld."

"We'd pay you tomorrow, if we had the money, you know that. We've always paid."

"Mrs. Woodruff, we've already lost six weeks' rent on this house. Others are prepared to pay a higher rent than the one you paid. They're waiting for you to get out. The papers have been signed. Do you want me to get the sack?"

"How long do we have?"

"Two weeks."

The muscle men from the furniture store didn't waste time talking. I came home to Livingston Road one day to find all the furniture gone. I found mother sitting on a stool, looking through the rain-washed windows. Streaks of snow marked the summit of Pendle Hill. The curtains (Jenny's curtains) had been drawn back. She didn't notice my coming. The muscle men must have caught her while she was washing her hair, for she wore a hand-towel wrapped round her head like a turban. Her head was lowered as if someone had struck her a blow. Tears streamed down her hollowed cheeks. I looked at her sad figure and thought how often she'd sung:

> I'm forever blowing bubbles, pretty bubbles in the air;
> Oh they fly so high, nearly reach the sky,
> Then, like my dreams, they fade and die.
> Fortune's always hiding. I've looked everywhere.
> I'm forever blowing bubbles, pretty bubbles in the air.

Poor Maggie, so many of her bubbles had burst. She had lost her father as a child; neglect had become her lot. The war had changed her man; the depression had ruined their livelihood. Tied to an industry of boom and bust, she'd lived on a precipice, always uncertain, fearful that our living might disappear altogether. Now the Livingston Road bubble - the best bubble of all - was to die too. No wonder she sat there looking totally vanquished.

I wept with her.

Two weeks later we put our scant possessions on a flatcart and, in the middle of the night, pushed it to a lodging house in Nab End. Out of shame we didn't want the neighbours on Livingston Road to see us go. I'd been avoiding Mr. Peek and Roger for days. I didn't want their sympathy. Now, when it came time to go, I couldn't face them. I didn't say good-bye. Yet I have never forgotten the man who shared his knowledge with me; I shall feel indebted to him forever.

The midnight flit from Griffin Street to Livingston Road had been a triumphal march. The journey through the streets to Nab End was like a funeral. We were all too miserable to talk. We'd been robbed of the only really decent living conditions we'd ever known. There wasn't one of us who didn't feel sad and shamed. "Who cares what people think," mother had said when we were rising. I knew in my heart that she cared deeply what people thought now that we were falling. She walked arm in arm with Jenny and Brenda with a guilty look on her face. Even the family clown, Gordon, held his tongue.

Although Gordon's parents took in Jenny and Gordon later on, no other relative offered help. Most of them didn't have anything to give.

Nab End was a come-down after Livingston Road; about as far as we could fall. It was worse than Griffin Street. At least we'd had our own cottage there. Nab End was chiefly lodging houses - all of them long past their prime and seedy looking - with vacant faces peering through dirty windows.

Six of us - mother and father, Jenny and Gordon, Brenda and
I - occupied one room. Bess was kept outside. It was the
cheapest thing we could get. Stacked with lodgers from cellar
to roof, the place reeked. It wasn't the usual haddock and
cabbage reek; it was a funny dead, musty smell. In Livingston
Road, which out of shame I never visited again, I had had a
room to myself and a garden to sit in. In Nab End there was
foul, crowded shelter, nothing more. Without the Lathams to
flee to, Bess and I would have been lost.

I was so offended by the move, that I couldn't think straight.
By then I was about fifteen and I had a lot of pride. It was a bad
dream from which I felt I would waken. Thank goodness
grandmother Bridget was not alive to see us in such squalor: the
damp bricks, the dust-covered, broken windows, the sputtering
gaslight, the peeling plaster and paint, the faded wallpaper, the
crowded, greasy rooms, the dim landings where we washed and
the shaky banisters. Toilets were shared in the yard. After
Livingston Road, the noise of the place was deafening.
Everybody spoke at a higher level - almost in a hoarse shout.
There was an incessant clamour throughout the building.
Doors were always being banged to. There was no such thing
as privacy. Everybody's business came through the walls.
Outside, the shouting of children went on all day. There was no
end to it.

An enormous, one-eyed man, with tattooed arms and a
bullock's neck ran the place - chiefly by bawling orders from the
bottom of the stairs. Gross and unclean, he looked as if he never
took his clothes off. Like the ceilings and the walls of the
lodging house, his bald head was covered with sweat. He had a
bad limp - 'the war' everybody said - and was forever
accompanied by a small, black Boston terrier. It had pricked
ears and bulging eyes. It was so silent and kept so close to the
man that one could mistake it for one of his boots.

Periodically the landlord and his mouse-like wife had fights
to the death; usually when we were about to go to sleep. As our
room was directly above theirs, we could hardly avoid the din.
The fights began with shouting and name-calling; there
followed the throwing of dishes, which led to a free-for-all.
There were such bangs and crashes that mother feared for the

329

woman's life. It did sound as if the brute was throwing his wife against the wall. There was a thud, followed by a deep groan, followed by silence; then another thud, followed by greater groans, followed by silence. Eventually, presumably when the combatants were lying on the floor unconscious, we were allowed to go to sleep.

As long as we were there, the woman and the dog survived. Sometimes the woman had a black eye, a split lip, or a puffed-up face, but nothing bad enough to stop her going about her daily business. The wounds on her husband's face showed that she was giving as good as she got. I couldn't make head or tail of them. Having fought half the night, they'd spend the next day cooing, laughing and chatting together like young lovers. Mother said it was ridiculous. "Rubbish," said father, "they're having the time of their lives."

The one redeeming feature about that dark hole was the sense of community among the poor wretches who lived there. They were like members of a great noisy family. They understood and sympathized with each other's hunger and desperation. They willingly shouldered each other's burdens. With nothing to lose, these people should have been revolutionaries and thieves. On the contrary, they were the most law-abiding people one could meet. Their luck was out; like ourselves, they'd gone on the dole; they'd then endured the Means Test, which - having assessed their non-existent resources - had either reduced or removed state aid altogether. There was no work to be had. Their reserves had been used up. Their families and friends either couldn't afford to help them, or had deserted them. Beyond the workhouse, which they all feared, there was no one else to whom they could turn. "But don't worry," they said, "times will change. We maun bide His will till work coom again." With childlike innocence, they honestly believed that they would climb back to the level from which they'd fallen. Against all the misfortunes of their earthly lot they clung to the promise of heavenly salvation. God was their only balm.

Every night, the Catholics among them went down on their knees on the sanded floor in one of the rooms to implore the Virgin to intervene on their behalf. We heard the drone of voices throughout the house:

Remember, O most gracious Virgin Mary, that never was it known that anyone who fled to thy protection, implored thy help, or sought thy intercession, was left unaided. Inspired with this confidence we fly unto thee, O Virgin of Virgins, our mother. To thee we come, before thee we stand, sinful and sorrowful. O mother of the word incarnate, despise not our petition, but in thy mercy hear and answer. Amen.

They showed infinite patience. Nothing got better; nobody seemed to hear or answer them; the world remained pitiless. Yet they always made their nightly appeal: "Remember, O most gracious Virgin Mary..." They answered the skepticism they detected in my eyes with: "Mary can't be expected to answer every supplicant at once."

A spindly, bright-faced Irishman with silver hair led them in prayer. He'd been the 'boots' at the local railway hotel and, having spent his life working for a pittance, had fallen about as far down the ladder as he could. I don't know how he got to Nab End. All I know is that it seemed wrong for a good man to end his life in such circumstances. I didn't know what a saint was supposed to look like, but every time I saw the Irishman in the house or on the street, he made me think of a saint. He radiated serenity and peace. When later in life, I learned about 'abiding grace and inner peace,' I thought about him. Mother had a beautiful face, but it wasn't a saint's face. There was agony on it and the agony stayed there until father got a job and she escaped from Nab End to Polly Street by the railway line. Polly Street wasn't much better than Nab End, but at least we had a small weaver's cottage to ourselves.

———<o>———

It was while we were at Nab End that my brother Dan married Christine Bailey. It was a quiet wedding.

Christine had met Dan while he was working away from Blackburn as a 'devil.' She didn't seem to object to soot, and fell deeply in love with him.

Mother was not happy about Christine at first. She was not prepared to have her Dan marry somebody just because the girl said she was pregnant.

"If he's put her in t' family way, then he's got to marry her," said father.

"How do you know she's in t' family way?" mother retorted.

"Grieves will tell you," father answered.

He did.

Christine was about two months pregnant. Mother bowed to the inevitable. The wedding took place.

Against all odds, Dan and Christine lived happily ever after.

About this time I was pulled in at the Darwen Brick Works by friends as a junior labourer. I was just sixteen. It was a temporary job, which I was glad to get. With a gang of others, my job was to stack the bee-hive shaped kilns with unbaked bricks ('green bricks'). The bricks were cut automatically, loaded onto pallets, and then dried before being fired with gas. Days later we'd take out the finished product. We used sacking to cover our hands; the alternative was suppurating blisters.

We also helped at the grinders, where the clay was crushed and forced through holes in the pan bottom, or at the pugmills, where a column of clay was forced through a die onto the cutting table. I learned early on not to hustle. At the Darwen Brick Works, slow and steady was the rule.

After several months there wasn't much I didn't know about bricks. Day after day, morning, afternoon and night, I handled the bricks. Bricks that went into kilns, bricks that came out of kilns. It wasn't the sort of thing I wanted to do for the rest of my life. Yet, by the standards of those days, I had a good job. I could keep Bess with me. I had young, enjoyable work mates, who roared at each others' jokes and the accounts of their weekend escapades. The foreman, soft-voiced Arthur Dimbleby, was a pleasant change after Mr. Grimshaw. For a foreman he had unusually pleading eyes.

Best of all, I loved the moors where - because of clay - the works were sited. Most of the time, I worked out of doors where I could hear the birds and see the fells. Every morning and every night, wet or fine, with Bess running alongside, I rode for the best part of an hour across the moors to and from Blackburn on a borrowed bike. I'd stop to give Bess a chance to swim in a water-filled clay pit. In the spring and summer, the evening colours were so captivating that I often regretted it when the outskirts of Blackburn came into sight.

It's amazing what you'll do when you're poor. It was across those moors, at the end of a day's work, that I brought a kitchen sink all the way to Blackburn. I got a faulty one from the brickworks at a give-away price. The trouble began when I tried to take my give-away sink home. With Bess at my side, I trudged the whole six miles from Darwen to Blackburn, up and down hills, fighting to keep the slippery, forty-pound basin on the handle-bars. It was an ordeal. On more than one occasion, I was tempted to abandon the wretched thing by the wayside. I was drenched with sweat when I got home.

Arthur Dimbleby was a quiet father figure whom we all respected. Well-built, tough, skilled, he had a benign face that was often crinkled in a huge grin. He'd join us for a game of cards, or pitch and toss, at midday, or he'd sit with us on a plank supported by trestles, and yarn. He was always ready to join us in placing a small bet on the horse races at Aintree. One day he got talking about London where he'd worked when he was younger. His stories excited us. "It's the place for young uns like you," he said. "I'd be off to the South like a shot if I was your age."

Mr. Dimbleby's talk about London put all kinds of ideas into my head. It fired me up. I knew that my job at Darwen was insecure. I never knew when I got there in the morning whether I'd still be working for them at night. It kept me on edge. Later on, I talked to Mr. Dimbleby about London again. I didn't mention Betty Weatherby.

"It'll do you no harm to try to get a job there," Mr. Dimbleby said. "You can always come home. I still know one or two people down there. I might be able to give you a hand." A few days later, he showed me a letter he was about to send to a Mr. Dent at the Bow Bridge Iron Foundry in Bow, East London. It said that I was a good labourer who needed a job, and could he help? Weeks passed without hearing anything from Mr. Dent.

"Give him a chance," was all Mr. Dimbleby said when I asked him if he'd had any news.

Chapter XXI

Politics

As I did not work Saturday mornings at the Darwen Brick Works, I kept in touch with the world by spending some time reading the newspapers and magazines in the Blackburn Public Library reading room. One had to get there early because it was always full. Some of the unemployed workers just sat there with vacant, watery eyes daydreaming, killing time, glad to be off the cold streets. Others stared blankly at the ceiling or leafed aimlessly through the magazines. Still others stood before the high reading stands to which the newspapers (minus the sporting pages to discourage betting) were fastened. Few readers studied the 'Vacancies' column any more. A real job didn't have to be advertised; it was fought over.

The only woman there was the mousy librarian with eye-glasses who invariably had a cold. She always wore a blue pullover and a pleated, blue skirt. In really cold weather she put on a quilt-sized shawl that covered everything except her head. She was usually hidden behind a glass partition. On the polished counter at which she sat stood a large unneeded 'No Smoking' sign. Even when cigarettes were selling at five for twopence, few of the workers had money to smoke. Other notices demanded 'Silence.' One gained the librarian's attention by rapping hard on the glass. Earlier encounters and raised eyebrows had taught me that this was a foolish thing to do. The wise thing was to get a seat with your back to the hot pipes, keep your head down, and ask for nothing.

On one particular Saturday morning I was lost in my reading when I became aware of a thin, gaunt man standing behind me.

"After you with the *Herald*," he said.

I began to yield my place.

"No rush," said the stranger. "I can read something else while I'm waiting."

At that moment the sound of a band drifted in from the street as a procession made its way to the square. To satisfy our curiosity, we both hurried to the door to see what was afoot. It was cold out there and we wasted no time in getting back. We talked some more together in hushed tones. The man introduced himself as Peter Shad. He was in his thirties. He had a plain, pasty face with a small nose. His eyes protruded slightly; they had an intense look. He was dressed like the rest of us: cap, muffler, coat, clogs. He was an unemployed weaver.

I next saw Peter Shad one Sunday evening when I was wandering across the half-darkened town square. One could pick up a copy of left-wing newspapers there, such as the *Daily Worker*, the *Labour Leader* and the *Daily Herald*. There were little knots of people standing about, talking politics. Many of them were at a loss for something to do. To my surprise, Mr. Shad was standing on a box haranguing a large crowd. His excited face was lit by an acetylene lamp hanging above his head. Behind him, flapping in the breeze, was the Red Flag bearing the hammer and sickle. I simply couldn't believe it. As most of what he was saying was being drowned out by the drums and cornets of the Salvation Army band, which blared its way back and forth across the square, I pushed through the crowd until I stood directly in front of him.

For the next hour I stood there while Mr. Shad hurled thunderbolts into the crowd. "Theft! Theft!" he shouted. He really got hotted up. Everything he said rang with conviction. There was so much fire in him that no one dared interrupt him.

He opened my eyes to what was going on in Lancashire. "Those who say that things will buck up, those who tell us to wait and see are fools," he yelled. "Capitalism has taken whatever profits it can out of Lancashire, and has gone elsewhere. Fortunes have been made here, but we've never enjoyed them."

Mr. Shad took a deep breath. "That's what free enterprise is all about," he went on, "to make a fortune and then clear off, leaving the dirt behind. The problem is not cotton, it's capitalism. It will let Blackburn rot. It will let you rot. If more profit can be made in China, the capitalists will drop you and sweat the Chinese. They'll eat each other for gain."

There followed another thunderbolt. "Capitalism can never be changed. It can only be destroyed. To say that the rich have an obligation to the poor is tripe. Love does not make the world go round, money does. To the capitalist, making money is the only virtue. Drive the money changers from the temple!" he yelled. "The enemy is greed. You work for less and less while the usurers take more and more. There will be no peace on earth until the working class destroys the masters and the money bags - the financiers. Private ownership of our mills and our lives must go."

After wiping the sweat off his forehead, the speaker was off again. The crowd stood entranced. "Not love, but hate is what matters - hatred of the capitalist class. It's madness to think that you can make a deal with the bosses. No capitalist is going to give up a good thing without a fight. The bosses have to go."

Mr. Shad was now vigorously beating one hand against the other. "Only when the capitalist class has been overthrown" - here he struggled with an imaginary object and threw it to the ground - "only when we have robbed them of the ability to exploit others, can there be true social justice. All power to the people!" he ended.

The spell broken, the crowd stirred. Here and there, there was a gentle rumble of approval. Among us, any man who could hold a crowd like that was respected.

Mr. Shad struck me as a man who really believed what he was saying. He was ready to die in the people's cause. Except for the policeman, who stood to one side, a lamp on his belt, impassively watching, and making a note, I'm sure most of the audience felt as I did. The meeting ended with Mr. Shad singing the 'Internationale':

> Oh, comrades, come rally,
> For the last fight let us stand,
> The Internationale,
> Unites the human race...

It filled me with hope. We were going to fight and win a better life.

In a subdued tone, as if they weren't quite sure if they could get away with it - and with an eye on the policeman - two or three others sang with him. To one side, several youths, the worse for drink were singing the parody of 'The Red Flag':

> The people's flag is palest pink.
> It's not as red as you might think.
> We've been to see, and now we know,
> They've gone and changed its colour so.
> While cowards flinch and traitors sneer
> We'll go on drinking bitter beer...

I had hoped to speak to Mr. Shad when he was through, but he deliberately ignored me. His eyes said 'piss off!' He quickly furled his flag and was lost in the crowd.

The following Saturday morning I encountered him once more in the reading room. I could hardly believe that this was the same fellow who had held the crowd spellbound in the town square. He crossed the room to speak to me.

"Keep clear of me on the streets and on the square," he warned in a low voice. "Recognize me only here. Elsewhere it is dangerous for you to be seen with me. Capitalist repression is growing. Moseley's Black Shirts will appear in the square any day. When you're older you can make up your own mind about communism." (The British Fascist Movement had been launched in October 1932 by Sir Oswald Moseley.)

That Saturday morning, with Mr. Shad as my tutor, I began my education in political economy. Every Saturday thereafter, almost without fail, he arrived and fished books out of his deep pockets. He also gave me a glossy magazine depicting life in

Russia. We knew that bringing books into the reading room was forbidden. We sat at a table in a corner with our backs to the other readers, talking in whispers. Chiefly he whispered and I listened. He first went over the *Communist Manifesto*, explaining its inner meaning. I was overwhelmed by it. Why hadn't I heard of it before? It was almost a hundred years old. How right Marx had been to say that the working class had nothing to lose but its chains. Anybody who lived at the bottom of the heap in Blackburn knew that.

Mr. Shad was a born teacher. Whenever I got lost - as I often did - he started all over again. He had infinite patience, infinite generosity.

What I found difficult to swallow was his need to hate the bosses. He wanted me to hate with all my mind and all my heart. Grandmother Bridget had taught me not to hate. Hate will rot you, she'd said.

"Must we really hate the bosses?"

"You can't fight evil without hating it. Tell me, do you hate sin and the devil?"

"Oh, yes."

"If you had the chance to kill the devil, would you?"

"Oh, yes." I hadn't forgotten the statue of St. Michael fighting the devil at St. Peter's School.

"Well," he concluded, "the devils are the bosses; they won't go away peacefully. Rotten societies have to be toppled. That's what history is all about."

For several months, I met Mr. Shad every Saturday morning in the library. Like grandmother Bridget, and Mr. Peek, he seemed honestly concerned with my education. I looked upon him as my teacher. He aroused in me an interest in what was going on in the world. Now and again he gave me a copy of the communist newspapers, the *Daily Worker*, or the *Young Worker*, but he didn't push them onto me.

The only person to whom I said anything about Peter Shad was Harold Watkins. My Saturday morning meetings in the Public Library I decided to keep to myself. One Sunday night Harold went with me to hear Shad. One moment we were waiting for him, the next moment there was the box, the lamp, the flag and the speaker. People quickly gathered; you could almost feel the growing rustle of attention. He started quietly, so that we were forced to listen carefully. As he warmed to his subject, a new note entered his voice. The voice grew in pitch and volume until it echoed from the surrounding buildings. With the speech done, and the questions answered, Mr. Shad disappeared as mysteriously as he'd come. He simply melted into the crowd.

Harold marvelled at him. The look in his eyes told me that he was just as spellbound as I. There was magic in Shad's words. He got our blood up. We believed him when he said that Russia was a worker's paradise: that it was the only country in the world where no one went hungry, where no one was out of a job, and where no one could exploit the workers for profit. His stories about the Russian workers' paradise turned our heads.

We believed him when he said that the Russian Revolution was a great light beckoning the workers of the world. We believed him when he said that the revolution was coming in Britain. We believed him when he said that the world couldn't wait until capitalism died of its own weaknesses; it had earned the sentence of death and should be got rid of. We believed him when he said that religion was 'the opium of the people.' He was so eloquent, so persuasive, that we couldn't do anything else but swallow everything he said - hook, line and sinker. Not for a moment did we worry about how the revolution would be achieved. We didn't ask him and we wouldn't have thanked him for the details. It was the vision that mattered.

I knew Mr. Shad for quite a while, yet there was a side of him about which I knew nothing. I'd no idea where he lived. He always left the library before me. By the time I'd got to the door, he'd gone. He never mentioned a wife or children. The only thing I knew about him was that he didn't sleep well. He talked about becoming a weaver in Brazil.

I don't know whether he ever reached Brazil. The last I saw of him was during a brawl on the square. He had predicted that Oswald Moseley's Blackshirts would turn up and they did. Having tried to deafen him with their shouts, the Fascists suddenly seized his flag. Shad fought back and was knocked to the ground. Most spectators backed away. The struggle for the Red Flag ended with Peter Shad in possession of a bare flag pole.

Apart from the shouting, the affair was all over in minutes. The communists were simply swept aside.

As Mr. Shad got to his feet, a policeman arrested him for 'disturbing the peace.' I had seen the same copper at many meetings. There was a struggle in which Shad must have lost self-control, for he struck the officer across the face with the flagpole. With witnesses present, that was lunacy. The policeman could have struck him, but it was a criminal act to strike back. The moment the officer released his grasp, Shad swung round and disappeared in the crowd. Peter Shad had become 'a fugitive from justice.'

A warrant was issued for his arrest. It startled me out of my clogs when I saw his picture in the paper under the name of Arthur Cray. Why had he called himself Peter Shad when his name was Arthur Cray? Or was it? Harold and I puzzled over the matter so much that we didn't know what to think. Try as I might, I could not think badly of him.

I was left in no doubt what the reading room librarian thought of him. "Born trouble maker, I'd say," she whispered primly. "Tell them anywhere. Good riddance. You needn't think I didn't notice you two plotting and planning in the corner there - breaking all the rules. I thought several times of having you thrown out. From now on you'll have to watch your step."

I went to the square the next night to see if I could learn anything from those who used to sing the 'Internationale.' No one appeared. Peter Shad (or Arthur Cray) had left my life as mysteriously as he had entered it.

A man was found drowned in the canal about this time. It was in the paper. They said he had protruding eyes. No one claimed the corpse. Could it have been Peter Shad? I sat with the paper in my hands in the corner of the library where I had first met him and wondered. I became so curious that for several weeks I went on trying to find one or other of the faces that I'd seen alongside Shad on the square. None of them ever showed up. Where Peter Shad had stood with his Red Flag, the Fascist Black Shirts now gathered.

—◦—

Shad's disappearance left Harold Watkins and me in a quandary. We were lost without him. His talk of the Russian Revolution had fired us up. As there was nothing for us in Blackburn, we decided to write to the Russians and offer to go to Russia as weavers. All the things that Mr. Shad had told us about, and that we'd seen in the Russian magazines that he'd given us, we'd go and see for ourselves. I couldn't weave as well as Harold - I was at that time working at the brick works - but provided we could work together as a team, we'd manage. I trusted Harold, we'd grown up together. I knew he wouldn't let me down.

But then came the problem: how does one write to the Russians? I sought the advice of the librarian. Her spectacles jumped off her nose when I whispered, "How can I get in touch with the Russians?"

"The Russians?" she whispered, frowning. "In heavens name, what would a good Blackburn boy be doing writing to the Russians? Don't you know they're godless atheists!"

"I'm just curious," I whispered, guardedly. "I want to learn what's going on."

"Curiosity killed the cat," she hissed.

Had I gone on and told her that Harold and I intended to go to Russia, she would, I'm sure, have fainted dead away.

As there was no Soviet Embassy in Britain at the time (the British had accused the Soviets of spying) she gave me the address of the Russian Trade Legation in London.

It was one thing to get an address, another thing to know what to say. Harold and I anguished over our letter for some time. Clumsily, my first effort began "Dear Sirs," which Harold thought ridiculous.

"Communists don't call each other 'dear' or 'sir'."

I substituted 'Comrades,' which pleased him. He also took out my reference to Peter Shad. Eventually we agreed to send the following note:

> Comrades,
>
> We are two unemployed Blackburn weavers. We are both skilled, fit, and in our teens. We believe in the Russian Revolution and want to share it with you. Can you find us a job so that we can come to Russia and see it for ourselves? If

you will write to the above address, we are free to come any time.

> Fraternally,
> Harold Watkins,
> William Woodruff.

Very deliberately, we stuck a stamp on the envelope and took it to the main post office. A great change came over me as I slipped the envelope into the black mouth of the red letter box. All the way home we talked about what might happen. Would the Russians write or would somebody come in person? How would we get there? Well, that was up to the Russians. Anyway, we were determined not to turn back.

We never heard a word. Peter Shad's dream of a great and glorious new life in Russia was denied us. Perhaps the letter was removed from the mail by the police, or both the Russians and the police had more important things to do.

-------◄○►-------

With our Russian options closed, we gave more thought to our political futures. Not long after Peter Shad had disappeared, and our Russian venture had died, I decided to join the Youth Labour League. With a 'red' scare on in Britain (there'd been one earlier in 1924-1926 when a number of communists had been sent to jail) it wasn't the time to join the Communist Party, which had been in existence in Britain since 1920. Anybody who put Russia before Britain was run down. Even in the trade unions, those suspected of being a bolshie were rooted out.

Harold and I took every opportunity to hear the important politicians who spoke in town. Blackburn square is where I heard all the best speakers of the land. MacDonald, Snowdon, Henderson, Clynes, Thomas and Churchill all spoke there. Some like MacDonald, Snowdon and Clynes were intensely religious. They were always saying God this and God that. I'm sure none of them had read Marx.

One night I listened to Winston Spencer Churchill. The audience was belligerent from the start because of the role he had played in breaking the General Strike in 1926. He was a bald-headed figure standing on a box, wagging an admonitory finger at the crowd. "Hang on to India," he advised. "Take no notice of that little fakir, Gandhi." We knew he was talking rubbish. Even those of us whose living depended on it had the common sense to realize that we couldn't go on ruling hundreds of millions of Indians. We didn't agree with his intention to hang on to Ireland, either.

Gandhi and Churchill seemed to follow each other around. In 1931 Gandhi spent three days visiting the Lancashire textile industry. He was a little, bespectacled, ascetic figure, with a white shawl and a homespun loincloth, skinny legs and clumsy wooden sandals. He was greeted warmly. The antiquated condition of the Lancashire textile industry did not escape him. "The machinery in the Bombay and Ahmadabad mills," he said, "is one hundred percent more efficient."

Eager to make my way in the labour movement, I began to make speeches on the square for the Labour Party. At first the speeches only lasted a couple of minutes, and I was told what to say. With Blackburn streets full of unemployed, and things getting worse every day, there was no shortage of topics and audiences. I talked about the dole, the slump in the basic industries, and the need to tax the rich.

I found public speaking unnerving. The moment I got on the box, I became tense. A five minute stint had me running with sweat. Harold was much better at it than I was. His speeches were more compelling. My maiden speech was attended by an audience of two, one of them a wild, half-clothed figure who kept shouting that the Day of Judgement had arrived. His interruptions grew louder, the longer I spoke. "For God's sake, shut up, you silly little bugger," he finally shouted right in my face. Sunday night audiences on Blackburn square were even more aggressive. Hecklers roughed me up in no time. Their purpose was to get me rattled. I had been warned that if they did, they'd chop me up into little pieces. They made no allowance for age.

I couldn't have survived these ordeals had I not had the help of Elsie Briggs, whom I met at one of these meetings. She swore that I was the worst speaker she'd ever heard, and that she was going to improve me or die.

Elsie Briggs was a spinster in her thirties, who lived round the corner from us in Polly Street. She was a small woman dressed in black. I never saw her face clearly because she wore a cap pulled down over her eyes. Her mouth was puckered around a pipe, which she smoked incessantly. She was one of the few spinners in town who seemed to be able to hang on to a job.

Her widowed father ran a fruit and vegetable shop in one of their downstairs rooms. I cannot imagine what the old man made out of it. There was one other member of the family, Charlotte - also a spinner - who was a couple of years younger than Elsie. She was disfigured by smallpox.

Elsie began her coaching by standing me before a stained, body-length mirror in her bedroom. I was told to address a circle she had drawn above the mirror on the wall. Throwing my arms about, I repeated the short speeches which she had written for me, and which I'd memorized while cycling home from the brickworks. In these speeches, politics were incidental. All she cared about was elocution.

I didn't get halfway through any of them because she never let me. "It won't do! It won't do!" she'd interrupt, while blowing smoke in my face. "I won't own you on the square if you talk like that. You sound like a gobbin. You'll be lucky if you're not lynched."

Elsie was pure Lancashire: blunt, aggressive and sarcastic. She could also be grim and ironic. She was not the slightest bit interested in whether I liked her or not. She treated me as if I were daft. Life with Elsie was hell.

"Start again!" she commanded in a deep mannish voice. "Look at your hands! Face the crowd! Take that silly grin off your face. You've nothing to grin about." The punching and kneading never stopped.

I wondered if she wasn't trying to torture me. There was a touch of sadism in Elsie Briggs. Yet when she removed her black cap and I could see her gray eyes, I saw only loneliness. Charlotte swore that her sister had a heart of gold. She might have had, but I didn't see any evidence of it. Not once did I see her smile. No wonder her father threw me a look of sympathy whenever I entered the shop. I hope Elsie didn't treat him as she treated me.

One night, I complained to Charlotte. "I'm thinking of chucking it, Elsie is inhuman."

"It's the war. Elsie's never been the same since her bloke got killed on the Somme. That's why she wears black. I wouldn't chuck it if I was you. She needs you as much as you need her. Why drop it now when you're improving? I know she says you're only middlin', but, secretly, she thinks you're coming on real gradely."

Charlotte was right. If I hadn't been improving, I wouldn't have put up with Elsie. But I was getting better. I wasn't as good as Harold, or as assertive as Peter Shad had been - probably never would be - but I was getting that way.

Whenever I spoke on the square, Elsie Briggs took up a position right in front of me, puffing on her pipe, umbrella in hand. She revelled in the heckling I got. The more I was ribbed, the more some crank in the crowd annoyed me, the more she cheered. The involuntary movements of her head and shoulders told me that she was enjoying every minute. Yet there was a point beyond which criticism of me was not allowed to go. At that point Elsie would turn upon my tormentor, umbrella raised.

Elsie's torture didn't stop Harold and me from building all kinds of dream worlds in Britain, as previously we'd built them in Russia. "You know, Billy," he said to me one night after listening to one of my speeches, "I've been thinking about you. When I become Prime Minister, I shall appoint you as Foreign Secretary." Harold had a droll humour, but I knew he was serious. I was impressed. As an expression of thanks, I bought him a black pudding on the way home.

Chapter XXII

The Bitter Years

When I left school in 1930, and began to look for a full-time job, half the workers of Blackburn were on the streets. The entire output of the Lancashire textile industry had been halved since 1914. Because it depended upon the export trade, our town was hardest hit. The number of workers in the mills in 1930 had shrunk to a tenth of what it had been before the war. The poor were not only going hungry; they were pawning their bedding for a meal. Some of them finished up on straw and sacking, their 'bed of sorrows.' A diet of fish-head soup and haddock was all that kept many of them going. The medical journal, *The Lancet*, reported that people in the depressed areas of Blackburn were literally dying of starvation. The birth rate declined; the infant mortality rate was higher in Lancashire than in the rest of the country. The maternal mortality rate rose. Things must have been desperate because the money lenders thrived. Sickness wasn't feared for sickness' sake, but because of the threat of destitution.

Throughout the spring and summer of 1932, there were pitched battles between unemployed workers and the police in London, Manchester, Birkenhead and Glasgow. In Belfast demonstrators had been shot and killed. In Rochdale the army had been called out. Street fights were common. In desperation, the unemployed decided to make a direct appeal for help to parliament and the king.

In the fading light of a wintry afternoon at the beginning of October 1932, Harold Watkins and I watched a column of ragged hunger marchers form up to begin the long trek from Blackburn to London. We had joined the crowd in the town square to give them a send-off.

"We're goin' to tell t' king that we need work and food," one of the marchers told us. "You'll see, 'e'll understand. Once 'e knows what's 'appening in Lancashire, matters will be put right, there's no doubt. After t' king, we'll tell parliament. The guvernment will sit up when they 'ear from us. It isn't going to be easy. But who cares if it puts matters straight again, eh?"

Just before their departure the Blackburn contingent was joined by a small group from Jarrow, which had missed the main Northumberland, Durham and Teeside contingent going south through Yorkshire. With the light fading, the Jarrow men, each with a blanket over his shoulder, came marching into the square with a springy step. Some had regular walking sticks, others carried ash rods. Most were young. Although they'd been on the road several days, their faces were still bright. They wore cloth caps and mufflers. Their belongings hung on their backs. The Blackburn people gave them wedges of bread, steaming tea and tator-hash. I helped to pour the tea. While they ate, a fellow with a banjo sang:

> I'm a four loom weaver as many a one knows;
> I've nowt to eat and I've worn out me clothes.
> Me clogs are boath broken and stockings I've none.
> Tha'd scarce gie me tuppence for a' I've gotten on.
>
> Owd Billy o't Bent he kept telling me long,
> We might have better times if I'd nobbut howd me tongue.
> Well I've howden me tongue till I near lost me breath,
> And I feel in my heart that I'll soon clem to death...

Our Margaret declares if she'd clothes to put on,
She'd go up to London to see the great mon,
And if things didna alter when there she had been,
She swears she would fight wi' blood up t' th' een.

I'm a four loom weaver as many a one knows;
I've nowt to eat and I've worn out me clothes.
Clogs we ha' none nor no looms to weave on,
And I've woven myself to t' far end.

The Jarrow marchers had never been so far from home. The idea of going to London had fired them up. "Nothing between here and London can be worse than what we're already going through," they said. Three-quarters of Jarrow's labour force was out of work. Some had been out for years.

Despite all the talk of hunger marchers being nothing but communist riff-raff, these men were a good-natured, law-abiding lot. I doubt there was a revolutionary among them. Some of them had just been to church to receive communion before setting out. They'd fasted all day before receiving the Host.

In the late afternoon the Blackburn and Jarrow men formed up together. They seemed a bit clumsy and shy at getting into line. Someone ordered the column forward. With their heavy boots and laced-up clogs ringing on the cobblestones, the marchers moved off. They were going to march all night. The fellow at the end of the column waved his lamp.

"Good luck!" we shouted.

After little more than a month they were back, thinner than ever, their blankets and their boots and clogs worn out. London had wanted to get rid of them, and had sent them home by train. The police had seen them off. The London labour movement didn't have the resources to feed every fellow who took it into his head to talk to the king. We greeted them at the station and heard their story. In London, they had repeatedly been run down by the mounted police. It had been like a battlefield. They hadn't seen the king, or Ramsay MacDonald the Labour prime minister, or anybody of any consequence. They'd been fobbed off at every turn; promised all kinds of remedies.

They told us that there'd been big meetings in Hyde Park and Trafalgar Square at which contingents from all over the north - including the women's contingent from Yorkshire - had participated. Labour members of parliament had addressed them and poured oceans of praise upon them. They'd said that thanks to the hunger marchers, the complacency of the government would now be broken. The marchers could return to their homes, knowing that something would be done to give them food and jobs. The speakers had promised to work night and day. A manifesto had been approved calling upon the government to abolish poverty and provide work. A million-signature petition was to be presented to parliament. In the end, nothing was done. Bitterest pill of all, the police had seized the petition.

It didn't surprise me to see the marchers come home again. Peter Shad had hammered it into our heads that Pilgrimages of Grace get nowhere. It was bargaining from weakness; the weak get nothing, he'd said.

Harold Watkins and I were in a teashop in Bank Top when the hunger marchers from Northumberland, having spent a night in Blackburn, went by on their way home. Their clogs and boots pounded the snow into a dark slush. Fragments of paper-thin ice filled the gutters.

"Like the rest of 'em, they've been banging t' head against a brick wall," Harold said, jerking his cap in the direction of the marchers. "They look licked."

"What do you expect? They've been shoutin' so that somebody would hear 'em. Better than sufferin' in silence."

"Nobody gives a damn about the weak shouting. When will people learn?"

"These poor devils 'ave a real grievance, Harold."

"Of course. They wouldn't have marched all the way to London if they'd 'ad a job and their bellies were full. You'd have never heard from 'em if they'd been getting three meals a day. They felt helpless, with nothing to loose. For all the notice that was taken of 'em, they might as well have stayed home and marched round the park. Some of them got a broken head for their troubles. The toffs don't give a damn. They don't know what we're putting up with, and if they did they wouldn't care.

Lancashire's no longer part of England. So much for 'This blessed plot, this realm, this earth, this England,' that we learned at school."

"You've got a point, Harold. Paper says there are two Englands: one with an unemployment rate of six percent, the other with sixty."

I thought of my own family. I'd had years to think about them. The Watkins family was the same. They were all hard workers, all law-abiding. None of them were feckless, or habitual drunkards. Their needs were extremely simple. Yet, no matter how much they worked and saved and schemed, their lot got worse. Even if they got a job, it would be sure to die on them before they'd had a chance to pay off their debts.

"What do we do, Harold?"

"I don't know. I do know that hunger marches aren't going to make any difference. It's not a genuine grievance they need; it's power. Anybody who goes on a hunger march, carrying a petition that 'humbly prays' is asking for trouble. Somehow they've got to get power in their hands."

"How?"

"Turn the toffs out of parliament and put the workers in. We've got to send our own man. Bradford did it nearly thirty years ago."

"But the workers vote for the toffs. They won't vote for their equals. Lancashire voted overwhelmingly for MacDonald when he deserted the workers for the bosses in 1931. You know what happened when we pushed Pat Murphy as our Labour candidate."

"As long as the workers go on doing that, they're going to go on marching like those poor, pinch-faced sods out there."

———

It says a lot for the Lancashire unemployed that they didn't revolt. They certainly had grounds for it. Some of them had been out of work for almost a decade. Many of them felt unwanted, of no use to anyone, living in vain.

Some of the things happening in the industrial areas of Britain in the 1920's and 1930's were not only wrong, they passed all understanding. Government aid through the dole seemed to be deliberately aimed at breaking the spirit of anyone who was proud, thrifty, honest and upright. How could anyone 'genuinely seek work' when there was no work to seek; or accept a Means Test, which seemed designed not only to lower an already low standard of living, but also to break up family life - the only thing some of the poor had got left. Some of the regulations were mean and villainous, if not downright cruel. Hardship could be borne; meanness and cruelty had to be fought.

There was no end to the madness. Blackburn was a town that at one time had clothed much of the world; yet in the worst years of the depression we didn't have enough clothing to cover our backs. We Blackburnians bought Japanese shirts and cottons at half British prices because we didn't have enough money to buy our own products.

Blackburn was close to some of the richest coal seams in the world, yet because we couldn't afford coal, we were reduced to burning cinders. We stuffed miserable little perforated cans with coal dust, which we burned in our hearths during the coldest days and nights. The family sat over them like a lot of crows. Refusing to put up with the cold, we stole the wooden railings of the rich. We wrenched them away, one after another as we went by, and stuffed them under our jackets. Whole fences disappeared. Special guards had to be mounted on coal shipments. Any railway truck full of coal, left standing overnight in the railway sidings, was empty by morning. Local cinemas advertised warmth not films. For threepence you could keep warm, be entertained, and forget the bleak world outside.

The system was inhuman. So inhuman that it could throw people out of work on Christmas Eve, casting them off like old clothing, or give them a cheap bottle of sherry as a reward for fifteen, thirty, forty or even fifty years' work in the mills. My father brought such a bottle home. He put it on the kitchen table and - with the rest of us - sat and stared at it. Then, without a word, he picked it up, opened the kitchen door, and flung it against the alley wall. There must have been factory owners - other than Terence Peek - who felt a social obligation to the workers and to the industry, but in all my sixteen years in Blackburn I didn't know one. My family knew as much about the factory owners as they knew about our landlords - nothing. Pounds, shillings and pence, not human relations, dominated our lives.

Meanwhile newspaper advertisements were persuading the rich to take Union Line cruises to Madeira, First Class £20, Second Class £15; and to buy bed-side phones with extension cords; "Why Get out of Bed to Answer the Phone?"

No wonder that the bottom dogs were brought up to sing:

> It's the rich that gets the pleasure,
> It's the poor that gets the pain.
> Ain't that a blinkin' shame...

Cotton made unbelievable fortunes for some people in Britain, but not for the working class. At one time, the Lancashire spinning town of Shaw was said to be 'the richest town in England.' But they measured it by millionaires to the square mile. Fat lot of use that is to the working man.

Perhaps things were not quite bad enough for revolution. Perhaps, as Mr. Peek believed, revolution wasn't in the British workers' blood. He used to say if the workers wanted a revolution, they'd have to import it. Muddlers and tinkerers don't make revolutions. Perhaps because poverty in Britain was so highly localized in Wales and the North of England, it could be contained. Perhaps the dole helped to save the country from upheaval. Perhaps religion helped. Strong non-conformists and Roman Catholics don't sit well with communism. No matter how bad things got, the British did not become a people of guns and armed risings. Except among the toffs, there never was widespread talk of the workers seizing power by force. The workers were too law-abiding for that. Fiery extremists, such as Peter Shad, who really did believe in pulling the mighty down, were called 'reds' or bolshies and kept out.

One thing that did help to turn the country away from violence was the way in which the poor helped each other through the hard times. No wonder we sang, 'It's the Poor what Helps the Poor.' There was a lot of pitching in, a lot of making do and a lot of pluck. Too little has been made of working-class solidarity and community spirit. It wasn't the dole that saved

Britain from revolution, it was the nature of the British working class. The British toffs will never know how lucky they were.

Moreover, the workers didn't revolt as Peter Shad had told them because they didn't live in his world of blood and fury. The poor are by nature meek. It took a lot to get their blood up. It took even more to get them out onto the streets. The beatings they'd had since 1920 had undermined their confidence. They thought of life as a bit of a muddle that would sort itself out in time. Not least, they didn't revolt because they never lost hope. Even the poor devils I'd known in the Nab End lodging house didn't lose hope. For a Lancashire man or woman to lose hope was to lose life. As indeed they did. The number of suicides rose. Sometimes they took their life only hours after being laid off. "Ead in t' oven' was most commonly used.

I refused to believe that the dire conditions in which we lived were, as Sister Loyola used to say, 'an act of God calling for heroic fortitude and passive endurance.' Nor did I believe that material poverty was spiritually cleansing. Material poverty was no more a virtue to me than spiritual poverty. Peter Shad had taught me not to swallow the 'act of God' business, or to suffer in silence. Those ideas were put abroad by the toffs to keep the working class down.

Our choice was either to overthrow the system as Shad had urged, or escape from it altogether. Harold and I had tried unsuccessfully to escape to Russia. We'd also talked about emigrating to Fall River where my father's brothers lived. But the fare was beyond us. Failing Russia and America, we decided to escape to London. The more we thought about London, the better it seemed. But where would we find a job in London? Mr. Dimbleby had talked about helping me. But he had produced nothing tangible. With no other options open, we waited and stagnated. Everything in Blackburn hung like wet washing on the line, dead. It was like waiting for a storm.

Meanwhile we Lancastrians neither revolted nor whined. Instead, those who could, took to the fields and the hills. Things weren't so bad when it was getting warmer and summer was at hand. Some of my best days in Blackburn, before I got the job at the Darwen Brick Works, were those when I was unemployed. Provided I got something to eat, I could wander about all day. I didn't have to get back for anybody. Nobody owned me. There was no work tomorrow; no clocking in. There were times when we even laughed at our plight. As Gracie Fields, our Lancashire comedienne, used to say, "It's so bad, luv, laughing is all that's left." It is hardly surprising that we sang and tap-danced the American song:

> I can't give you anything but love, Baby,
> That's the only thing there's plenty of, Baby,
> Dream a while, scheme a while,
> You're sure to find happiness, and I guess
> All those things you've always wished for,
> Gee, but I guess I like you looking swell, Baby,
> Diamond bracelets, Woolworth doesn't sell, Baby,
> Till that lucky day, you know darn well, Baby,
> I can't give you anything but love.

Little wonder that I should have decided to try my luck elsewhere. As things got worse and worse, Harold and I finally made up our minds to leave.

———◦———

In the spring of 1933, Mr. 'Sharabang' Fisher married Mrs. Beatty. Mr. Fisher's ailing wife and 'Up-and-at-em' Beatty had both died in 1932. There had always been a close connection between the two families. With a complete invalid on her hands, Mrs. Beatty had been relying on Mr. Fisher for years. He had done all the fetching and carrying. Old 'Up-and-at-em' had just faded away. He'd been in that basket dribbling for the best part of fifteen years. His mind had never left the trench in France where Mr. Fisher had picked up what was left of him so long ago. We thought it wonderful that Mrs. Beatty could at long last live a fuller life. They were married at St. Philip's and the reception was at St. Philip's Hall where my gang used to steal meat pies. It was a crowded wedding followed by a really good send-off.

The joy of the Beatty-Fisher wedding was marred by the death of Mr. Peek. I learned of Mr. Peek's death by chance long after he had been buried. Chain-smoker that he was, he had accidentally set his bed alight and had died from burns. He didn't finish his book - the book that was to save the world. I was so appalled with the news that I felt I must sympathize with Roger, who by now had lost both parents. Agnes Peek had lingered on for a year or so after her attack of tetanus and then had died of other things.

I was on the point of returning to Livingston Road when I learned that, following their father's death, the Peek children had left town. That was the last I heard of them.

I took my leave of Rosie Gill in a manner that neither of us had expected. One evening, shortly after the Beatty-Fisher wedding, Rosie Gill was rushed to the infirmary with acute appendicitis. While I was visiting the Gill house to inquire about Rosie, a nurse came in and told Gill that following surgery somebody had given Rosie fish and chips and that she was dangerously ill. Mr. Gill and I hurried to the hospital. He was beside himself. With me trying to keep up with him, he barged past everybody at the hospital who got in his way. "Here, hang on! Where do you think you're going?" the nurses called after him.

When we got to the ward a commotion was going on. There were doctors and a priest around Rosie's bed. Nurses were running in and out with slop basins and towels. There was a strong smell of methylated spirits. One of the doctors was taking Rosie's pulse. The priest was administering the Last Sacrament. I'd stood by a number of Catholic deathbeds in my sixteen years. I knew that in the fifth chapter of James it is said: "Is anyone sick among you? Let him bring in the Priests of the Church; and let them pray over him, anointing him with oil in the name of the Lord..." I knew what it meant. With tears pouring down his face, Mr. Gill made the sign of the Cross.

Rosie lay like a corpse, her eyes dead and staring. Her lips were blue; her body was drenched with sweat. Her long, curly hair lay tousled across the pillow. Her faded amulet of Mary and Christ crucified - the one she'd shown me years before - rested on the sheet. There had been times when I thought something might develop between Rosie and me, but it hadn't. We were always running in and out of each other's houses and meeting at dances, but we knew without saying it that we wouldn't be anything closer than good friends.

As I stood and stared at the scar on her left temple, it all came back, flooding my mind. I remembered how we'd been fooling around in the Ribble one summer's day in our early teens; and how Rosie had finished up bashing her head on a rock at the bottom of a water hole. I got her out of the Ribble as she'd got me out of the Blakewater earlier - dripping with blood. Somehow I'd managed to get her over the bridge into Ribchester, where Rosie's blood-stained towel, which I'd wrapped around her head, caught the attention of a policeman. He took us to a doctor who stitched up Rosie's wound. Then, without so much as by your leave, the policeman and his mate collected our bikes from the high bank of the river and, with Rosie, Bess and me quaking in the back of the police car, wondering what on earth was going to happen to us, drove us back to Blackburn. They were nice all the way. Poor old Gill almost swallowed his teeth when we drew up outside his front window - the one which still displayed a bowl of 'Virginia fresh tobacco.' I pushed my bike home afterward puzzled. I'd no idea that the police could be so kind. It changed my view of them.

Now Rosie was lying at death's door. The doctors and the priest, all of whom knew Willie Gill, moved aside as he bent over his child. Rosie made no response to his quiet pleadings. The older of the two doctors beckoned Mr. Gill away from the bedside. With a hand on Willie's shoulder, he began talking to him quietly. I caught snatches. "It's too late... You'll have to face it... It can happen at any moment." One of the nurses began to draw a curtain around Rosie's bed. All I could think of was Rosie helping me out of the Blakewater river when I'd been thrown in head first. I wished I could have rendered comfort unto her in her last moments, as years before she had rendered it unto me. Instead, I stood there helpless, holding on to the weeping Willie Gill.

Rosie died a few minutes later. She was just sixteen.

I knew she was gone when I saw the nurse cover Rosie's face, and the priest beckoned us to begin the 'De Profundis.'

"Out of the depths I have cried to Thee O Lord," the priest began almost before we had time to take up our positions at the foot of the bed. I wasn't sure that Willie was going to respond until I heard his faltering, "O Lord, hear my voice." He spoke like a child, lips trembling, too afraid to be heard.

One of the nurses quickly followed: "And let Thine ears be attentive to the voice of my supplication."

And so in hushed tones, with the priest leading, we went on together until the end: "May she rest in peace, Amen."

Several times I'd stood with mother and her work mates while Patrick Murphy had said the same prayer for a dead mill-hand. Whether you make the appeal among silent looms or in a hospital ward makes no difference.

I took Willie Gill home. As he stumbled through his doorway, he turned and placed a hand on my shoulder.

"They've killed my child, Billy," he sobbed.

Chapter XXIII

Good-bye, Lancashire

At long last, having talked the subject to death with Harold Watkins, I made up my mind to leave Lancashire and go to London. I decided to risk my chance by going to Mr. Dimbleby's friend, Mr. Dent at the Bow Bridge Iron Foundry, with a letter of recommendation from Mr. Dimbleby. Better to make up my own mind than have the Brick Works make it up for me.

As the time for my departure approached, I became more and more excited. I'd been promised a ride in a lorry from Manchester to London by another friend of Mr. Dimbleby's, Mr. Tomkins. It would cost me five shillings instead of the twenty-five charged by the railway. Failing the Bow Bridge Iron Foundry, I'd look for work somewhere else in London. Provided I could find a job to hang on to, Harold would join me in about a month's time. After that we'd fight it out together.

My going to London was not only a matter of finding a job, it was a matter of adventure. I used to stand at the railway level-crossing close to Polly Street and watch the trains chugging their way south. As I leaned over the gate, I wondered what the people of the south were really like. Were they like us? With Betty Weatherby in London, I had a compelling reason to go and find out. Meanwhile I was afraid that somebody would learn of my plans and stop me from going. Only Mr. Dimbleby at the brickworks, my sisters Jenny and Brenda and Harold knew that I was leaving. I didn't tell the Latham's. I knew Madge would be against my going off on my own. I decided I'd write to them as soon as I'd landed a job in London.

At this time, Harold had become the Blackburn agent of the ACDO laundry soap company. It was a little job with big aspirations. He drove a motorcycle three-wheeler with a plywood box at the back shaped like a block of soap with the words MIRACULOUS, ACDO LAUNDRY SOAP, painted all over it. He was going to hang on to this job until he could join me in London.

Harold's parting gift to me was a day-long trip through the Trough of Bowland. We took two girls with us with whom we'd clicked on the 'chicken run' the week before. The 'chicken run' was the way to meet girls. Harold and I had walked backward and forward on a parade out Whalley way until we had 'clicked.' Clicking meant that the girls had responded to our greeting and that they were prepared to stop and talk. These two girls were game enough to come with us for the lark. They turned up with cheery faces.

We rode in Harold's delivery van. Harold sat up front with goggles and gloves revving up the engine. With the mustache he'd begun to grow, he looked dashing.

"Does your boss know we're taking his bike?" I asked, as the two girls and I climbed into the windowless trailer.

"He does and he doesn't."

"What do you mean, he does and he doesn't? You're not risking your job to give us a treat, are you?"

"Now there you go again, Billy, .taking the blackest view. Who's to know? This van is too small to be seen."

"But Harold, it's the only block of soap on three wheels on the road."

My fears for Harold's future were not lessened when I learned from a chance remark later that the ACDO company was also paying for the petrol.

Once we got under way, Harold shouted and pointed at what we were meant to see. "Look at those trees! Have you ever seen a cliff like that! What a wonderful view of the lake!" Although it was impossible for the girls and I to see anything, being thrown about in the trailer, we took everything in our stride, laughing all the way. We laughed when we had to get out and push the bike up the steep fells. We laughed when we noticed that our hands and clothing smelled of ACDO soap. We didn't know which was worse: the fumes from the bike or the smell of soap. We laughed harder still when we ate meat pies we'd bought at Clitheroe that had a decided ACDO flavor.

After much shouting from the girls and myself, Harold stopped and we unravelled ourselves and got out of the soap bubble to see the sights. Not even the cramp in our legs stopped us from appreciating the beauty of the Trough of Bowland on a clear day. Sitting on the grass, with our backs against the trailer, we marvelled at the great vistas, at the seeming limitless expanse of the high moors and the windy fells - ridge after ridge with not a sign of human habitation. We watched the light, fair-weather clouds scudding in from the Irish Sea. We heard the curlew's lonely cry and the tumble of the streams. We smelled the lemon-scented gorse. We were exhilarated by the heights and by the air. This was the Lancashire I would remember when choice and fate had carried me far away: a great expanse of wild hills and moorland brooding against the sky; a land of vivid green valleys and beckoning dales; the blue haze of distant fells with strands of water shining in the sun. Even after the gas works, the railways, and the steam-driven factories had done their worst, the north of England would always remain for me a wild, lovely place.

And then, on full throttle, we were off again, bouncing and rattling up and down the dusty, winding lanes, through half-sleepy villages with thatched cottages, gray-stone churches and solitary spires pointing into the bright summer sky. Several times we had to stop for a shepherd and his flock. The bleating tide of bobbing black and white heads swept around us and held us in its grip. The smell of sheep and dust settled on us like a heavy mist. It took a couple of collies to get us free.

———◆———

I took leave of mother the next day without telling her what I was up to. I was afraid that there would be a scene and she would attempt to stop me from going. After all, I was the last of her brood to fly away. Mother had a way of knowing what was going on. Unlike father, who lived in another world, there was a bond of understanding between us. We didn't have to declare our love. The hug I gave her told her all she wanted to know. Poor Maggie, she was always having to deal with people who ran away: her husband, her daughters, her sons. Running away seems to have been a recurring theme with the Woodruffs. But then, it was also true of the Kenyons; Bridget and Maggie had both run away. Questing seems to have been in the blood of both families.

I didn't think father would be interested in my departure, so I didn't say anything to him either. Not that there was enmity between us. His silence at times may have been hard to bear, but it was something that we'd got used to. It wasn't that he just stopped talking, or didn't want to talk to us. It was more gradual than that. He just drifted off into a world of his own: of work, flowers and birds. It was a happy disengagement from the more immediate matters going on around him. I respected him for what he was: an honest and a courageous man. I don't think he feared anything, not even hunger or death. He was quite content to plod along as a member of the 'lower orders' as long as the 'upper orders' left him alone. If he held a grudge against anyone, we never heard of it.

At least he set me the example of being a good worker. All he wanted was a fair day's pay for a good day's work. After returning from the war in 1918, he never sought money for money's sake; he never took an unearned pound; he never earned much beyond what he needed to survive. His sights were not high - he had become almost devoid of ambition; ambitious people worried him; he thought that in scrambling after their own self-interests they were likely to damage all those around them. To the end he remained a plain and a poor man.

I had felt for him as I watched the cotton industry collapse under his feet. More than any of us, he had believed that it would never die. Mother said that it had been his secret wish that Dan and I should be weavers alongside him. It was not to be.

Although I didn't have a job to go to, and had neither friends nor a place to stay in London, Jenny and Brenda did nothing to dissuade me from leaving. I could tell from her eyes that Jenny was not as sure as Brenda about my going to London, but her doubts and fears remained unspoken. Both my sisters promised to explain to mother what I was up to when I had gone. I promised to write.

Elsie Briggs was the last person I said good-bye to. There was no emotion or sentiment about our parting; we just shook hands.

She turned aside when I tried to thank her. "You're a bit better speaker than you were," she said. I guardedly agreed.

She knew I was much better; but she didn't want to take credit for it.

"I'm sorry I won't be the best speaker in Lancashire. I know that was your goal."

She gave me the only smile I'd ever seen on her face. It warmed me through. "It's best that you should go. There's nothing here for you. Go and show London what you can do."

"Thanks, Elsie." I gently lifted her cap and, dodging her pipe, gave her a peck on the cheek.

Worst of all was the parting from Bess. It was the only thing that brought tears. Brenda was to care for her. Brenda and her husband Dick were fond of the dog, and I knew that Bess liked them. Harold promised to bring Bess to London when he joined me. It had been my original intention to take Bess with me. "You must be out of your mind," Harold had said, "taking a dog when you don't have a bed. What are you thinking about? First get your bed; I'll bring the dog."

I was persuaded. It was all arranged. When I said good-bye to her, Bess looked at me with unforgiving eyes and whined.

Harold saw me off at the station for Manchester. From that station, built in the 1840's, Blackburn cottons had been sent to the whole world. It was quiet and looked run down now. It was the station to which my family had come on their return from America in 1914. With thousands of other Blackburn men, my father had gone to war from the same platform, and had come home again, gassed. From here I'd made my trips to Bamber Bridge, to Little Blackpool and Big Blackpool. From where I stood Jenny and Gordon had gone off on their honeymoon. A year ago, I'd met the ragged hunger marchers here on their return from London.

There was a drizzle about. I wore a cap, a coat and rough trousers. I had toyed with the idea of buying my first hat, but considering my resources had decided against it. My worldly possessions, including my two pairs of overalls and my only suit - the suit I got for Jenny's wedding - I carried in a small, battered cardboard suitcase. The suit had been let out as far as it would go, and was still a bit short in the arms and legs, but it would have to do. Also in my bag was a pullover, a shirt, socks, a face cloth, soap and a razor. Despite Madge Latham, who had introduced me to underclothing, I wore and took no underwear. With other odds and ends, my pockets contained my worldly wealth, five pounds, a watch, a comb, a handkerchief and a knife.

Neither Harold nor I said much on the platform. There were unusually awkward pauses. I couldn't think of anything interesting to say and I was glad when the train came and we shook hands and said good-bye. I waved to him from the window. The engine gave a shrill whistle, there was a puff or two of steam, the carriages lurched forward and slowly slid out of the station. I was off. Tat-tattat, tat-tattat the wheels went. I looked through the rain-streaked window at streets and buildings and smoking chimneys that I knew so well. I should have been excited, instead I felt sad - as sad as the clouded, melancholy sky.

It was dusk by the time I found Mr. Dimbleby's friend in Manchester. I had been told to be at a garage by the central bus station not later than six, and to ask for Mr. Tomkins. It was ten minutes from the hour when I hurried into the cavernous depot.

As I entered, a bundled figure of a man, wearing a box-like cap, a muffler and a coat that reached down to his boots, left a little office in one corner and walked toward me. He had a blank, scrawny face.

"You the young 'un for London?" the bundled figure asked, eyeing my valise.

Putting on a bold look, and trying to sound older than my sixteen years, I said I was.

"Well then," he went on - ignoring my 'are you - er - Mr. Tomkins?' - "don't muck abaht; jump in, we've got a long way to go."

As he didn't tell me whether he was Mr. Tomkins or not, I henceforth thought of him as Mr. Bundle.

I put my suitcase in the back of the lorry among crates of machine parts, and clambered into the cab. It smelled of petrol. It was unbearably warm. However, the great hole in the canvas above the door on my side told me that I'd better enjoy the heat while I'd got it. Mr. Bundle took some time to adjust the controls, then he got out and swung the starting handle at the front, at which the engine sprang into life.

Shortly after six, with a blaring of the horn, we rumbled from the garage in the direction of the London Road. At first, Mr. Bundle's constant crashing of gears and screeching of brakes unnerved me, but I got used to it. I also accustomed myself to his explosive sneezes. "Oh, oh, oh," he'd call out before shaking the cab with an "atchooo!" I feared that he would lose control of the wheel, but he didn't. Instead, we clattered, rocked, and sneezed our way past the groaning trams into the open countryside.

Curled in my corner, trying to avoid the gale now blowing through my side of the cab, I continued to watch the headlights as they ran before us, piercing the gloom. Periodically, other vehicles danced toward us out of the night, filling our cab with a blinding light. Now and again I saw the skeleton of trees in the background, the hazy lights of towns.

It was just as well that Mr. Bundle remained silent, for I had enough on my mind. As I watched the road, all kinds of thoughts raced through my head. I was overwhelmed at the idea of going all the way to London. For a sixteen-year-old who had hardly been out of his town, London seemed a long, long way. When I thought of Bess or mother, I was overcome with a great sadness. Only when I was on the London road did I realize that I should have brought Bess with me. I shouldn't have listened to Harold . I'd allowed myself to be talked into the idea. I'd betrayed Bess. I felt like bursting into tears.

At that moment Mr. Bundle followed a sneeze by pointing through the windscreen. "See that?" I looked. "For London," he said. It was the London train, a long string of lights slipping across the dark valley floor before us.

"More comfortable like that."

"Oh, yes," I agreed, a catch in my voice.

"Tha mustn't take it badly," he said, glancing at me. "If tha falls flat on thi face in London, tha can allus cum 'ome 'gin wi' me."

"Tha kind."

The truth was that now that I was running away I had lost the desire to do so. While I didn't feel like jumping out and running back, had there been a steady job, or a steady girl to run back to, I might have done.

There must have been periods in Lancashire's history when it was possible to live a fairly contented life as a weaver without having to look elsewhere for a living. But that had not been my experience. The Lancashire I had known was a long story of broken work and broken pay; of being overworked or having no work at all; of being paid so badly that the whole family had to work or nobody ate; with only a narrow margin separating us from sinking altogether. I was sixteen when the hunger marchers returned to Blackburn. I had lived through the worst years Lancashire was to endure. By then I didn't need anybody to explain to me, as Mr. Peek had done, that the Lancashire cotton industry had been dealt a fatal blow. I had no job to go back to. Best I could hope for was pick-and-shovel work. I either sought a better living elsewhere, or I lived from hand to mouth, forever paying 'something off,' forever 'carrying over,' forever worrying where the next meal was coming from - as the rest of my family did. London was the lure, but I might not have gone there had hard times and Betty Weatherby not made up my mind.

My great-grandfather Arne had come to Lancashire when the name of Blackburn was about to be known world-wide. Now the Lancashire cotton industry was dying - as was our pride and our loyalty to cotton. An industry that treats its workers, especially its defenseless women and children as inhumanely as cotton textiles had done, must die unsung. All my life I have been puzzled why we Lancastrians should have been so good at inventing machines, at starting an industrial revolution that transformed the entire world, yet so bad at human relations. In my whole sixteen years in Lancashire I had heard nothing but 'us'n' and 'them.' The gulf dividing capital from labour was never bridged.

It didn't cross my mind that in going to London I might be jumping from the frying pan into the fire. The obvious dangers accompanying my mad-cap scheme didn't penetrate my thick head. I never thought of discomfort or danger. The fact that I had no idea where I would sleep the next night, or the one after that, added spice to the adventure. Somehow the solution to all my problems would be found at the end of the road that lay before me. I was blindly optimistic of the outcome.

I didn't hold it against anybody that I had to go. Because of what grandmother Bridget had taught me, I didn't hate anybody for it. I envied, but I can't say I ever hated the rich. That is one conversion Peter Shad had not succeeded in making.

Least of all did I blame Lancashire, the county of my birth. Regardless of the fact that Lancashire had not offered me much of a living, I was proud to be a Lancastrian, especially to be a Blackburnian. Blackburn was not just another Lancashire town; Blackburn had been the greatest weaving center in the world. It had been the pioneer, the seed-bed of inventions in power weaving. It was unique. East Lancashire had developed the greatest concentration of manufacturing industry there had ever been. Without the textile industries of Lancashire and Yorkshire there would have been less 'Rule Britannia' in the world.

Whatever else Lancashire had denied me, it had left me with a love of individual liberty and freedom. Lancashire had given me the liberty to run as wild as I wanted. I had always had the freedom to run from dark streets and alleyways into the open rolling countryside. Liberty and freedom were in the bones of my people. Lancashire folk might be rough and ready, but they were never servile. Servile people didn't take it upon themselves to walk out as I was doing. At least Lancashire had left me free to reject my birthplace.

My heritage was joyful as well as bleak. I knew not only the squalor of a factory town, I also knew the unforgettable beauty of the surrounding fields, moors, hills and craggy fells. I shall never forget the long, joyful summer days playing on the banks of the Ribble; the hectic winter flights down icy hillsides on homemade sleds, or the happy hours spent flying a linen kite in the ever-present north wind. These things are rooted in my mind, they are part of my blood. More than anything else, it was the river, the rushing streams, the wind, the hills, and the moors that made me what I am. They are with me forever.

As a Lancashire boy running wild, I'd never known boredom. There had always been something to do. I had never had the time or need to ask, "who am I?" I was a weaver's son, somebody close to the bottom of the social pile; somebody who could not evade reality; somebody who had been brought into daily contact with the conditions of labour; somebody who had been blessed by constant challenge: the challenge of poverty, the challenge of making do; even the challenge of a harsh climate and a cold north wind.

There was nothing dishonourable in all this. Hard times had bred resourcefulness and self-reliance. I knew by experience how to take setbacks. I also knew that nobody owed me a living. I took it for granted that in life I'd have to shift for myself. Lancashire schools hadn't taught me much. What schooling I had received was deplorable. But I had at least been taught common sense and how to survive; I wasn't quite the greenhorn I looked and sounded.

No, all things considered, I was lucky to have been born and reared in Lancashire; doubly lucky to have been born poor.

"Tha leaving Lancashire," my friend said, as he slammed in the gear. "Cheshire's at top of 'ill."

"Good-bye Lancashire," I said, a frog in my throat..

MY EARLY LIFE

WINSTON CHURCHILL

Packed with adventure and incident, Winston Churchill's first twenty-five years included night marches, cavalry charges, skirmishes on the North West Frontier, a dangerous escape from a Boer prison-camp, and, to avoid any moments of longeur, a visit to the Cuban war. As both correspondent and soldier he was present at the epic battle of Omdurman and at the relief of Ladysmith. But *My Early Life* is more than just an adventure story: it is an elegiac evocation of the so-called Golden Age before 1914, while revealing the unhappiness of a child who was surrounded by so much grandeur.

Churchill's biographers agree that this is the best written and most enjoyable of all his many books.

There can be few who could play on all the strings – humour, headlong excitement, quiet irony, melancholy regret for vanished customs and glories, love of sport, the pleasures of friendship – with such a sure hand.
The Times

He has enjoyed writing it as much as he enjoyed living it, and he is able to convey this enjoyment to the reader, who shares it with him to the full.
Duff Cooper, The Spectator

Written with extraordinary vivacity and power. Mr Churchill may or may not be a model politician; he was certainly a model war correspondent.
Henry Nevinson, New Statesman

ISBN 0-907871-62-3

A SQUARE OF SKY

Memoirs of a wartime childhood

JANINA DAVID

At the age of nine Janina David was leading a sheltered life with her prosperous Jewish family in Poland. One year later they were all facing starvation in the Warsaw ghetto. In her memoirs of a wartime childhood Janina David describes the family's struggle against insurmountable odds. When it became clear that none of them was likely to survive, the thirteen-year-old girl was smuggled out of the ghetto to live with family friends – a Polish woman and her German-born husband. When this place became too dangerous, she was sent with false identity papers to a Catholic convent, where she lived in constant fear of being discovered.

She has the artist's gift for knowing exactly what to say and what to leave out. She doesn't dwell on the atrocities, and there is no trace of bitterness or self-pity.
Miriam May, The Observer

Miss David has three valuable gifts: her remarkable memory for detail, a sense of restraint, and a true writing talent.
Nicholas Carroll, The Sunday Times

It is more than 400 pages long, and impossible to put down.
Caroline Moorehead, The Independent

'The resilience of the human spirit' may seem too glib a phrase in relation to the extreme sufferings of others. It is nevertheless an awesome reality. And it has never been illustrated more poignantly, or with such courageous dignity than in *A Square of Sky*.
The Times Literary Supplement

ISBN 0-907871-17-8

TRAVELS WITH MYSELF AND ANOTHER

MARTHA GELLHORN

'I was seized by the idea of this book while sitting on a rotten little beach at the western tip of Crete, flanked by a waterlogged shoe and a rusted potty ... This is not a proper travel book: it is an account of my best horror journeys, chosen from a wide range, recollected with tenderness now that they are past.'

Must surely be ranked as one of the funniest travel books of our time – second only to *A Short Walk in the Hindu Kush* ... It doesn't matter whether this author is experiencing marrow-freezing misadventures in war-ravaged China, or driving a Land Rover through East African game-parks, or conversing with hippies in Israel, or spending a week in a Moscow Intourist Hotel. Martha Gellhorn's reactions are what count and one enjoys equally her blistering scorn of humbug, her hilarious eccentricities, her unsentimental compassion.
Dervla Murphy, The Irish Times

Spun with a fine blend of irony and epigram. She is incapable of writing a dull sentence.
The Times

Miss Gellhorn has a novelist's eye, a flair for black comedy and a short fuse ... There is not a boring word in her humane and often funny book.
The New York Times

ISBN 0-907871-35-6

WALLED GARDENS

Scenes from an Anglo-Irish childhood

ANNABEL GOFF

W alled Gardens is a journey both into a time and a place –
the South of Ireland in the 1940s and 1950s. The author
describes a childhood outside the main currents of the 20th
Century; her parents still went fox-hunting and horse racing and
relied on readily available servants from a vast and inexpensive
work-pool. At the same time they had no central heating, no
television, and the roof leaked. Like many other Anglo-Irish
families they attempted outlandish and impractical schemes to
maintain deteriorating driveways and crumbling houses. Her
father was a witty baronet born into a generation down on its
luck; the author observes how his marriage to her beautiful
mother gradually falls apart. This is an affectionate yet
unsentimental memoir of a transitional generation, one born too
late to benefit from the last years of the Ascendancy, but too early
to integrate into the mainstream of contemporary Irish life.

Vividly entertaining ... written with a quality of mercy added to the
acute perceptions of a child.
Molly Keane, The Spectator

Beautifully written ... A unique character and flavour, which is
extraordinarily well conveyed.
William Trevor, Irish Times

Her descriptions of places and people are evocative, sometimes moving,
and sometimes very funny.
Isabel Colegate, Washington Post

ISBN 0-907871-42-9

A STATE OF FEAR

Memories of Argentina's nightmare

ANDREW GRAHAM-YOOLL

For ten hair-raising years, Andrew Graham-Yooll was the News Editor of the Buenos Aires Herald. All around him friends and acquaintances were 'disappearing'. Although the slightest mistake might have caused his own disappearance, he didn't shrink from getting first-hand experience of this war of terror; he attended clandestine guerilla conferences, helped relatives trace the missing, and took tea with a torturer who wasn't ashamed to make the most chilling confessions.

It is one of the most affecting books I have ever read.
Nicholas Shakespeare, The Times

Mr Graham-Yooll's brilliant book is the portrait of a society that seems on the edge of final dissolution.
Raymond Carr, The Spectator

I have never read any book that so conveys what it is like to live in a state of permanent fear.
Graham Greene, The Observer

A State of Fear will appeal equally to those who relish a sophisticated, understated, real-life thriller, to students of Argentinian politics, to anyone interested in psychology of terrorism used as an instrument of government and to all readers who enjoy supremely good writing for its own sake – whatever the subject.
Dervla Murphy, Good Book Guide

ISBN 0-907871-36-4

THREE CAME HOME

A woman's ordeal in a Japanese prison camp

AGNES KEITH

When the Japanese swept through Borneo in 1942, Agnes Keith was captured with her two-year-old son. Even though keeping notes was a capital offence, she wrote a diary on the backs of labels and in the margins of old newspapers, which she buried in tins or sewed inside her son's home-made toys. Unlike many other narrators of camp life, Agnes Keith gives an honest and rounded description of her Japanese captors. The camp commander, Colonel Suga, was responsible for a forced march which killed all but three out of 2,970 prisoners; yet he regularly took children for joy-rides in his car, stuffing them with sweets, and sent them back to camp with armfuls of flowers from his garden.

This is one of the most remarkable books you will ever read.
John Carey, The Sunday Times

No one who reads her unforgettable narrative of the years she passed in Borneo during the war can fail to share her emotions with something very like the intensity of personal experience.
The Times Literary Supplement

Three Came Home should rank with the great imprisonment stories of all times.
The New York Herald Tribune

A truly remarkable book.
David Holloway, The Sunday Telegraph

ISBN 0-907871-26-7

SCUM OF THE EARTH

ARTHUR KOESTLER

At the beginning of the Second World War, Koestler was living in the South of France working on *Darkness at Noon*. After retreating to Paris he was imprisoned by the French as an undesirable alien, even though he had been a respected crusader against fascism. "A few years ago we were called the defenders of liberty – now we have become the scum of the earth". He was luckier, though, than many innocent refugees who were handed over to the Nazis for torture or execution. *Scum of the Earth* is more than the story of Koestler's survival among these horrors: it is also a description of what happens when a nation loses its honour and pride.

A memorable story, vivid, powerful and deeply searching.
The Times Literary Supplement

This is a book in a thousand, by far the best book to come out of the collapse of France.
The Guardian

Koestler's personal history of France at War. It is, I think, the finest book that has come out of that cauldron.
New York Herald Tribune

One of the greatest books to come out of the Second World War ... Life in the camps is illuminated by a writer whose humanity, optimism, and intelligence shine on every page.
The Observer

ISBN 0-907871-07-0

THE HONOURED SOCIETY

The Sicilian Mafia observed

NORMAN LEWIS

Epilogue by Marcello Cimino

Norman Lewis describes how, after Mussolini came close to destroying the Mafia, the U.S. army returned them to power in 1944. Henceforth they infiltrated every aspect of Sicilian life, corrupting landowners, the police, the judiciary, and even the church. In one of the most astonishing chapters, the author tells the story of how an eighty-year-old priest, Padre Camelo, led his monks on escapades of murder and extortion, frequently using the confessional box for transmitting threats.

One of the great travel writers of our time.
Eric Newby, The Observer

This book has not a dull moment in it; it is indeed imbued with that quality of terribilita which Giuliano himself was said to possess.
The Spectator

It is deftly written, and every page is horribly absorbing.
The Times

The Honoured Society is the most penetrating book ever written on the Mafia.
Time Out

PUBLISHED BY *ELAND*

NAPLES '44

An Intelligence Officer in the Italian labyrinth

NORMAN LEWIS

Norman Lewis arrived in Naples as an Intelligence Officer attached to the American Fifth Army. By 1944 the city's inhabitants were so destitute that all the tropical fish in the aquarium had been devoured, and numbers of respectable women had been driven to prostitution. The mafia gradually became so indispensable to the occupying forces that it succeeded in regaining its former power. Despite the cruelty and suffering he encountered, Norman Lewis writes in the diary, 'A year among Italians has converted me to such an admiration for their humanity and culture that, were I given the chance to be born again, Italy would be the country of my choice'.

A wonderful book.
Richard West, The Spectator

As unique an experience for the reader as it must have been a unique experience for the writer.
Graham Greene

Here is a book of gripping fascination in its flow of bizarre anecdote and character sketch; and it is much more than that.
J. W. Lambert, The Sunday Times

The best single British memoir of the Second World War.
Geoffrey Wheatcroft, Daily Mail

One goes on reading page after page as if eating cherries.
Luigi Barzini, New York Review of Books

ISBN 0-907871-45-3

AN INDIAN ATTACHMENT

SARAH LLOYD

An *Indian Attachment* is part travel book, part love story.
Because of Sarah Lloyd's relationship with a placid, beautiful,
opium-addicted Sikh, she spent two years in rural India, first in a
remote mud-built Punjabi village, and then in the impoverished
community of a dubious holy-man. Here she lived in a minute
brick hut, with living expenses of only fifty pence a day. No
other outsider has been able to write so convincingly about the
plight of Indian villagers.

Travel writing will never be the same again.
Anne de Courcy, Evening Standard.

A remarkable achievement: beautifully written, sympathetic without
being starry-eyed ... lots of real wisdom and sensitivity and delicious
quiet humour.
Dervla Murphy, Times Literary Supplement

Sarah Lloyd has produced a rare and important document. Without
abandoning her Western critical faculties, she has written
sympathetically, as an insider, of life as the vast majority of Indians
know it. In this sense, *An Indian Attachment* is the *truest* book about the
subcontinent today that I have read.
Geoffrey Moorhouse

An Indian Attachment is harder to put down than any thriller.
John Mellors, London Magazine

A remarkable book ... a traveller's tale, a love story, and, above all, a
brilliant exposé of village India.
John Keay, Sunday Telegraph

ISBN 0-907871-12-7

A REED SHAKEN BY THE WIND

GAVIN MAXWELL

The Marsh Arabs were one of the most isolated communities in the world. Few Europeans had travelled in their territory, a mass of tiny islands among the swamps of Southern Iraq. One of the few was the legendary explorer, Wilfred Thesiger, who agreed to let Gavin Maxwell accompany him on a journey to the marshes. Thesiger was well known and liked by the reed-dwellers, and Maxwell describes his daily tending of their wounds, 'stitching away like a tailor at dog bites and pig-gores'.

For Maxwell himself the journey was eventful; he was charged by a wild-boar, he was a witness to family feuds, and by making a pet of an otter, began his famous relationship with that breed. But, more than just a collection of enthralling tales, *A Reed Shaken By the Wind* is a moving and valuable record of a unique community that is now being deliberately destroyed.

This is prose close to poetry, written by a man of great perception and understanding.
W.O. Douglas, New York Times

An unusual and exceptionally good travel book.
John Freeman, New Statesman

He enriches his reader with shock upon shock of delight.
Times Literary Supplement

It is not too much to say that the author has produced an almost perfect book of travel.
New Yorker

ISBN 0-907871-37-2

THE
UNDEFEATED

GEORGE PALOCZI-HORVATH

Afterword by Agi Argent

George Paloczi-Horvath was born in 1908 into the feudal nobility of Hungary. Despite his privileged background, he came to realize that his family's wealth was based on the exploitation of a brutalized peasantry. By the 1930s he was an active anti-Nazi; by 1941 he was forced to flee the country. Returning after the war, he became a dedicated communist; but this didn't prevent him from being arrested, tortured and imprisoned by the communist regime. He spent 1,832 days in prison, many of them in the solitary confinement of underground prison cells. In 1954 he was eventually released; but after the Hungarian Revolution he was forced to escape with his wife and baby for sanctuary in Britain.

In its power to enlighten, to inform, and to shock, *The Undefeated* ranks with Arthur Koestler's *Darkness at Noon*.
The Atlantic Monthly

This autobiography is what the anti-Fascist autobiographies of the Thirties tried to be, but failed ... it will be a true classic of life in the totalitarian age.
J.E.M. Arden, The Spectator

I have read dozens of books which described prison and torture in the communist world, but I cannot remember being so distressed and moved as by this account.
Nicholas Carroll, The Sunday Times

As if Lewis Carroll and George Orwell had taken turns to rewrite each other's masterpiece.
C.M. Woodhouse, The Observer

ISBN 0-907071-22-4

THE PEOPLE OF PROVIDENCE

A housing estate and some of its inhabitants

TONY PARKER

Over a period of eighteen months Tony Parker interviewed the residents of an ordinary housing estate in South London. He listened to an assorted mixture of personalities – including a vagrant, two policemen, an often-convicted fence who was the mother of five children, a pro-flogging magistrate, a local doctor, and a 75-year-old widower who spent 'an hour or two in bed each week with one or other of about twelve different ladies I meet at our church'. The inhabitants of 'Providence' opened their hearts, revealing all their quirks, emotions and prejudices. These interviews prove that extraordinary stories are found not only in deserts and jungles: even amid the bleak sprawl of South London, Tony Parker discovered a community that is diverse and enthralling.

All these brief lives read with a marvellous vivacity. I have never previously reviewed a book which was constantly filched away by my children. We can all learn from it. Mr Parker has peopled a world with a texture sometimes achieved in the grandest and simplest fiction, hardly ever in the reporting of fact.
Philip Whitehead, The Listener

One of the most original, absorbing books I have read this year.
Hilary Spurling, The Observer

More conventional researchers could usefully learn from Tony Parker. As a set of vignettes, it is a triumph.
Peter Willmott, Times Literary Supplement

ISBN 0-907871-57-7

ASK SIR JAMES

The life of Sir James Reid, personal physician to Queen Victoria

MICHAELA REID

In a dark cupboard of her house, Michaela Reid, the granddaughter-in-law of Sir James Reid, discovered 40 pocket diaries and 31 of his large scrapbooks, as well as some 200 letters and notes from Queen Victoria. From this remarkable unpublished material, the author spent five years writing the life of the man who enjoyed unparalleled intimacy with the Queen during the last years of her life.

Although Sir James was never allowed to see her undressed, or approach her with a stethoscope, he was habitually summoned four or five times a day, and quickly became her trusted confidant, privy to all the most intimate aspects of her court and family life. It was he who was responsible for persuading Princess Christian to give up her opium addiction; he also had to cope with John Brown's alcoholism, as well as informing his unruffled royal employer about her Indian secretary's gonorrhea.

The doctor's memoirs have left us an unusually vivid portrait of the Queen, who was eccentric and stubborn, and yet at the same time perceptive, endearing, and warm-hearted..

This biography is especially absorbing.
The Times

An exceptionally well-constructed biography.
Kenneth Rose, Sunday Telegraph

This is an engaging story, well told.
Alan Bell, Literary Review

260 pages of narrative, and never a dull one.
Denys Forrest, The Tablet

ISBN 0-907871-30-5

ELAND

53 Eland Road
London SW11 5JX
Fax 020 7652 5055
Email: travel@travelbooks.co.uk

All our books are printed on fine, pliable, cream-coloured paper. Since 1984 they have been sewn as well as glued. This gives larger margins in the gutter, as well as making the books stronger.

We take immense trouble to select only the most readable books, and therefore many readers collect the entire series. If you haven't liked an Eland title, please send it back to us, and we will refund the purchase price.

If you want to be sent our catalogue, please write to us at the above address.